THE PINKERTON CASEBOOK

The Editor

Bruce Durie has been a paper-bag salesman, bus conductor, research scientist, journalist, broadcaster, Director of the Edinburgh Science Festival, museum director, senior academic and manager at various universities.

His books (fiction and non-fiction), plays and screenplays include a number of bestsellers on internet and e-business subjects, popular local history and Victorian detective novels, including *The Murder of Young Tom Morris* (2003) and *Dick Donovan: The Glasgow Detective* (2005).

He lives in Glasgow with his teenage son, and teaches at the University of Strathclyde.

THE PINKERTON

ADVENTURES OF THE ORIGINAL PRIVATE EYE

CASEBOOK

WE NEVER SLEEP

ALLAN PINKERTON
EDITED BY BRUCE DURIE

MERCAT

Mercat Press
www.mercatpress.com

First published in 2007 by Mercat Press
Mercat Press is an imprint of Birlinn Limited, West Newington
House, 10 Newington Road, Edinburgh EH9 1QS
www.mercatpress.com

ISBN 13: 978 1 84183 116 9

Typeset in Cheltenham BT
Printed and bound by Bell & Bain Ltd.

⊰ Contents ⊱

Allan Pinkerton, 1860

⊰ Introduction ⊱

Allan Pinkerton (21 August, 1819—1 July, 1884)

Everyone knows the name of Allan Pinkerton, detective and spy, best known for creating the first detective agency. He is synonymous with the image of the private detective, and his story has the added allure of the Wild West, mail train and bank robberies, plus the tracking down of outlaws, irredeemable Confederate bandits and con-men.

Beyond that, Pinkerton's story descends into the fog of myth. I imagine myself pitching the screenplay of his life to a smoke-filled roomful of cigar-clamping Hollywood movie producers in the following terms:

> Born in poverty in Glasgow; father a policeman disabled in a riot; set off for a new life in America; shipwrecked but recovered; set up a business near Chicago; discovered some men burying counterfeit cash, put them under surveillance and had them arrested; became an agent of the law and set up the first detective agency; helped Lincoln win the Civil War and prevented that president's assassination; protected express trains from banditry; hunted down robbers; finally brought the infamous James Gang to book; pacified the Irish and the communists bent on disrupting American society; set up the beginnings of the FBI's criminal records system; cruelly disabled by a stroke but turned to writing, and produced a slew of thrilling stories that captivated America and the wider world; his legacy carried on by his sons in the agency that still bears his name. Cut to square-jawed, resolute men in suits and gunbelts, facing down the bad men. Pinkerton's story is the American Dream.

Then I see myself translated to a more, shall we say, reflective environment—a lecture, perhaps, before the Society For Tearing Down Reputations—and pulling out a left-liberal crowd-pleaser:

> Originally a poverty-stricken chartist in Glasgow, he evaded the clutches of the establishment by a hasty marriage and emigration; once in America became instrumental in setting up Lincoln's spy network and helping slaves escape to the North and Canada; had his undoubted surveillance and intelligence skills suborned by the government and became its blunt weapon in the interests of big business—massacring the associates of Jesse James, who were only trying to protect themselves against the depredations of a revengeful North, beating down legitimate voices of protest such as the Molly Maguires and organised labour unions, targeting and harrassing socialists, gypsies and others; unashamed self-publicist who was cruel and domineering towards his workers and family; architect of all that is sinister in America's covert agencies. It's the American Dream gone bad.

Of course, and isn't it always thus, the man is far more complex and his story is other than what it seems. The documented 'facts' are contradictory. The interpretations based on them proceed, often, from prejudice. Much of what we know of Allan Pinkerton comes from his own telling, which is not always reliable or, at best, had an agenda. (In his defence, many of his early records were destroyed in the disastrous fire which overtook Chicago in 1871.) There are sections of American society today where the very mention of Pinkerton causes strong men to take off their hats, look heavenwards with a tearful eye and intone his name in a breathless, reverential whisper, such as used to be reserved for George Washington and Randolph Scott. Then there are places, notably in Missouri but more generally in the South, where they can barely bring themselves to say 'Pinkerton', and not without spitting in the dust. A friendly if somewhat insistent Southern gentleman offered to take me in his 4x4—Confederate flag, gun rack, hounddogs, the lot—to see the place where old Mrs James had her arm blown off by the Pinkertons. He was not amused when I suggested that she had capitalised on this mercilessly and sold guided tours of the house where her son, Jesse, was shot in the back, waving her stump for emphasis while collecting the entry fee. Mention that Pinkerton was a once a socialist, and you'll find yourself lynched in almost any town, county or city in America. The heart is pure, but the neck is red.

This book, then, is a collection of Pinkerton's 'own' writings (and the reason for the rabbit's ears there will become clear), which certainly have historical interest, and if they lack strict literary merit they are firmly in the canon that later produced the pulp novel. The selection has been made on the basis of intrinsic interest, importance, illumination, relevance and, ultimately, whim. It is also an excuse to examine what is 'known' (again!) about the man and his life through his own eyes, with some perspective thrown in.

Allan Pinkerton was, born in the Gorbals, Glasgow, Scotland, on 21 July or 21 August 1819, to William Pinkerton and his wife Isobel McQueen. That much we can be almost sure of, because an entry appears in the Old Parish Records, showing his birth on the 21 (it is unclear what month this refers to) and baptism on 29 August. Some biographies date his birth to the 25th, and his mother's name is variously spelled Isobel, Isabell etc. in other records (a common occurrence in the days when no one cared that much, provided it sounded right). His birthplace, on the corner of Rutherglen Loan and Muirhead Street, did not survive into the twentieth century and is now overtaken by Old Rutherglen Road. It is not the site of Glasgow Central Mosque, as is often claimed—that was raised on the land occupied by Thomson's Mill, where Allan's mother and half-sisters worked—but, more appropriately, is now occupied by the offices of the Procurator Fiscal (chief prosecutor) for Glasgow and Strathkelvin, and one day someone will find it appropriate to nail a plaque to its wall or erect a statue pointing this out. The 1841 Census for St James Parish, Gorbals, shows a family of four at Little Dowhill, consisting of William (aged seventy), a weaver; Isabella (fifty-five); Robert (twenty-five), a journeyman blacksmith; and Allan (twenty), a journeyman cooper (barrel maker). If the ages look suspiciously rounded, that's because they were—the 1841 census rounded down the age of everyone over fifteen to the nearest five years.

The various published accounts of Pinkerton's early life speak of chaos and poverty. William was a home handloom weaver, whose first marriage (probably irregular but no less valid) to Isabel Stevenson was 'acknowledged' in 1791, and whose second 'marriage' to Isobel MacQueen or McQuin, or some variant, is unrecorded. William and his two wives had at least eleven children (six surviving to adulthood) from his first daughter Love in 1792 to Allan in 1819, and including the unruly James (1796). William—himself one of at least eight—is variously said to have died in 1826, 1828 or 1833, yet he appears upright and breathing in 1841. Disentangling all that is a matter for another time and place. However, the matter of William being 'the first sergeant in the Glasgow police' and the circumstances of his injury, are worthy of investigation.

Glasgow indeed had a police force from 1800 (the first in Britain, despite what the London Met will say), but William Pinkerton does not seem to have been part of it, nor was he the 'first sergeant'—that singular honour belongs to one Donald MacLean. He does seem to have secured a position as a 'trusty' (locker-up) at Glasgow City Jail. William was certainly built for the robust policing of the day: unusually tall for the time at over six feet, and grim of countenance. Possibly, William had supplemented his weaving income as one of the 'Charlies' (nightwatchmen-cum-streetsweepers) who evolved in 1808 in to a regular police force in the Gorbals, which was then a separate burgh. The Gorbals men, however, would be drafted in to help Glasgow at times of need—Hogmanay, the Glasgow Fair holiday and major gatherings. References in some biographies to William's tenure as a police sergeant and an earlier career in the Black Watch (the 42nd Highland Regiment) are a confusion with Allan's elder half-brother, William (born 1803) who did both of those things. The ex-army 'Big Hielan' Polis' is something of a fixture in Glasgow's history, right up to the 1960s. It was said of them that they preferred to arrest miscreants in Hope Street or Bath Street, as both were easier to spell than Sauchiehall.

Even Allan Pinkerton's own writings (mostly in letters to his son) are shot through with inaccuracies and erroneous or imprecise dates. He is wrong about the marriages of his three half-sisters and speaks of being brought up in a household of two families crowded into two rooms, when by the time he was five only his parents and elder brother were still alive or living there. This matters, because if we cannot take the details in his most intimate correspondence at face value, what worth can be place on any of his later statements?

The confusion over his father's injury and death is a case in point. As we have seen, William was still alive in 1841. The poet, Oliver Wendell Holmes, no less, has him paralysed during a chartist riot in 1829 and dead in 1833, the dates now enshrined in the *Dictionary of American Biography*; Sigmond Lavine, writing in 1963, kills him off in 1829; James Horan, writing in 1967, has William die in a riot of 1827; and Dr James Mackay seems to accept a date between 1831 and 1833, based on the numinous evidence of missing records from that date.

And what of the said chartist riot? Granted, Scotland had seen some ferment ever since 1816, with the workers rising up against the Corn Laws, restrictions on union activities and low wages. In 1819 a wholly merchant-class special constables force was formed and the cavalry was on alert. Rumours flew about daily that thousands of French troops were on their way to aid the workers (as if they weren't busy enough at home with the Bourbons and yet another revolution) and there were a few Ealing-comedy uprisings of cottage weavers, one of which culminated in the execution of Keir Hardie's grandfather and therefore set the scene for the eventual founding of the Labour Party. But of large scale riots in Glasgow in the late 1820s there is not a single record. In any case, the very term 'chartism' only originated in 1838 with the publication of the *People's Charter*, and was a reaction to the half-hearted electoral reforms of 1832 rather than a wages movement. The whole story may be another invention of the fertile fictive brain of Allan Pinkerton.

Whether fatherless or not, Allan left school aged nine (he says) and went to work as a runner for a pattern maker. Then at twelve, when old enough for an apprenticeship, he went to McCauley the barrel-makers to learn to be a cooper. Nine or ten was not an unusual age to leave school, and the Scottish system being what it was, he would have had a better grasp of the three Rs than many sixteen-year-old school-leavers today. By 1837 he had his journeyman's ticket, the same year Princess Victoria got her Queen's ticket. They both picked a bad year. The 1832 Reform Act and an economic downturn persuaded the mill owners to cut wages by half and the workers to down tools for three

months in protest. This sparked mass meetings and the formation of
the National Radical Association. The High Sheriff of Lanarkshire
(which was the county containing the part of Glasgow north and east
of the Clyde) panicked, pressed the button on all-out class war and arrested five members of the Cotton Spinners' Union for treason. A year
later, John Collins of the Birmingham chartists arrived in Glasgow
like a missionary and plans were made for an event on Monday
21st May on Glasgow Green. This was no storming-the-Bastille
exercise; a procession of more than seventy unions, with forty-odd of
their marching bands, arrived ready for a day of speechifying to be
followed by a 'soireé'. It was a gala, and anywhere between 30,000
(Tory estimate) and 200,000 (Radical estimate) turned up for a
rather orderly meeting.

The young Pinkerton took part in the organisation of various social
reform schemes to do with poverty, housing, sanitation and—interest-
ingly in the light of his later career—slavery. But whether he actually
attended the occasion at Glasgow Green is in doubt, because he spent
a lot of 1838 tramping the roads of southern Scotland and northern
England to find cooper's work. His journeyman's ticket was a ticket
to independence (in its guise of unemployment) whereas the young
Queen Victoria had taken over the family business.

Come the end of 1838 the general enthusiasm for radicalism had
waned somewhat, but Allan Pinkerton joined the Glasgow Universal
Suffrage Association and became a director. Like most idealistic mass
movements in Scotland, as soon as such a body is established it springs
apart like shrapnel. The Reformed Church ended up in splinters, its
various secessions themselves fragmenting even more; Jacobites became
Catholics on one hand and Episcopalians on the other; and likewise
radicalism soon found itself in factions concerned variously with tem-
perance, Irish Home Rule, the various flavours of emerging socialism,
violence versus non-violence and sundry other anarchies. The idealistic
Pinkerton met and was influenced by George Julian Harney, an associ-
ate of Marx and Engels and later founder of the *Democrat* and *Red
Republican* newspapers. This led him to participate in the unholy mess
that was the Newport Rising on 4 November 1839. Had he and the
other Glasgow men there been arrested, Pinkerton would have found

himself transported to Australia. Instead, he got back to a Glasgow to find his Association in the hands of a middle-class tea merchant and a rather well-off steam engine mechanic. Virtually accused of financial improbity with the Association's finances (and held liable for its debts, as a director), Pinkerton engaged in an exchange of frankly libellous letters to newspapers and resigned to set up his own Northern Democratic Association. He espoused physical force as the road to Reform, and watched with some satisfaction as the Suffrage Association fell to pieces.

At a fundraiser in 1841, organised by Allan, a young soprano sang and captivated him. She was an apprentice bookbinder from Paisley called Joan Carfrae, and they started 'winching'. There was more ferment on the way, though. A poor harvest and a harsh winter prompted a wave of emigration that had the newspapers fretting about what would now be called a 'brain drain', as the skilled and talented headed for Canada and the Unites States, to be replaced by Irish who couldn't afford an Atlantic crossing and headed for the west of Scotland instead.

The Pinkerton myth talks of pursuit by the police, a tip-off by a sheriff's officer who knew his father, a hasty marriage followed by flight on a ship just ahead of the hue-and-cry. He may have been disillusioned by the failure to win universal suffrage (he was almost ninety years ahead of his time in that) and the internecine strife of chartism and radicalism. But the simple explanation may be that Allan sought a better life for his new wife in Quebec. At least one of his brothers was already in North America, and while there were certainly arrests of militants in Glasgow, there is no evidence that Pinkerton was sought.

The 'secret wedding' fantasised by Horan was in fact celebrated on the 13th March 1842 in Glasgow Cathedral, after proclamation of banns for the previous three Sundays, and along with a number of other couples. Joan, it should be noted, was only fifteen and both she and Allan are given as residing in Glasgow (though neither did) which might suggest they were lying low, but possibly only from Mr and Mrs Carfrae. It then took them almost another month to 'flee' aboard a ship, on 8 April.

All of this has a point. Socialist, working-class radical, despiser of the establishment and rebeller against authority and its police lackeys, economic migrant and romantic—would the younger Allan Pinkerton recognise the alleged strike-breaker and persecutor of the left and the immigrants of later years? Is there, in fact, much connection between the two?

There are subsequent tales of a storm, a shipwreck off Nova Scotia and the loss of all their possessions—including a brand-new wedding ring—to predatory natives, and the decision to forget Canada in favour of a bustling, brawling frontier town just developing on the shores of Lake Michigan. Chicago, it was called, and it was fast becoming the place where everything was packaged up for the drive west to open up new country. What Chicago used was barrels, so what Chicago needed, clearly, was a barrel-maker. Some fellow Scots told Pinkerton that Lill's Brewery in the downtown area was hiring coopers, and soon Lill was hiring Allan.

However, the independent-minded Glaswegian in Pinkerton knew that the way to make money was with his own shop, so he headed for a small Scots-dominated township called Dundee in Kane County, Illinois, some forty miles to the west, where he established a cooperage business. Fed up with paying top prices for barrels shipped from Chicago, the local farmers were soon patronising 'Pinkerton's One and Original Cooperage of Dundee', as his shingle proudly proclaimed. It rapidly became a ten-man factory. Here, Pinkerton showed his mettle and his credentials by running down a gang of counterfeiters while out scouting for lumber to make into barrels. Appointed a Deputy Sheriff of Kane County in 1846, he was also made a full-time investigator for Cook County, with its headquarters in Chicago. Pinkerton organised a force of detectives along with Chicago attorney Edward Rucker to capture thieves who were stealing railway property—the team which developed into the North-Western Police Agency, and later Pinkerton's National Detective Agency of which Allan took sole charge in 1853. Their logo was a wide open eye with the motto 'We Never Sleep'. This was at a time when most of America's towns and cities—even the largest—had unqualified law enforcement officers. Pinkerton's agents took on the most difficult cases, from money and property thefts to attempted coups and murder.

But the agency's speciality was capturing thieves who targeted express companies. In 1866 Pinkerton's captured the principals in the theft of $700,000 from Adams Express Company safes on a train of the New York, New Haven and Hartford Railway, and recovered all but $12,000 of the stolen money. But his real break came in February 1861, when he uncovered evidence of a plot to assassinate President-elect Abraham Lincoln while arriving in Baltimore on the way to Washington. Pinkerton's advice was to keep going without a stop. In April, as a direct result of coming to the attention of the new president, Pinkerton received a suggestion from General George B. McClellan to organise a military information system in the southern states. This became the US Secret Service, which Pinkerton headed throughout the Civil War, under the *nom de guerre* of Major E. J. Allen.

Before engaging with the Union Army, Pinkerton had developed a series of investigative techniques still used today, including 'shadowing' (close but covert surveillance) and 'assuming a role' (now called undercover work). Pinkerton's agents, following his precepts, and on occasion 'Major E. J. Allen' himself, worked undercover as Confederate soldiers and sympathisers, in an effort to gather military intelligence. He was succeeded as Intelligence Service chief by Lafayette Baker. Pinkerton went back to pursuing train robbers, but also worked to stem what he saw as the infiltration by secret terrorists of labour organisations.

In 1869 Pinkerton suffered a stroke which left him partially paralysed, and he handed over the management of the agency to his sons, William Allan (b. 1846) and Robert (1848-1907). Meanwhile, the agency went from strength to strength. James McParlan, one of his men, lived among the Molly Maguires in Pennsylvania in 1873-76 and secured the evidence which led to the breaking up of the criminal organisation.

But Pinkerton himself was not idle. He turned his hand to crime writing—between *The Expressman and the Detective* in 1874 and a memoir, *Thirty Years a Detective* in 1884, Pinkerton produced an output to rival Muddock's Dick Donovan.

He established the archetype of the extra-legal hero in a lawless world, and used a style of dispassionate descriptions and short sentences that echo down through Philip Marlowe and Sam Spade to

James Elmore. It is no coincidence that Dashiell Hammett was an ex-Pinkerton man. Nothing notable happened in American detective-story fiction between Edgar Allen Poe and the end of Victoria's century (except perhaps, the works of Anna Katharine Green) and Pinkerton's memoirs dominate. Closer to the zeitgeist of the contemporary America than Poe ever was, Pinkerton alludes slightingly to novels and stage plays featuring detectives. By the time the classic dime-novels appeared, chronicling the 'cases' of Nick Carter, Old Sleuth, King Brady and their ilk, Pinkerton was at the end of his life. Needless to say, he never heard of Dick Donovan or his follower in popularity, Sherlock Holmes. But he had certainly read the first true English detective story, the exploits of Inspector Bucket in Dickens's *Bleak House*.

The books (see page xx) were ostensibly based on his and his agents' exploits, and some were published, possibly even written, after his death. On the other hand, Allan Pinkerton was a meticulous administrator. If anyone had written his later books, an accounting entry would exist that showed payment for such a service. None has come to light.

Far from being any sort of literary pursuit, they were entirely intended to promote his detective agency and at least some of them must have been produced by hired ghost writers. Pinkerton joined a long and honourable tradition—Homer did PR for the Mycenaeans; Shakespeare did PR for the Tudors; and Thackeray did PR for a Mediterranean cruise company. At least Allan Pinkerton was doing it on his own behoof, and for no-one's coin but his own, considerable though that was.

No one in their right mind thinks that Leslie Charteris wrote all the *Saint* books or doubts that Sexton Blake, Dixon Hawke and the rest of that multi-serialed crew were the effusion of many a pen, and Tom Clancy doesn't even pretend any more, so why not the 'Pinkerton' *oeuvres*? Nonetheless, the books published under his name doubtless reflect his thoughts and values. They are also in part a chronicle of the impact the Scots made on opening up the Big Country (and importing various criminal speciality acts in the process).

Meanwhile, Pinkerton's agents were developing a reputation for heavy-handed anti-labour involvement. This tarnished the high moral image of Pinkerton's Detective Agency for years afterwards. They went from being the ones who 'always got their man' to being seen as a right-wing, Tong-like arm of big business and against the freedom of the honest workers and their right to organise. So where did his own political sympathies lie? His early life would suggest dissent, with left-liberal and free-thinking icing on the wha's-like-us Scottish black bun. Union and anti-slavery sympathies during the American Civil War also indicate a libertarian persuasion (but let's not forget that the South was Democrat and Lincoln was a Republican). Later business activities point towards a predilection for market mega-capitalism, with tinges of anti-Irish, anti-Jewish, anti-ne'er-do-well, anti-minority and anti-communist (as it would later be called) sentiment. Like his countrymen Adam Smith and John Muir, Pinkerton can be read both ways, and is frequently recruited to the cause of either side who, in the interest of reinforcing their own prejudices, can read him selectively and with the reassuring bias of certainty at a distance. In fine, Pinkertson was a classic Presbyterian utilitarian—we might be poor, but by God, we're miserable. To be fair, Pinkerton himself admits to enjoying a good whisky and a cigar, although gambling was a life-long abhorrence.

Perhaps Pinkerton had come full circle from Glasgow radical suffragist to friend of the capitalist bosses. Whatever the truth of that, his agency was certainly involved in strike-breaking and other anti-labour activities during the late-nineteenth and early-twentieth centuries, including: the Pullman Strike (1894); the Wild Bunch Gang (1896); the Ludlow Massacre (1914); the La Follette Committee (1933-37). A once-popular song went:

> 'Hear the poor orphans tell their sad story
> Father was killed by the Pinkerton men.'

All of this was after his death. During life, though, the Pinkerton detectives protected replacement workers and property of that other famous alleged strike-breaker and fellow-Scot, Andrew Carnegie. Pinkerton's personal involvement in it may have been minimal, but probably reflected his philosophy (his 1878 title *Strikers, Communists, Tramps and Detectives* is a bit of a give-away). Frankly, Pinkerton himself had often been guilty of less than fastidious tactics. When his agents, in pursuit of Jesse James, firebombed his mother's house, the explosion, as we have heard, blew off one of her arms and killed a child.

In his extremely popular *The Molly Maguires and the Detectives* (1877), Pinkerton gave a book-length account of his agency's work against the semi-secret and somewhat sinister group of Irish coal miners organisation in Philadelphia, mainly drawn from agent James McParlan's clandestine activities. The protagonist comes over as almost selling his soul to get the job done, and Pinkerton tells us that the private detective should become 'one of the order, and continue so while he remains in the case before us. He should be hardy, tough, and capable of labouring, in season and out of season, to accomplish, unknown to those about him, a single absorbing object.' Commitment to the task was clearly a prerequisite in his eyes, and as the writings in this book show, he applied that ethic to himself just as much as he required it of his agents.

Pinkerton died in Chicago, Illinois on 1 July, 1884 at the grand not-too-old age of almost sixty-five, and was buried in Graceland Cemetery, Chicago. In the way of these things, he had developed an infection after biting his tongue when he slipped on a sidewalk. (Twenty-seven years later Jack Daniels, the whiskey magnate, would die from septicaemia after he broke a toe from kicking his safe in anger. I don't know why both of these tragedies are funny; they just are.) At the time of Pinkerton's death, he was busy developing a system to centralise all criminal identification records, the precursor of the database now maintained by the Federal Bureau of Investigation.

In 2000, the Pinkerton National Detective Agency celebrated one-hundred and fifty years of service (now as Securitas) and to mark the anniversary, donated a huge archive to the Smithsonian Institute in Washington, DC. This included, a press release rather breathlessly tells us, 'photographs, drawings and documents on Jesse James, the Hole-in-the-Wall Gang, the Missouri Kid and Butch Cassidy. The archives document the history of the nation's early law enforcement.'

Allan Pinkerton became a member of the Military Intelligence Hall of Fame. As with Bentham, his fellow utilitarian, he should have been stuffed and mounted, and a suitable place for his mummy would be in the front hall of the FBI building in Washington. Here he could remind the cuckoo-children of J. Edgar Hoover that their country was hard won, carved from lawless, raw geography and unbridled opportunity, yet not at the expense of civil liberties, whatever today's Patriot Act might be assumed to say. The South eventually won the American Civil War, extracting out of the North, by way of reparations, everything they had wanted in the first place. The Irish, the Jews, the Africans and the Hispanics came to dominate America. Big business lost out to worker power.

If Pinkerton had only set up his detective agency and laid the groundwork for all sorts of police and surveillance procedures that came after, his place is history would be assured; but his literary legacy is also crucial. Pinkerton leaves us one man's impression of a country at its birth, the taming of the Wild West, great cities emerging from a collection of frontier shacks. Pinkerton's America is a society busy painting nineteenth-century European ways onto a new and largely blank canvas. In the same way, Pinkerton wasn't constrained by existing literary mores, and found a new voice that ranks in importance with Poe, Twain and Ned Buntline. We could, in an idle moment, debate how deeply Pinkerton's work influenced the growing dime novel market, between Harlan Halsey's 'Old Sleuth' going strong from 1872 and Nick Carter starting his adventures in 1886, after Pinkerton's death. We could muse on the idea that Pinkerton was writing at exactly the right time—dime novel and detective magazine sales slumped in the late 1890s as motion pictures emerged, and the new genre of pulp fiction adventure stories was targeted specifically at adult readers. And we could also discuss whether the pieces in this book were written with business promotion rather than public entertainment in mind.

Either way, Pinkerton's stories laid the foundations in America for one of the defining literary genres of the early twentieth century, and every Sam Spade, Philip Marlowe and Race Williams that followed.

Here's looking at you, kid.

Note: These stories have been edited. Typographical mistakes have been corrected. British spellings and modern punctuation have been adopted.

⊰ A Partial Bibliography ⊱

History and Evidence of the Passage of Abraham Lincoln from Harrisburg, Pa., to Washington, DC, on the Twenty-second and Twenty-third of February, 1861 1868

The Expressman and the Detective 1874

Claude Melnotte as a Detective and Other Stories 1875

The Detective and the Somnambulist; The Murderer and the Fortune Teller 1875

The Model Town and the Detectives: Byron as a Detective 1876

The Mollie Maguires and the Detectives 1877

The Spiritualists and the Detectives 1877

Mississippi Outlaws and the Detectives 1878

Strikers, Communists, Tramps and Detectives 1878

The Gypsies and the Detectives 1878

Bucholz and the Detectives 1878

Criminal Reminiscences and Detective Sketches 1879

Mississippi Outlaws and the Detectives; Don Pedro and the Detectives; Poisoner and the Detectives 1879

Bank-Robbers and the Detectives 1881

Professional Thieves and the Detectives 1881

The Spy of the Rebellion 1883

The Rail-Road Forger and the Detectives 1883

The Burglar's Fate and the Detectives 1884

The Spy of the Rebellion 1884

Thirty Years a Detective (memoir) 1884

Published Posthumously

A Double Life and the Detectives 1885

A Life for a Life; or, The Detective's Triumph 1886

Cornered at Last: A Detective Story 1892

This piece, the first account by Pinkerton of his earliest commissioned case, takes place in 1847 but was published three decades later. It is worth bearing in kind that the relative value of the dollar between then and now is such that someone carrying around $2,000 then would have to carry $40,000 or $50,000 now, and it was worth ten times that much in terms of the average unskilled wage.

⊰ How I Became a Detective ⊱

On the romantic Fox River—called the Pish-ta-ka in the original Potawatamie language—and about thirty-eight miles northwest of the city of Chicago, is located the beautiful village of Dundee. It has probably at this writing a population of three thousand inhabitants and is one of the brightest and most prosperous towns of Illinois.

The town was originally settled by a few sturdy people, the hardy Scotch, as its name would indicate, as also that of the splendid little city of Elgin, but five miles distant, and who occupied to some extent the outlying farms, so that the place and community, while never accomplishing anything remarkable in a business way, has had a steady, quiet growth, has lived its life uninterruptedly and peacefully, and possesses the pleasantest evidences of steady prosperity and constant, quiet happiness.

If this would be easily observed by the visitor, its beautiful location would attract still greater attention.

Before you, looking up-stream, you would see at your feet the rapid river which has just leaped the great dam from which the mills and manufactories are fed, and, above this, stretching and winding away into the distance like a ribbon of burnished silver, it would still be seen, gliding, along peacefully with a fair, smooth bosom, wimpling fretfully over stony shallows, or playing at hide-and-seek among the verdure covered islands, until the last thread-like trail of it is lost in the gorges beyond. To the right, just beyond the little basin which holds

1

its part of the village, rise huge hills from which here and there issue forth beautiful springs, while now and then a fine roadway, hewn out between, leads to the Indian Mounds and the splendid farms beyond. To the left, over the opposite portion of the village, the eye ranges over a succession of elevations dotted with handsome residences and embowered by gardens, with the hills and the uplands beyond, as well as the highway, or 'river road', threading along in and out of sight among the tree covered bluffs; while, facing about, you will see the river moving peacefully along, until lost in the valleys and their forests below.

The town rests there on the banks of this beautiful stream, and between the guardian hills upon either side, like twin nests where there is always song and gladness.

In the time of which I write, however, all this was different; that is, the town was different. The river ran down like a silvery ribbon from among the islands just the same; the splendid hills were all there crowned with fine forests as they are now; but the town itself did not contain probably over three hundred inhabitants all told, the business portion only consisting of a few country stores, a post office, a blacksmith, a shop or two, a mill, and two small taverns able to accommodate a few travellers at a time, but chiefly depending for their support upon the custom of the farmers who straggled into the village on rainy days, 'election time' or any other of the hundred and one occasions which mark out events in the lives of back-country people.

There was then one rough bridge across the river, built of oaken beams and rude planks in a cheap, common fashion; and at either end of this were clustered, each side of the street, all the stores and shops of the place, save one.

That shop was my own; for there I both lived and laboured, the 'Only and Original Cooper of Dundee'.

This shop was the farthest of any from the business centre of the village, and stood just back of, and facing, the main highway upon the crest of a fine hill, about three hundred yards distant from the bridge. It was my home and my shop.

I had straggled out here a few years before, and by industry and saving had gradually worked into a comfortable business at my cooper's trade, and now employed eight men. I felt proud of my success

2

because I owed no man, had a cheery little home, and, for the early days when it was pretty hard to get along at all, I was making a comfortable living.

My cooper-shop and house were one building—a long, one-story frame building with a pleasant garden about, some fine old trees near, and always stacks of staves and hoop-poles quite handy. At one end we lived, in a frugal, but always cheery way, and at the other was the shop, where, as nearly all my hands were German, could be heard the livelong day the whistled waltz, or the tightly-sung ballad, now in solo, now in chorus, but always in true time with the hammering of the adz and the echoing thuds of the 'driver' upon the hoops as they were driven to their places.

This was my quiet, but altogether happy, mode of life in the beautiful village of Dundee, in the summer of 1847, at which time my story really begins; but, to give the reader a better understanding of it, I will have to further explain the existing condition of things at that time.

There was but little money in the West, which was then sparsely settled. There being really no markets, and the communication with eastern cities very limited, the producer could get but little for his crops or wares. I have known farmers in these times 'hauling', as it was called, wheat into Chicago for a distance of nearly one hundred miles, from two to five streams having to be forded, and the wheat having to be carried across, every bag of it, upon the farmer's back, and he not then able to get but three shillings per bushel for his grain, being compelled to take half payment for it in 'truck', as store goods were then called.

There was plenty of dickering, but no money. Necessity compelled an interchange of products. My barrels would be sold to the farmers or merchants for produce, and this I would be compelled to send in to Chicago, to in turn secure as best I could a few dollars perhaps, and anything and everything I could use, or again trade away. Not only did this great drawback on business exist, but what money we had was of a very inferior character. If one sold a load of produce and was fortunate enough to secure the entire pay for it in money, before he got home the bank might have failed and the paper he held have become utterly worthless. All of these things in time brought about a most imperative need for good money and plenty of it, which had been met some years before where my story begins, by several capitalists of Aberdeen, Scotland, placing in the hands of George Smith, Esq., also an Aberdonian, sufficient funds to found a bank in the Great West.

Milwaukee, then a city of equal importance with Chicago, was chosen as the point, and the Wisconsin Legislature, in 1839, granted a charter to the institution, which was known as The Wisconsin Marine and Fire Insurance Company, which, in its charter, also secured banking privileges.

But a few years had elapsed before the bills of this institution gained a very wide circulation throughout the Northwest. Branch agencies were established at Chicago and various points in the West, as also an agency for the redemption of the bills at Buffalo; and at the time of which I write, Chicago, having taken rapid strides to the front, had in reality become the central office, although the Wisconsin organisation and Milwaukee headquarter were still retained.

Many reasons obtained to cause these bills—which were of the denominations of one, two, three, five, and ten—to be eagerly sought for. The company were known to have large and always available capital at command; its bills were always redeemable in specie; and with the personal character of George Smith, who stood at the head of the concern, there was created an almost unequalled public confidence in it and its management. In fact, the bills soon became known far and wide as 'George Smith's money', and 'as good as the wheat', the farmers would say.

Smith himself was a Scotchman of very decided and even erratic character; and the old settlers of Chicago and the West have many an interesting incident to relate of his financial career. One, serving for many, to give an idea of the peculiarities of the man, and showing how he gained a great reputation in those times and that section, is as follows:

The almost immediate popularity of 'George Smith's money' caused considerable envious feeling; and the officers of several other western banking institutions sought as far as possible by various means to prevent the encroachment upon their business.

At one time a small bank near the central part of Illinois, in order to assist in the depreciation of this particular money, began the policy of refusing to receive the Wisconsin Marine and Fire Insurance Company's bills at par, which for a time caused in certain sections considerable uneasiness among the holders of those bills.

The quiet Scotchman in Chicago said never a word to this for some time, but at once began gathering together every bill of this bank he could secure. This was continued for several weeks, when he suddenly set out alone and unattended for Central Illinois, being roughly dressed and very unpretentious in appearance.

Reaching the place and staggering into the bank, he awkwardly presented one hundred dollars in the Fire and Marine bills, requesting exchange on Buffalo for a like sum.

The cashier eyed him a moment and then remarked sneeringly:

'We don't take that stuff at par.'

'Ah! ye dinna tak it, then?'

'No,' replied the cashier; '"George Smith's Money" is depreciating rapidly.'

'Then it's gaun down fast, is it?' responded Smith, reflectively.

'Oh, yes; won't be worth fifty cents on a dollar in six months!'

'It'll be worth nae mair than fifty cents? An' may yours be worth a huner' cents on a dollar, noo?'

'Certainly, sir, always, If you should happen to have ten thousand dollars' worth about you at the present time', replied the cashier, as he gave the stranger another supercilious look, 'you could get the gold for it in less than ten seconds.'

'Then,' said the travel-stained banker, with a very ugly look in his face, as he crashed down a great package upon the counter containing twenty-five thousand dollars in the bills of the opposition bank, 'Mister George Smith presents his best respects tae ye, and would be obleeged tae ye if ye wad gie him the specie for this'. This shrewd stroke of business policy had its legitimate effect. The bank in question could not instantly redeem so large a sum, and opposition of an unfair character in that and other directions, through the notoriety given this practical humiliation, was effectually ended.

In countless other ways this early Western financier established credit and compelled respect, until, as I have said, 'George Smith's money' was as good as the gold throughout the entire western country, and this fact, in time, caused it to be taken in hand by eastern counterfeiters.

This brings me again to the main part of my story.

Just afternoon of a hot July day in the year mentioned, a gentleman named H. E. Hunt, then keeping a small general store in, and now a wealthy merchant at Dundee, sent word to my shop that he wished to see me immediately at his place. I was busy at my work, bareheaded, barefooted, and having no other clothing on my body than a pair of blue denim overalls and a coarse hickory shirt, my then almost invariable costume; but I started down the street at once, and had hardly reached Hunt's store before the proprietor and myself were joined by a Mr. I. C. Bosworth, then another storekeeper of the village and now a retired capitalist of Elgin, Illinois, the place previously referred to.

'Come in here, Allan,' said Mr. Hunt in a rather mysterious manner, leading the way to the rear of the store, while Bosworth and myself followed; 'we want you to do a little job in the detective line'.

'Detective line!' I replied, laughing; 'why, my line is the cooper business. What do I know about that sort of thing?'

'Never mind now,' said Mr. Bosworth, seriously, 'we know you can do what you want done. You helped break up the 'coney men' and horse-thieves on 'Bogus Island' and we are sure you can do work of this sort if you only will do it.'

Now the reference to breaking up the gang of 'coney men' and horse-thieves on 'Bogus Island' calls for an explanation.

I was actually too poor to purchase outright a wheel-barrow-load of hoop-poles, or staves, and was consequently compelled to cut my own hoop poles and split my own staves. In the pursuit of this work I had found a little island in the Fox River, a few miles above Dundee, and but a few rods above the little post-town of Algonquin, where poles were both plentiful and of the best quality and one day while busy there I had stumbled upon some smouldering embers and other traces indicating that the little island had been made quite common use of. There was no picnicking in those days—people had more serious matters to attend to—and it required no great keenness to conclude that no honest men were in the habit of occupying the place. As the country was then infested with coin-counterfeiters and desperate horse-thieves, from the information I gave, the sheriff of that county (Kane) was able to trace the outlaws to this island, where subsequently I led the officers who captured the entire gang, consisting of men and women, securing their implements and a large amount of bogus coin; while, in honour of the event, the island ever since has been known as 'Bogus Island'.

Upon this faint record Messrs. Hunt and Bosworth based my claim to detective skill, and insisted on my winning new laurels, or at least attempting to do so.

'But what is it you wish done?' I asked, very much preferring to return to the shop, where my men and their work needed my attention.

Mr. Hunt then explained that they were certain that there was then a counterfeiter in the village. They both felt sure he was one, although they had no other evidence save that the party in question had been making inquiries as to the whereabouts of 'Old man Crane'.

Old man Crane was a person who from general reputation I knew well. He lived at Libertyville, in the adjoining county of Lake, not more than thirty-five miles distant, bore a hard character generally, and it was suspected that he was engaged in distributing for eastern counterfeiters their worthless money. Nearly every blackleg that came into the community invariably inquired for 'Old man Crane', and this fact alone caused the villagers to give him a wide berth. Besides this fact, but recently counterfeits on the ten-dollar bill of the Wisconsin Marine and Fire Insurance Company's bank had made their appearance, and were so well executed as to cause serious trouble to farmers and country dealers. Pretty positive proof had come to light that Crane had had a hand in the business; and the fact that a respectable appearing man, a stranger well mounted

7

and altogether mysterious, and also well supplied with money, had suddenly shown himself in the village, to begin quietly but searchingly making inquiries for 'Old man Crane', seemed to the minds of my friends to be the best of evidence that the stranger was none other than the veritable counterfeiter who was supplying such old reprobates as Crane with the spurious ten-dollar bills on George Smith's bank.

But this was curious business for me, I thought, as protesting against leaving my work for a will-'o-the-wisp piece of business, which, even should it happen to prove successful, would pay me nothing, I said: 'Now, see here, what do I know about counterfeiting?'

'Oh, we know you know enough about it!' they both urged anxiously.

'Why,' said I, laughing at the absurdity of the idea of turning detective, 'I never saw a ten-dollar bill in my life!'

And neither had I. There I stood, a young, strong, agile, hardworking cooper, not exactly green, perhaps—for I consider no man verdant who does well whatever he may have in hand—barefooted, bareheaded, dressed, or rather, almost undressed, in my hickory and denims, daring enough and ready for any reckless emergency which might transpire in the living of an honest life, but decidedly averse to doing something entirely out of my line, and which in all human probability I would make an utter failure of. I had not been but four years in America altogether. I had had a hard time of it for the time I had been here. I had heard of all these things I have mentioned concerning banks and money, but I had positively never seen a ten-dollar bill!

A great detective I would make under such circumstances, I thought.

'Come now, Allan,' urged Mr. Hunt, 'no time is to be wasted. The man is down there now at Eaton Walker's harness-shop, getting something done about his saddle.'

'But what am I to do?' I asked.

'Do? Well! Do the best you can!'

I suddenly resolved to do just that and no less; although I must confess that, at that time, I had not the remotest idea how to set about the matter.

So I began by strolling leisurely about the street for a few minutes, and then, villager like, sauntered into the saddlery shop.

Eaton Walker, a jolly, whole-souled, good-hearted fellow, was perched upon his bench, sewing away, and when I entered merely looked up from his waxed end and nodded, but made no remark, as my being in his place was a very common occurrence.

There was the usual quota of town stragglers loafing about the shop, and looking with sleepy eyes and open-mouthed at the little which was going on about the place.

I passed, as I entered the shop, a splendid horse hitched outside. It was a fine, large roan, well built for travelling; and in my then frame of mind I imagined from a casual glance that it was a horse especially selected for its lasting qualities, should an emergency require them to be put to a test. The owner of the animal, the person who had caused so much nervousness on the part of Messrs. Hunt and Bosworth, was a man nearly six feet in height, weighed fully two hundred pounds, was at least sixty five years of age, and was very erect and commanding in his appearance. I noticed all this at a careless glance, as also that his hair was dark, though slightly tinged with gray, and his features very prominent. His nose was very large, his mouth unusually so, and he had a pair of the keenest, coldest small gray eyes I have ever seen, while he wore a large, plain gold ring on one of the fingers of his left hand.

I made no remark to him or to any person about the place, and merely assumed for the time being to act a village loafer myself. But I noticed, without showing the fact, that the man occasionally gave me a keen and searching glance. When the work had been completed by Walker, I stepped outside and made a pretence of being interested, as any country gawky might, in the preparations for the man's departure; and was patting the horse's neck and withers as the stranger came out with the saddle and began adjusting it, when I carelessly assisted him in a free-and-easy country way.

There were, of course, a number of people standing about and a good deal of senseless chatting going on, which the stranger wholly refrained from joining in; but while we were both at work at the saddle, he said, without addressing me, but in a way which I knew was meant for my ears: 'Stranger, do you know where old man Crane lives?'

I took my cue from the manner in which this was said, and followed it to the best of my ability. I was now as certain as either of my friends that the man was a blackleg of a dangerous order, whatever his special line of roguery might be. We were both busy at the saddle on the side of the horse where there were the fewer loungers, and being close together, I replied in the same tone of voice: 'Cross the river to the east, take the main road up through the woods until you come to Jesse Miller's farm house. Then he will tell you; but if you don't want to ask'—and I put considerable meaning into this—'hold the road to the northeast and inquire the direction to Libertyville. When you get there you will easily find the old man, and he is as good as cheese!'

He then said in the same cautious voice as before:

'Young man, I like your style, and I want to know you better. Join me over the river in some ravine. I want to talk to you.'

'All right,' I rejoined, 'but you better let me go ahead. I'll have to go up to the shop first and put on my boots and hat. I'll be as quick as I can, and will start on first. Then you follow on, but not too closely. I'll be up in some of the gorges, so we can talk entirely by ourselves. But I'll tell you the truth, stranger', said I, rather indifferently, 'upon my word, I don't care very much about going, because I've already lost too much time at the shop to day.'

He had by this time finished saddling his horse, but he continued adjusting and readjusting things so as to gain time to say what he wished; and to my intimation that I cared very little about leaving my work, he responded:

'Don't fail to join me. I'll make it worth something to you!' He then added flatteringly: 'You're as good a man as I've met lately.'

I then moved forward to fasten the reins, and he edged along towards me, asking carelessly: 'Do you know John Smith of Elgin?'

'I know all the Elgin John Smiths,' I replied. 'Do you mean the gunsmith?'

'Yes', he answered tersely.

'Well, I know John,' I continued, 'that is, he has repaired my gun and shotgun several times; but he might not remember me. I never had much talk with him.'

'He's a square man,' replied the stranger. 'I'm his uncle. I came up from Elgin this morning. Smith didn't know just where Crane lived. He told me that he traded here and that the boys were over here a good deal, so that I would be likely to find somebody here who could readily direct me to his place.'

'Well,' I said rather curtly, 'we've talked too much already. It won't do. I'll join you over the river soon.' With this I carelessly walked away towards my shop, and at some little distance turned to see the stranger now engaging Eaton Walker in conversation with an evident purpose of gaining time.

'Well,' I thought, as I hastened on, 'there's no doubt now. This man is certainly a counterfeiter. John Smith is always loaded down with it. He gets it from old Crane; and this man at Walker's is the chief of the gang travelling through the West to supply these precious rascals. But then,' it suddenly occurred to me, 'what business of mine is all this? Good gracious! I've got a lot of barrels to make, my men need attention, and everything is going to the old Harry while I am playing detective!'

But having got this far my will had been touched, and I resolved to carry the matter through, whatever might be the result. While putting on my hat and boots hastily, Hunt and Bosworth came in, and I quickly related what I had learned.

Looking down the hill, we could see the stranger slowly moving across the bridge, and as I was starting in the same direction my friends both urged:

'Now, Pinkerton, capture him sure!'

'Oh, yes,' I replied, 'but how am I to get at all this?'

'Why, just get his stock, or some of it, and then we'll have him arrested.'

'Oh, yes,' said I, 'but, by thunder! it takes money to buy money! I've got none!'

'Well, well, that's so,' remarked Mr. Hunt; 'we'll go right down to the store. You drop in there after us, and we'll give you fifty dollars.'

All this was speedily done, and I soon found myself over the bridge, past the horseman, and well up the hill upon the highway.

It was a well-travelled thoroughfare, in fact, the road leading from all that section of the country into Chicago; but it was in the midst of harvest-time, and everybody was busy upon the farms. Not a soul was to be seen upon the road, save the stranger and myself, and almost a Sabbath silence seemed to rest over the entire locality. The voices of the birds which filled the woods in every direction were hushed into a noon-day chirping, and hardly a sound was to be heard save the murmuring of the rills issuing from the sides of the hills and from every nook in the gorges and glens.

I confess that a sense of insignificance stole over me, originating doubtless from the reflection caused by this silence and almost painful quiet; and I could not but realise my unfitness for the work before me. There I was, hardly more than a plodding country cooper, having had but little experience save that given me by a life of toil in Scotland and my trip to this country, and no experience of things in this country save that secured through a few years of the hardest kind of hard work. For a moment I felt wholly unable to cope with this keen man of the world, but as I was gaining the top of the hill I glanced back over my shoulder, and noticing that the horseman was following my instructions to the letter, I reasoned that, from some cause, I had gained an influence over this stranger, or he thought he had secured such a one over me, as would enable me, by being cautious and discreet, to obtain a sufficiently close intimacy with him to cause the disclosure of his plans and possibly ultimately result in his capture.

I had now reached the top of the hill, and taking a position which would permit of my being seen by no person save the horseman, I waited until he had approached near enough for me to do so, when I signalled him to follow, and then struck into the woods over a narrow trail about two hundred yards to a beautiful little opening on the banks of a purling brook, leaping down the descent towards the river from a limpid spring a few feet above the spot I had chosen for the interview.

But a few moments elapsed before the stranger, dashing in over the trail in fine style, leaped from his horse with a good deal of dexterity for a man of his age, and carelessly flinging the bridle

rein over the limb of a small sapling, passed me with a smile of recognition, proceeded to the spring, where he took a long, deep draught,
and then returning to where I was seated upon the velvety greensward,
threw himself carelessly down upon the ground beside me.

There we two lay—the stranger with his keen, sharp eyes, and his
altogether careless, but always attentive manner, closely regarding me
and looking me over from toe to tip; while I assumed an equal care-
lessness, but was all intent on his every movement. I saw the handles
of two finely-mounted pistols protruding from his coat-pockets, and I
did not know what might happen. I was wholly unarmed, but I was
young, wiry, powerful and though I had nothing for self-protection
save my two big fists and my two stout arms, I was daring enough to
tackle a man or beast in self defence at a moment's warning.

After a moment's silence, he said:

'Well, stranger, I'm a man of business from the word "go". What's
your name and how long have you been about here?'

'My name's Pinkerton. I've been here three or four years, coopering some, and harvesting some; but coopering's my trade. You'd have
seen my shop if you had come up the hill. I manage to keep seven or
eight men going all the time. But times are fearfully hard. There's no
money to be had, and the fact is,' said I, looking at him knowingly,
'I would like to get hold of something better adapted to getting more
ready cash out of—especially if it was a good scheme—so good that
there was no danger in it. But what's your name and where did you
come from?' I asked abruptly.

He scarcely heeded this, and, Yankee-like, replied by asking where
I came from before locating in Illinois.

'From Scotland,' I replied, 'from Glasgow. I worked my way
through Canada and finally found myself here with just a quarter in
my pocket. What little I've got has been through hard work since.
But, my friend,' said I smiling, 'the talk is all on one side. I asked you
something about yourself.'

'Well,' he said, still looking at me as though he would read me
through and through, 'they call me "Old man Craig". My name is
Craig—John Craig, and I live down in Vermont, near Fairfield; got a
fine farm there. Smith, down here at Elgin, is a nephew of mine; and

old Crane, over at Libertyville, and myself, have done a good deal of business together.'

'Oh, yes,' said I nodding, 'I understand.'

'But, you see,' resumed the counterfeiter, 'this part of the country is all new to me. I've been to Crane's house before, but that was when I came up the lakes to Little Fort*, and when I got through with my visit there I always went into Chicago on the "lake road".'

'And of course you both stopped at the "Sauganash",' I said meaningly.

'Certainly we stopped there,' replied Craig musingly.

'I know that Foster's a man that can be depended on,' I remarked with considerable meaning upon the word 'know'.

'He's a square man, Foster is,' rejoined the counterfeiter; 'and, Pinkerton, I believe you're the right sort of a man too. I sold Foster a big pile the last time I was in Chicago.' And then quick as thought he said, looking me in the eyes: 'Did you ever "deal" any?'

'Yes, Mr. Craig,' I replied, 'but only when I could get a first-class article. I frequently "work off" the stuff in paying my men Saturday nights, when travelling through the country, and on the merchants here in Dundee, who have all confidence in me. But I wouldn't touch anything like it for the State of Illinois, unless it was as good in appearance as the genuine article. Have you something really good, now?' I concluded indifferently.

'I've got a "bang up" article,' said the stranger, quietly.

'But I don't know what you've got,' I persisted. 'I thought you were going over to old Crane's?'

'Well, so I was, Pinkerton; but I believe you're a good, square man, and I don't know but I had as soon sell to you as him.'

'I think you had better see Crane,' said I indifferently. 'He's probably expecting you, and as it's afternoon now, it would be a good idea for you to make the best time you can there'.

'How far is it?' he asked.

'Oh, thirty-five miles or thereabouts, and as you've got a good horse, you can make it by dark or before.'

* *The city of Waukegan, in Lake County, Illinois, was called 'Little Fort' by the early settlers.*

He rose as if undecided what to do, and without making any further remark at the time, took his horse to the spring and watered it.

He then returned, and again throwing himself down beside me, remarked carelessly:

'But I haven't yet showed you what I've got. Here are the "beauties",' and he whipped out two ten dollar bills, counterfeits on the Wisconsin Marine and Fire Insurance Company's money.

I looked at them very, very wisely. As I have already said; I had never seen a ten-dollar bill in my life; but I examined them as critically as though I had assisted in making the genuine bills, and after a little expressed myself as very much pleased with them.

They were indeed 'beauties', as the old rascal had said, and in all my subsequent detective experience I have hardly seen their equal in point of execution and general appearance. There was not a flaw in them. To show how nearly perfect they had been made, it is only necessary to state that it was subsequently learned that several thousand dollars in these spurious bills had been received unhesitatingly at the bank and its different agencies, and actually paid out and received the second time, without detection

'Come now, Pinkerton, I'll tell you what I'll do,' continued Craig earnestly; 'if you'll take enough of this I'll give you the entire field out here. The fact is Crane's getting old; he isn't as active as he used to be; he's careless also, and, besides all this, he's too well known'.

'Well,' said I thoughtfully, 'how much would I have to take?'

'Only five hundred or a thousand,' he replied airily.

'On what terms?' I asked.

'Twenty-five per cent, cash.'

'I cannot possibly do it now,' I replied, as though there was no use of any further conference. 'I haven't anywhere near the amount necessary with me. I want to do it like thunder, but when a man can't do a thing he can't, and that's all there is about it.'

'Not so fast, my man; not so fast,' answered the old rogue reassuringly. 'Now, you say these lubber heads of merchants down at the village trust you?'

'Yes, for anything.'

'Then can't you make a raise from them somehow? You'll never get such another chance to do business with a square man in your
life; and you can make more money with this in one year than any one
of them can in ten. Now, what can you do, Pinkerton?'

I assumed to be studying the matter over very deeply, but, in reality, I had already decided to do as the man wished; for I knew that
Messrs Hunt and Bosworth would be only too glad to have the matter
followed up so closely. Finally I said: 'I'll do it, Craig; but it won't
answer for you to be seen hanging about here. Where shall we meet,
and when?'

'Easy enough,' said he, grasping my hand warmly. 'I won't go
over to old Crane's at all. If he wants any of the stuff after this, he'll
have to come to you. I only let Smith have about one hundred dollars
in the bills, and that out of mere friendship, you know. When he wants
more, I'll make him come to you too. Now, I'll go right back down
there, and you can meet me at Smith's this evening.'

'Oh, no; no you don't, Craig!' I answered with an appearance of
deep cunning. 'I'm willing to take the whole business into my hands,
but I don't propose to have every Tom, Dick and Harry understand
all about the business from the beginning. I'll find my own customers,'
I concluded, with a protesting shake of my head.

'Well, that's best. You're right and I'm wrong. Where'll we meet?'
he asked.

'I've a capital place,' I replied. 'Do you know where the unfin-
ished Baptist Church and University are, down at Elgin?'

'Let me see,' he said, smiling. 'I ought to know. I'm a splendid
Baptist when I'm in Vermont—one of the deacons, as sure as you
live! Are they up on the hill?''

''Yes, the same,' I answered. 'It's a lonesome enough place to not
be likely to meet anybody there; and we can arrange everything in the
basement.'

'All right,' he acceded, laughing heartily, 'and the first time I write
my wife, damn me if I don't tell her that I dedicated the new Baptist
Church in Elgin, Illinois!'

I joined in this little moment at the expense of the Elgin Baptist
Church; and then Craig, who had begun to feel very cheerful and

friendly, went into quite a lengthy account of himself and his mode of operations.

As before stated, he said that he was located in Fairfield, Vermont. This location was chosen from the ready facility it offered for getting into Canada, should danger at any time present itself. He owned a large and fine place, and was legitimately engaged in farming, was wealthy, and had been a counterfeiter for many years, keeping two first-class engravers constantly employed, and he warmly invited me to visit him, should I ever happen that way, although it was morally certain at that time, to him as well as myself, that it would be a very long time before I began travelling for pleasure, and I received all this for what it was worth, but fervently promised him a call while mentally observing: 'Ah! my man, if everything works right, maybe that the call will come sooner than you are expecting it!'

What chiefly interested me, however, was what he told me concerning his mode of operations.

He said that he never carried any quantity of counterfeit money upon his person. This twenty dollars which he had shown me was the largest sum he ever had about him. This was simply and only a sample for use, as it had been with me. Should he be arrested not one piece of paper would be found which would not bear the most rigid inspection, although he had always upon his person about two thousand dollars in genuine money, chiefly in eastern bank bills. No person, understanding the condition of things at that time, could be persuaded to condemn a stranger in a new country and unfamiliar with its money, for having twenty dollars of spurious money in so large a sum as two thousand dollars.

I asked him why he did not pad his saddle with the bills and carry them with him, in this manner, for convenience. I made this inquiry, more than anything else, to draw from Craig his manner of supplying parties, and I was successful, for he immediately replied :

'No, that wouldn't do. To begin with, the horse would sweat the pad and badly discolour the bills, and, in the next place, somebody might be as curious as yourself, and rip open the saddle. Oh, no, no; I've got a better scheme than that. I've got a fellow, named Yelverson, as true as steel and as shrewd as a man can be made. He follows me like a shadow, but you will never see him. He is never seen by any living person with whom I have business. I simply show my samples and make the trade. I receive the money agreed upon from the buyer, and then tell him that I think he will find the specified sum in my money in a certain place at a designated time.

'He goes there, and never fails to find the bills. But Yelverson is not seen in the transaction, and, in the meantime, I have hidden my samples, as well as the money received by me, which might be marked, so that if there should be any treachery, nothing could be proven against me. I have a good deal of Canada trade, and it is all effected in this manner. Old John Craig is never caught napping, young man!'

The last remark was evidently made by the counterfeiter to give me to understand that though he had given me, or pretended to give me, very freely, his valuable confidence, that he was not a man to be trifled with in any particular, and I fully believed this of the man already.

I was satisfied that he had a good deal of the honour which is so frequently referred to as existing between thieves. There is no doubt but that this man always kept his word. In that sense he was honourable. This kind of honour was a necessity to his nefarious business, however, and I fail to perceive, as many sentimentalists do, where the criminal deserves the credit for being honourable when that peculiar quality is only used for the worst purposes, and is as much required by the criminal as the bread he eats.

It was now fully half-past one o'clock, and I suggested to the counterfeiter that we conclude our interview, as some stragglers might happen that way.

'You will be on hand, Pinkerton?' asked Craig as he rose from the grass.

'There's my hand on it,' said I quietly.

'And you'll bring enough money to take five hundred?'

'I'm certain I can raise that much,' I replied. 'But see here. Don't you come down through the village again. It will cause talk, and couple you with myself in the village gossip in a way that won't do for me at all.'

He agreed with me in this, and I then directed him to take what was called the 'upper road', past General McClare's old place, and having got this well fixed in his mind, agreed to meet him at the designated place in Elgin, at about four o'clock, bade him good-by and took my departure.

I hastened towards the village, and saw on my way, just as I was descending the brow of the hill, my counterfeiter friend well along the upper road, halting his horse to wave me a good-luck, or good-by, as it might be taken, to which I merely nodded a reply, and then made all possible speed to Mr. Hunt's store, where I quickly reported the result of my interview to Messrs. Hunt and Bosworth.

They were very gleeful over my success in working into the confidence of the counterfeiter, but both were rather apprehensive that the money was in the man's saddle, that Yelverson was a myth, and that possibly we had lost an opportunity of securing either. But I felt pretty certain that Craig would be on hand at Elgin according to appointment, and securing the required amount of money, one hundred and twenty-five dollars, and a bite of lunch, I set out on foot for Elgin. The place was only about five miles from Dundee, and five miles for me then was as nothing; so that, a few minutes before four, I was within the deserted structure.

I looked into every conceivable corner and cranny, but could discover the counterfeiter nowhere.

I passed outside and looked in every direction, but still he was not to be seen. Tired and worried about the whole matter, I retired within the basement, and had been sitting upon one of the loose timbers there but a few minutes, brooding over the loss of my day's work, and disgusted with the whole business, when Craig suddenly entered and smilingly greeted me.

'Why, helloa, Pinkerton, you're ahead of time.'

'I told you I would be here,' I replied.

'Well, did you bring the money with you?'

'Certainly I did. Here it is,' said I, counting out one hundred and twenty-five dollars as carelessly as though accustomed to handling comfortable sums of money.

He looked it over more carefully than suited me exactly. The act seemed to hold a faint trace of suspicion, but he found it to be in eastern bills and correct in every particular.

'Coopering must be pretty profitable work?' he remarked with a light laugh.

'Oh, fair, fair,' I answered, indifferently. 'Does pretty well when one can do some other quiet business along with it.'

'Oh, I see,' he said pleasantly. 'Now, Pinkerton, you go outside for a few minutes, and keep a sharp look out, lest somebody may be watching. Remain outside four or five minutes, and if you see no one by that time, come back.'

I went out as directed, but I could not but feel that I had placed myself in the man's power completely, as far as giving him a fair opportunity to abscond with my friends' money was concerned, and though a new hand at this kind of bellows, I determined to be as keen as he was shrewd. So, instead of leaving the building altogether, for the time mentioned, I started off for a little distance and, quickly returning up through a small ravine, took a position near an open window, just in time to observe my Baptist friend from Vermont placing something beneath a wide, flat building-stone in one corner of that portion of the basement where we had been together.

This much seen, I got away from the place as speedily as I could, and at once sought a small eminence near the building, and made a great pretence of keeping a close watch on the locality.

While thus occupied, I observed, out of the corner of my eye, that Craig had appeared at one of the entrances and was closely watching my movements. Apparently satisfied at last, he gave a low whistle, attracting my attention, of course, when he then motioned me to join him.

As I entered I told him that I had looked everywhere, but was unable to see any person about.

'That's all right,' he replied pleasantly, and then looking at me in a quizzical sort of a way, asked: 'Pinkerton, what would you think if I told you that Yelverson had been here during your absence outside, and left the five hundred in my bills?'

'Well, I don't know,' I answered. 'I'd almost think you'd got old Nick working along with you!'

'Perhaps I have, perhaps I have,' he returned quietly. 'Look under that stone over yonder.'

I went to the place indicated and, lifting the stone which from the outside I had seen him busied with, I picked up a neatly-made package.

'I think you will find what you bought inside it,' remarked Craig.

I opened the package, and found that it contained fifty ten dollar bills. They were the counterfeits but, as I have already stated, were most handsomely executed.

I make this open confession to my readers:

For a moment the greatest temptation of my life swept over me. A thousand thoughts of sudden wealth and a life free from the grinding labour which I had always known, came rushing into my mind. Here in my hands were five hundred dollars, or what professed to be, every one of them as good as gold, if I only chose to use it. The purchasing power of five hundred dollars then, the use which could be made of it, the large gain which would accrue from its judicious investment, were one and all ten times what they are now. What would it not purchase? Why, to my mind then it was a great fortune!

All this and more pressed upon me with such weight—the first and last time in my whole life—that with this struggle in my memory, while I have always been unshaken in my determination to never lose sight of a criminal when it once becomes my duty to pursue him, I can never think of one undergoing the first great temptation to crime whether he has resisted or fallen, without a touch of genuine human sympathy.

I am satisfied that this showed in my face somewhat, but was taken by him to indicate cupidity and eagerness at the prospect of large profits as his 'wholesale agent' in that section, and soon after probably stood me in good service.

We sat down upon one of timbers and chatted pleasantly for a time, during which he informed me that Yelverson had at once returned to Smith's, where his horse was stabled, and ere then was on his road toward Chicago, where he, Craig, should rejoin him on the next day, after passing the night at his nephew's.

My thought was to get the two together and nab them both, if it were in my power. I saw that I had no possible opportunity to do this in Elgin for, according to Craig's statement, Yelverson was well on the road to Chicago out of all danger of pursuit; and even should I cause Craig's arrest, from what I already knew of his character and habits, his conviction on my unsupported evidence would prove difficult.

Accordingly, while sitting there and chatting away with Craig, all these things were playing back and forth like a swift shuttle through my mind, with the following result.

'Look here, Craig,' said I, 'if you wouldn't be in too big a hurry about getting back home, I'll tell you what I'll do. I believe I could make arrangements to buy you out altogether.'

'Well, now that's a good idea, Pinkerton,' returned the counterfeiter thoughtfully, but evidently pleased at the proposition.

'How much have you got?' I asked.

'I haven't any,' he answered with a sly look, 'Yelverson has about four thousand dollars in the stuff, I believe.'

'All right,' I replied. 'Craig or Yelverson, it's all the same so I get it. Now I've been thinking that I could take a trip out to Naperville, in Du Page County, and St Charles, Geneva, Batavia, Aurora, and Oswego, in this county, and work off the greater part of what I've got, and while at Oswego see Lawyer Boyd who, I am certain, will take a share with me.'

'How long will this take you?' inquired Craig.

'I can't tell,' said I, 'not more than three or four days at the outside, I think.'

'Well, try and see what you can do. I would like to sell my horse and my entire outfit too, and go back by the lakes, if I can.'

'All right, Craig,' said I. 'I'm pretty sure that I can buy everything. I'll try hard, and think that if I can see Bill Boyd at Oswego, there'll be no doubt about our being able together to take everything you have.'

'Goodbye then,' said the counterfeiter, shaking my hand warmly. 'I'll spend the night with Smith, go into Chicago to-morrow, and wait there at the 'Sauganash' for you four or five days. But, mind you, be discreet!'

With this we parted, Craig going over the hills into the woods behind the town, to make some slight detour before rejoining the gunsmith, and I, with my five hundred dollars in counterfeit bills on the Wisconsin Marine and Fire Insurance Company's Bank, starting on foot for home, where I arrived just as the sun was setting behind the grand hills of Dundee, upon what I then felt was the most exciting and eventful day of my life.

Messrs. Hunt and Bosworth were on the *qui vive* of expectation, and listened to my recital with the greatest interest; but they both seemed apprehensive that the counterfeiter would not keep faith with me, and had probably set out from Elgin for some distant point as soon as I had started for home, and would leave us all in the lurch with five hundred dollars in counterfeit money on our hands for all our trouble and officiousness.

I confess that, being new to the business, I had some thing of a like fear, or distrust; but still, in revolving the matter in my mind, I could not but always come back to the first impression I had gained of my Vermont friend, to the effect that, criminal though he was, he was a man who, when he had passed his word, would be certain to keep it.

With a view of allaying the anxiety of my friends, and also satis-fying my own curiosity concerning the matter, I promised that early the next morning I would take some measures to deem definitely the whereabouts of the counterfeiter. And so, tired, partly discouraged, and fully satisfied in my own mind that I was not born to become a detective, I went home, and sought my bed with a feeling that the little cooper-shop, my good wife, and our plain homely ways were, after all, the best things on earth and altogether better than any other sort of life or attainments possible for man to secure.

Prompt to my promise, I was up betimes the next morning; and, after a hasty breakfast, secured a horse, and was soon rapidly canter-ing off in the direction of Elgin, where I arrived by the time the vil-lagers of the little town were stirring about their several avocations. I proceeded directly to the house of John Smith, the gunsmith.

Before I had reached the same, my spirits were measurably raised to observe, sitting there upon the rough porch shaded with roses and honeysuckles, the veritable gentleman from Vermont who had given us all so much uneasiness.

He was smoking his pipe and enjoying the morning as composedly as any man well could and, as I approached, looked up with a pleasant smile of greeting.

He advanced quickly to the gate, and grasped my hand heartily, saying quietly :

'Helloa, Pinkerton, what's up?'

'Only myself,' I answered jokingly.

'Have you got started out on your trip this early?' he inquired.

'Yes, I believe if anything's worth doing it's worth doing quickly and thoroughly. I'm on my way down the river to take in the towns I mentioned yesterday. I'll see Boyd tomorrow, get back as quick as I can, and meet you as agreed at the "Sauganash" in Chicago.'

'You'll do, you'll do,' said Craig encouragingly. 'I just thought I'd call on my way, shake hands with you, and show you I was at work carrying out my part of the agreement.'

'Glad you stopped, glad you stopped. Make as good time as possible, for I want to get through here and get back east. The church interests always languish while I am away,' he added laughing.

And so, with a cheery goodbye, we again parted. I rode away ostensibly for St Charles but, after getting some little distance from Elgin, took a detour and, riding through the little post town of Undina, reached Dundee some time before noon.

The information secured through this little ruse satisfied both myself and my Dundee friends that dependence could be placed upon meeting Craig in Chicago. This was what I most desired for, alone in the country, and not knowing what secret companions he might have near him ready to spring to his aid at the lifting of his finger, made an attempt at his capture, with my then inexperience, simply foolish and something not to be thought.

Three intervening days were passed in frequent consultations with Messrs. Hunt and Bosworth, very little attention to my casks and barrels, and a good deal of nervous plotting and planning on my own part and before daybreak on the fourth morning I had caught the last glimpse of the little village of Dundee, nestling like a bird by the gleaming river, and was speeding my horse at a brisk pace over the winding highway toward Chicago.

I arrived in that then thriving, but little, city during the early forenoon and my first move was to procure warrants for the arrest of both Craig and Yelverson as I had high hopes of now being able, by a little good management, to get the two men together and I easily secured the services of two officers, one of whom I directed to follow and watch the movements of Craig, which would undoubtedly, if there was any such person as Yelverson, bring the two men together. My idea was to then wait until they had separated and were so situated that immediate communication would be impossible, and thus capture Yelverson; while, after this had been effected, myself and the second officer would attend to Craig. But, as fine as all this looked in a plan, it was doomed, as the reader will observe, to prove merely a plan.

After all these arrangements were perfected, I went to the Sauganash Hotel. The officers were merely constables, and one was stationed outside the house, to follow Craig wherever he might go, or whoever might come in contact with him, should he be observed to meet any person with whom he might appear to have confidential relations; while the other officer was located inside the hotel, to cause Craig's arrest whenever the proper time arrived.

I wanted to bring things about so that I could capture the men with the money upon them, or in the very act of passing it; but circumstances and my own youth and inexperience were against me.

I had been seated in the office of the hotel but a few minutes when Craig entered, smoking a cigar. He saw me instantly, but several minutes elapsed before he saw fit to approach me, and I observed by his manner that he did not wish me to recognise him. He sauntered about for a time, apparently like one upon whose hands time hung heavily and, finally securing a newspaper, dropped into a seat beside me.

Some minutes even elapsed before he in any manner recognised my presence, and then he said, with his attitude such that no one could imagine him otherwise than deeply engaged with his paper:

'Have you got the money?'

'Yes,' I replied, quite as laconically.

'Well, I've an even four thousand now. The horse is sold so you pay me one thousand dollars, and in the course of an hour I will see that you have the package.'

'Craig,' I said, 'Lawyer Boyd, from Oswego, is here with me and you know these lawyers are sticklers for form. Now, he don't want to pay the money until we see the bills.'

'Why, he has seen what you had, hasn't he? You know that old John Craig's word is as good as his money, and that's as good as gold!' he replied with some warmth, and evidently nettled.

'If it was wholly my own affair, Craig, you knew it would be different. You know I would trust you with ten times this sum,' I replied reassuringly; 'but I've placed myself in this damned lawyer's power in order to keep my word like a man with you, and he insists like an idiot on having the thing done only in one way.'

'Well, I'll think the matter over, and see you here a half-hour or so later,' returned Craig.

We then adjourned to the bar, and partook of sundry drinks but I observed, without showing that I did so, that Craig was very careful in this respect. We soon parted, and I must confess that I began to have a presentiment that matters were beginning to look a little misty. I could not imagine what the outcome would be but that Craig had become suspicious of something, was certain.

I could not of course then know, without exposing myself, what was done, or how Craig acted, but I afterward learned that he seemed perplexed and doubtful about what he should do. He started out rapidly in the direction of the lake, suddenly halted, returned, started again, halted again, and then walked aimlessly in various directions, occasionally giving a quick look back over his shoulder as if to determine whether he was being followed.

Whatever he might have thought about this, at last he returned to the hotel with the air of a man who had determined upon something, and entered the office.

Not making any move as though he desired to see me, I soon moved toward him, and finally said:

'Well, Craig, are you going to let me have the money?'

He looked at me a moment with a puzzled air of surprise, the assurance of which I have never since seen equalled, and replied quietly: 'What money?'

I looked at him in blank amazement, and finally said 'The money you promised me.'

With a stolidity that would have made a Grant or a Wellington, he rejoined: 'I haven't the honour of your acquaintance, sir, and therefore cannot imagine to what you allude.'

If the Sauganash Hotel had fallen upon me, I could not have been more surprised or, for the moment, overwhelmed.

But this lasted but for a moment. I saw that my one plan had fallen to the ground like a house of straw. Yelverson had not been located; probably no counterfeit money could be found upon Craig; and there was only my own almost unsupported evidence as to the entire transaction, as the reader has been given it; but I also saw that there was only one thing to do, and that was to make Mr Craig my prisoner. I therefore said: 'All right, John Craig; you have played your game well, but there are always at least two at a really interesting game, and I shall have to take you into custody on the charge of counterfeiting.'

I gave the signal to the officer, and Craig was at once arrested but he fairly turned the tables upon me then by his assumed dignity and gentlemanly bearing. Quite a crowd gathered about, and considerable sympathy was expressed for the stately, gray-haired man who was being borne into captivity by the green-looking countryman cooper from Dundee.

Not a dollar in counterfeit money was found upon Craig, as I had feared. He was taken to Geneva, in Kane County, lodged in jail and, after the preliminary examination, admitted to bail in a large sum. While awaiting the arrival of friends to furnish the required bonds, he was remanded and it was soon noticed by the frequenters of the place that Craig and the sheriff whose apartments were in the jail building, had become very intimate. He was shown every courtesy and favour possible under the circumstances, and the result was that the community was suddenly startled to learn that the now famous counterfeiter had mysteriously escaped—leaving, it was said, the sheriff of Kane County considerably richer in this world's goods from the unfortunate occurrence.

This was the outcome of the matter; but though this great criminal, through the perfidy of an official, had escaped punishment, the affair was worth everything to the Wisconsin Fire and Marine Insurance Company in particular, and the entire West in general—it having the effect for a number of years to drive counterfeiters entirely from our midst.

The country being new and great sensations scarce, the affair was in everybody's mouth, and I suddenly found myself called upon, from every quarter, to undertake matters requiring detective skill, until I was soon actually forced to relinquish the honourable, though not over-profitable, occupation of a copper, for that of a professional detective, with the result and a career of which the public are fully acquainted; all of which I owe to 'Old John Craig ' and this my first detective case.

I cannot resist relating another incident characteristic of George Smith.

With all his business success, like Dickens' Barkis, he became considerably mean, and finally obtained the soubriquet, among his friends and acquaintances, of old 'Na!' on account of the abruptness and even ugliness with which he would snap out his Scotch 'na!' or no, to certain applicants for banking or other favours.

As soon as I had got Craig safely in jail, Messrs. Hunt and Bosworth, who had expended nearly one hundred and fifty dollars in the matter, saw that they had nothing left for their pains save the counterfeit five hundred dollars, and that even was deposited in the hands of the Kane County Court clerk; so it devolved upon me to go into Chicago, see George Smith and get from him, if possible, so much money as had been expended, and a few dollars for my own services.

So I took my trip, after a vexatious delay was admitted to the presence of the mighty banker, and tersely stated my errand.

He heard me all through, and then remarked savagely: 'Have ye nae mair to say?'

'Not anything,' I replied civilly.

'Then I've just this tae speak: ye was not authorised tae do the wark, and ye have nae right t' a cent. I'll pay this, I'll pay this; but mind ye, noo,' and he shook his finger at me in no pleasant way, 'if ye ever do wark for me again that ye have nae authorisation for, ye'll get ne'er a penny, ne'er a penny!'

In fact, it was hard work for the close-fisted Scotchman to be decently just in the matter, and I am certain the incident has been of service to me during these later years in causing prudence in all such undertaking.

And so much for 'honour among thieves'. The Maximilian Shinburn referred to is, in Pinkerton's words, 'alias Mark Shinburn, alias Mark Baker, alias Zimmerman, with half a hundred other aliases, a very brilliant and exceptional instance of a professional criminal having won considerable fame from a series of masterly bank and bond robberies, marvellous prison escapes, and the like, in America, and then crowning all by a final escape, sound and safely, to Belgium, where he has since lived an active, and, as far as can be learned, an honourable business life, being favoured with luxury and the pleasantest of life's surroundings'.

⊰ Burglars' Tricks Upon Burglars ⊱

Criminals not only are very ingenious in their schemes against the general public, but they frequently show considerable skill and a certain grade of quiet humour in well-laid plans against each other. An instance of the kind happened in this wise: in 1875, Scott and Dunlap—the famous bank robbers who robbed the Northampton National Bank of nearly a million dollars, and who are now behind the bars of the penitentiary of that State, through the efforts of my Agencies—had laid their plans to rob a certain up-town New York city bank.

George Miles, alias Bliss, alias White, the notorious Max Shinburne's old partner, and his party were concocting a like operation for relieving a down-town bank of its capital.

Now it was found by the Miles party that both banks were to be robbed in like manner, by that very popular method of 'bank-bursting', which consists of renting a room or rooms above those occupied by a bank and then, if possible, tunnelling through into its vaults or into the bank offices, and then breaking into the vaults in the regular manner.

Miles saw that, if the Scott-Dunlap gang should happen to first complete their job, the publicity given the method employed would set every bank officer in New York investigating the possibility of a like misfortune, and thus defeat his own purpose. He accordingly took two of his men, who were wholly unknown to the other party, provided them with complete police uniforms and clubs and, at a suitable time after nightfall, stationed them in hiding behind the up-town bank, and when the members of the Scott-Dunlap party approached the building 'to pipe it off', or take observations, they were of course recognised by Miles' policemen, who drove them away.

The Scott-Dunlap party were now in utter consternation. They felt certain that their scheme had been discovered, or at least that the officers of the bank had had their suspicions in the matter awakened, and certainly to that extent which would make their project impossible.

To put the matter to further test, on the succeeding night other of their men were instructed to 'pipe off' the place still more cautiously. But these too were discovered by Miles' vigilant but bogus police, given chase to, and unmercifully clubbed.

This delayed matters with Scott and Dunlap until Miles and his party, the chief members of which consisted of George Miles, 'Pete' Curly, and 'Sam' Perris, alias 'Wooster Sam', got everything ready for their attack on the down-town bank, which was located within one block of the First District police station and within the same distance of my New York office, at No. 66 Exchange Place.

In the meantime, it is thought, the Scott-Dunlap party had learned of the down-town scheme, and caused information to be given, and before the Miles party had got fairly at work they were pounced upon by the police,

A lively fight ensued, and, although considerable shooting was done, the entire party of burglars escaped, so that two great bank burglaries, where very probably hundreds of thousands of dollars in cash and bonds would have been secured, were prevented through nothing more or less than what was hoped to be a very excellent trick by one notorious set of rogues upon another.

Pinkerton wrote his own story (or had it written for him), and proactively shaped the public's perception of him. But he was not above defending his reputation too. Nor was he going to let a simple New York plod upstage him. The famous incident in which he thwarted a plot to assassinate President Lincoln on a night train was called into question, so Pinkerton had a collection of letters and statements testifying to his pivotal role privately printed by Rode & Brand of New York, and liberally distributed. Reproduced below is his introduction and, for its historical importance, the statement of Lincoln himself. The book also contains letters from those in the know—railroad officials, Lincoln's confidantes etc., including the Mr Felton and Hon. Norman B. Judd referred to. It is also by way of a testament to Timothy Webster, executed for espionage. This may have been the work that persuaded Pinkerton there was merit in publishing his experiences.

History and Evidence of the Passage of Abraham Lincoln

TO THE PEOPLE OF THE UNITED STATES CHICAGO, 8 JAN, 1868.

The question of the passage of Mr Lincoln, on the night of 22 February, 1861, from Harrisburg, Penn, to Washington, DC, the Capitol of the United States, is one of marked interest in history, and one upon which the people of this country and the world, ought to have correct information. Hitherto I have kept silent upon this subject and probably might have continued so much longer, but that historians are now writing up the important events of the last seven years a period the most exciting in the life-time of this nation up to the present stage of its existence, and I deem it proper to lay the following brief statement before the public in connection with this event. I am induced, more over, to take this step from the fact of the publication, in the second volume of Lossing's *History of the War of the Rebellion*, of a letter from John A. Kennedy, Esq., Superintendent of the Metropolitan Police of New York City, dated New York, 13 August, 1867, in which Mr Kennedy speaks of the acts of himself and his detective force, in discovering the plot for the assassination of President Lincoln, on his passage through Baltimore, en route to Washington, for inauguration as President. This letter has had so wide a circulation in the press of the United States that it will be unnecessary for me to insert the whole of it here. I merely desire to call attention to the following words:

'I know nothing of any connection of Mr Pinkerton with the matter.'

That is to say, Mr Kennedy knew nothing of my connection with the passage of Mr Lincoln from Harrisburg, via Philadelphia, to Washington, on 22 February, 1861. In this respect, Mr Kennedy spoke the truth: he did not know of my connection with the passage of Mr Lincoln, nor was it my intention that he should know of it. Secrecy is the one thing most necessary to the success of the detective, and when a secret is to be kept, the fewer who know of it the better. It was unnecessary for Mr Kennedy to know of my connection with that passage, and hence he was not apprised of it. I am aware that Mr Kennedy is a loyal man, and has done much service for the Union cause, but it was not necessary that every Unionist should be informed that Mr Lincoln was about to make an important movement. Therefore, the secret was imparted only to those whom it was necessary should know it. With this preface, my statement will be brief.

About the middle of January, 1861, I was in Philadelphia and had an interview on other matters with S. M. Felton, Esq., at that time President of the Philadelphia, Wilmington and Baltimore Railroad, in which Mr Felton mentioned that he had suspicions that the secessionists of Maryland were bound to injure his road, either by destroying the ferry-boat which carried the trains across the Susquehanna River at Havre de Grace, or by the destruction of the railroad bridges over the Gunpowder River and other streams. Mr Felton felt very desirous to protect his road from injury or obstruction by the 'secessionists' as they were at that time called, but afterwards more familiarly known as 'rebels', who were then busily engaged in plotting the treason which shortly afterwards culminated in open rebellion. Mr Felton well knew that the Philadelphia, Wilmington and Baltimore Railroad was the only connecting link between the great commercial emporium of the United States and the Capitol of the Nation, and appreciated fully the necessity of keeping that link unbroken. He desired that I would consider the matter fully and, promising to do so, I returned to my home in Chicago.

On the 27 January, 1861, I wrote to Mr Felton my views upon this subject. They were not given in connection with secession, but as to what detective ability might do to discover the plots and plans of those who might be contemplating the destruction of any portion of this great and important link between New York and Washington.

On 30 January, I received a telegram from Mr Felton, requesting me to come to Philadelphia, and take with me such of my force as might be necessary, with a view to commencing the detective operations to which I had alluded in my letter to him of the 27th.

On 1 February, 1861, I accordingly left Chicago with such of my detective force, male and female, as I thought adequate for the purpose required. We duly arrived in Philadelphia, and after consultation with Messrs. Felton and Stearns, of the Philadelphia, Wilmington and Baltimore Railroad, I repaired with my force to Baltimore and there established my head quarters.

While engaged in the investigations spoken of, as relating to the safety of the Philadelphia, Wilmington and Baltimore Railroad track, my self and detectives accidentally acquired the knowledge that a plot was in existence for the assassination of Mr Lincoln on his passage through Baltimore to Washington, to be inaugurated as President. The plot was well conceived, and would, I am convinced, have been effective for the purpose designed. This information was acquired by me while in the service of the Philadelphia, Wilmington and Baltimore Railroad, who were paying me for my services, and although I felt impelled by my sense of duty, and my long friendship for Mr Lincoln, (we both being old citizens of Illinois), to impart the same to him yet, knowing the loyalty of Mr Felton, I desired his acquiescence in so doing. I accordingly imparted the information of the plot to Mr Stearns, and through him to Mr Felton, and received from both these gentlemen the authority to impart the facts to Hon. Norman B. Judd, the warm and intimate personal friend of Mr Lincoln, who was accompanying the President-elect on the tour from Springfield to Washington.

Nothing further, I believe, is necessary from myself on this affair, as the evidence which accompanies this statement is all that is necessary to show how far I speak truthfully. It would be egotistical on my part to parade before the public my acts. I hold proofs in addition to those, which are now furnished to the public, in my possession. A few words more, and those only in relation to one who is now dead, a martyr to the cause of the Union, who lies in unhallowed soil,

'Unwept, unhonoured and unsung'.

I allude to Timothy Webster, one of my detective force, who accompanied me upon this eventful occasion. He served faithfully as a detective amongst the secessionists of Maryland, and acquired many valuable and important secrets. He, amongst all of the force who went with me, deserves the credit of saving the life of Mr Lincoln, even more than I do. He was a native of Princeton, New Jersey, a life-long democrat, but he felt and realised, with Jackson, that the Union must and should be preserved. He continued in my detective service, and after I assumed charge of the secret service of the Army of the Potomac, under Major General McClellan, Mr Webster was most of the time within the rebel lines. True, he was called a spy, and martial law says that a spy, when convicted, shall die. Still, spies are necessary in war, ever have been and ever will be. Timothy Webster was arrested in Richmond, and upon the testimony of members of a secesh family in Washington, named Levi, for whom I had done some acts of kindness, he was convicted as a spy, and executed by order of Jefferson Davis, on 30 April, 1862. His name is unknown to fame; but few were truer or more devoted to the Union cause than was Timothy Webster.

With this statement, I herewith subjoin the following letters, which are proof of my participation in the passage of Mr Lincoln from Harrisburg, via Philadelphia, to Washington, on the night of 22 February, 1861. As I have before said, it was unnecessary that

Mr Kennedy should know aught of the movement that was going on, and I did not advise him of it; although I am informed that he was on the same train and occupied the third berth in the same sleeping car from that where Mr Lincoln lay on that eventful night of his passage to Washington from Philadelphia.

MR LINCOLN'S STATEMENT.
Extract from Lossing's *History of the War*, Vol. 1, page 278.

'Mr Judd, a warm personal friend from Chicago, sent for me to come to his room (at the Continental Hotel, Philadelphia, 21 Feb). I went, and found there Mr Pinkerton, a skillful police detective, also from Chicago, who had been employed for some days in Baltimore, watching or searching for suspicious persons there. Pinkerton informed me that a plan had been laid for my assassination, the exact time when I expected to go through Baltimore being publicly known. He was well informed as to the plan, but did not know that the conspirators would have pluck enough to execute it. He urged me to go right through with him to Washington that night. I didn't like that. I had made engagements to visit Harrisburg, and go from there to Baltimore, and I resolved to do so. I could not believe that there was a plot to murder me. I made arrangements, however, with Mr Judd for my return to Philadelphia the next night, if I should be convinced that there was danger in going through Baltimore. I told him that if I should meet at Harrisburg, as I had at other places, a delegation to go with me to the next place (Baltimore), I should feel safe and go on. When I was making my way back to my room, through crowds of people, I met Frederick Seward. We went together to my room, when he told me that he had been sent, at the instance of his father and General Scott, to inform me that their detectives in Baltimore had discovered a plot there to assassinate me. They knew nothing of Mr Pinkerton's movements. I now believed such a plot to be in existence.'

There follow extracts from Pinkerton's somewhat vainglorious and self-justificatory 1888 volume, grandly entitled The Spy's Rebellion; *being a true history of the spy system of the United States' army during the late rebellion revealing many secrets of the war hitherto not made public. (Written under the nom-de-plume of Major E. J. Allen, Chief of the United States Secret Service.) The preamble to the tale of the attempted assassination of Lincoln is noteworthy for a number of reasons, not least that America had, at the time, a three-party political system.*

⊰ The Spy's Rebellion ⊱

In 1858, the famous contest between Abraham Lincoln and Stephen A. Douglas for the United States Senatorship from Illinois took place, and during its progress absorbed public attention throughout the country. The two candidates indulged in open discussions of questions of public policy, which were remarkable for their brilliancy and for the force and vigour with which their different views were uttered.

It was during this canvass that Mr Lincoln made the forcible and revolutionizing declaration that: 'The Union cannot permanently endure half slave and half free'. Mr Lincoln was defeated, however, and Mr Douglas was returned to the Senate, much against the wishes of those Democrats who desired the unlimited extension of the institution of Slavery.

In the following year occurred the slave insurrection in Virginia, under the leadership of that bold abolitionist, John Brown. The movement was frustrated, however, and John Brown, after a judicial trial for his offence, was sentenced to be hung. Up to the day of his execution he remained firm in the belief that he had but performed his duty toward enslaved humanity, and he died avowing the justice of his cause and the hope of its ultimate success.

All of these occurrences tended to engender a spirit of fierce opposition in the minds of the Southern leaders. The growing sentiment of abolitionism throughout the North, and the manifest disposition to prevent its increase or extension, aroused the advocates of Slavery to a degree of alarm, which led to the commission of many actions, both absurd and unjustifiable.

The year of 1860 opened upon a scene of political agitation which threatened to disrupt long united associations, and to erect sectional barriers which appeared almost impossible to overcome.

In April, 1860, the Democratic National Convention assembled in Charleston, South Carolina, for the purpose of nominating a candidate for the presidency. During its session loud and angry debates occurred, in which the Southern element endeavoured to obtain a strong endorsement of the institution of Slavery, and of the right to carry slaves into the territories of the United States. They were met by the more conservative portion of the party, who desired to leave the question to be decided by the States themselves. After a prolonged discussion the majority of the Southern States withdrew their delegates from the convention, and the remainder proceeded to ballot for a candidate of their choice.

After a protracted sitting, during which several ballots were taken and no decided result obtained, the convention adjourned, to meet in the city of Baltimore on the eighteenth day of June succeeding. Stephen A. Douglas of Illinois, received a large percentage of the votes that were cast, but failed to obtain a sufficient number to secure his nomination.

The withdrawing delegates organised a rival convention, but, without transacting any business of a decisive character, also adjourned, to meet in Baltimore at a date nearly coincident with that of the regular body.

On the nineteenth day of May, the Constitutional Union (being the old American) party held their convention in the city of Baltimore, and nominated John Bell of Tennessee, for President, and Edward Everett of Massachusetts, for the Vice-Presidency,

The Republican Convention was held on the sixteenth day of May, in the city of Chicago, and upon the third ballot nominated Abraham Lincoln of Illinois, for the office of President, and Hannibal Hamlin of Maine, for the second office. This convention also adopted a platform very pronounced upon the subject of Slavery, and which was calculated to give but little encouragement to the extension or perpetuity of the slave-holding power.

On the eighteenth day of June the regular Democratic Convention assembled, pursuant to adjournment, in the city of Baltimore, and named Stephen A. Douglas of Illinois, and Herschel V. Johnson of Georgia, as their standard-bearers in the political conflict that was to ensue.

On the twenty-eighth day of the same month the seceding delegates met in the same city, and after pronouncing their ultra views upon the question of Slavery, nominated John C. Breckinridge of Kentucky (then the Vice-President of the country), and General Joseph Lane of Oregon, as the candidates of their choice.

The lines of battle were now drawn, and from that time until the election, in November, a fierce contest was waged between the opposing parties. Never before in the history of parties was a canvass conducted with more bitterness or with a greater amount of vituperation. The whole country was engrossed with the gigantic struggle. Business interests, questions of finance and of international import were all made subservient to the absorbing consideration of the election of a national President.

The Southern 'Fire-eaters', as they were called, fully realised their inability to elect the candidates they had named, but strove with all their power to prevent the success of the regular Democratic nominees, and when at last the day of election came, and the votes were counted, it was found that the Republican party had been victorious and that Abraham Lincoln had been elected.

In many portions of the South this result was hailed with joyful enthusiasm. The anti-slavery proclivities of the successful party was instantly made a plausible pretext for secession and the withdrawal of the slave-holding States from the Union was boldly advocated.

The same power that threatened in 1856, in the words of Governor Wise of Virginia: 'that if Fremont had been elected, he would have marched at the head of twenty thousand men to Washington, and taken possession of the capital, preventing by force Fremont's inauguration at that place', was again aroused, and an open opposition to the Republican inauguration was for a time considered.

The absorbing and exciting question in the South was: 'Would the South submit to a Black Republican President and a Black Republican Congress?' and the answer to the question was a loud and decisive negative.

Among the bolder advocates of secession the election of Mr Lincoln was regarded with pleasure, and meetings were held in Charleston, rejoicing in the triumph of the Republican party. Secession and disunion were loudly advocated, and the slave oligarchy of South Carolina regarded this event as the opportunity to achieve her long-cherished purpose of breaking up the Union, and forming a new confederacy, founded upon the peculiar ideas of the South.

Says Horace Greeley: 'Men thronged the streets, talking, laughing, cheering, like mariners long becalmed upon a hateful, treacherous sea, when a sudden breeze had swiftly wafted them within sight of their looked for haven, or like a seedy prodigal, just raised to affluence by the death of some far-off, unknown relative, and whose sense of decency is not strong enough to repress his exultation'.

Open threats were made to withdraw at once from the Union, and these demonstrations seemed to find sympathy among other nations than our own, and soon foreign intrigue was hand and glove with domestic treason, in the attempt to sap the foundations of our government, and seeking peculiar advantages from its overthrow.

It is unnecessary to detail the various phases of this great agitation which, firing the Southern heart with the frenzy of disunion, finally led to the secession of the Southern States. Various compromises were attempted, but all failed of beneficial result.

The 'masterly inactivity' of the administration contributed in no small degree to the accomplishment of this object, and in the end the Southern Confederacy was organised and Jefferson Davis was elected as its President. The Palmetto waved over the custom-house and post-office at Charleston; government forts and arsenals were seized by the volunteers to the Southern cause, and on February 1st, 1861, the Federal mint and custom-house at New Orleans were taken possession of by the secessionists.

The removal of Major Anderson from Fort Moultrie to the more secure stronghold of Fort Sumter, in Charleston harbour, had been accomplished, and as yet no measures had been taken by the government to prevent further demonstrations of a warlike character on the part of the Southern Confederacy. The administration remained passive and inert, while every effort was being made to calm the public fears of hostilities, and the organisation of an open revolt.

The city of Baltimore was, at this time, a slave-holding city, and the spirit of Slavery was nowhere else more rampant and ferocious. The mercantile and social aristocracy of that city had been sedulously and persistently plied, by the conspirators for disunion, with artful and tempting suggestions of her future greatness and advancement as the chief city of the new government.

If a Confederacy composed of the fifteen slave-holding States was organised, Baltimore, it was urged, would naturally be the chief city of the new Republic. In time it would become the rival of New York, and occupy to the Confederacy the same relations which New York does to the Union, and would be the great ship-building, shipping, importing and commercial emporium.

These glittering prophecies had not been uttered without effect. The ambition of the aristocracy was aroused. Already they saw the ocean whitened with her sails, and the broad domain of Maryland adorned with the palaces reared from her ample and ever-expanding profits. Under these hallucinations, their minds were corrupted, and they seemed eager to rush into treason.

Being a border State, Maryland occupied a position of particular importance. Emissaries were sent to her from South Carolina and elsewhere, and no effort was spared to secure her co-operation in these revolutionary movements. It is to be regretted that they were too successful, and the result was that the majority of the wealthier classes and those in office were soon in sympathy with the rebellion, and the spirit of domestic treason, for a time, swept like a tornado over the state.

Added to the wealthier classes was the mob element of the city of Baltimore, reckless and unscrupulous, as mobs generally are and this portion of her community were avowedly in full accord with the prospective movement, and ready to do the bidding of the slave power. Between these, however, there existed a great middle class, who were loyally and peacefully inclined. But this class, large as it was, had hitherto been divided in their political opinions, and had as yet arrived at no common and definite understanding with regard to the novel circumstances of the country and the events which seemed to be visibly impending.

The government of the city of Baltimore was under the control of that branch of the Democracy who supported Breckinridge, and who had attained power under a popular cry for reform, and it was soon learned that these leaders were deep in the counsels of the secessionists.

The newspaper press was no small factor of this excitement; their utterances had much to do in leading public opinion, and through their efforts 'to fire the Southern heart', many were led to sanction the deeds of violence and outrage which were contemplated.

Especial efforts had been made to render Mr Lincoln personally odious and contemptible, and his election formed the pretexts of these reckless conspirators, who had long been plotting the overthrow of the Union. No falsehood was too gross, no statement too exaggerated, to be used for that purpose, and so zealously did these misguided men labour in the cause of disunion, and so systematically concerted was their action, that the mass of the people of the slave States were made to believe that this pure, patient, humane, Christian statesman was a monster whose vices and passions made him odious, and whose political beliefs made him an object of just abhorrence. This was the condition of affairs at the dawning of the year 1861.

The events about to be related have been for a long time shrouded in a veil of mystery. While many are aware that a plot existed at this time to assassinate the President-elect upon his contemplated journey to the capital, but few have any knowledge of the mode by which the conspiracy was detected, or the means employed to prevent the accomplishment of that murderous design.

Considerations which affected the personal safety of those who actively participated in this detection, precluded a disclosure at the time, but that such a conspiracy existed no doubt can be entertained. Now, however, that the dark clouds have passed away, and the bright sunshine of an enduring peace is throwing its beneficent rays over a united country, the truth may be disclosed, and a desire to peruse a hidden page of history may now be gratified.

Early in the year 1861, I was at my headquarters in the city of Chicago, attending to the manifold duties of my profession. I had, of course, perused the daily journals which contained the reports of doings of the malcontents of the South, but in common with others, I entertained no serious fears of an open rebellion, and was disposed to regard the whole matter as of trivial importance. The same tones had been listened to before, and although the disunionists had hitherto never taken such aggressive steps, I was inclined to believe that with the incoming of the new administration, determined or conciliatory measures would be adopted, and that secession and rebellion would be either averted or summarily crushed.

At this time I received a letter from Mr Samuel H. Felton, the president of the Philadelphia, Wilmington and Baltimore Railroad, requesting my presence in Philadelphia upon a matter of great importance. From his communication it appeared that rumours were afloat as to the intention of the roughs and secessionists of Maryland to injure the road of which he was the President. From what had already been learned, it was feared that their designs were to prevent travel upon the road either by destroying the ferry-boats which then carried the trains across the Susquehanna river at Havre de Grace, or by demolishing the railroad bridges over the Gunpowder river and other streams. This road was the great connecting link between the metropolis of the country and the capital of the nation, and it was of the utmost importance that no interruption should be permitted to the free communication between Washington and the great cities of the North and West.

This letter at once aroused me to a realisation of the danger that threatened the country, and I determined to render whatever assistance was in my power towards preventing the successful operation of these ill-advised and dangerous men.

I lost no time, therefore, in making my arrangements, and soon after receiving Mr Felton's communication, in company with four members of my force, was upon the train speeding towards Philadelphia. Upon arriving in that city, I went directly to the office of Mr Felton and obtained from him all the information he possessed of the movements and designs of the Maryland secessionists. I also had a consultation with Mr H. F. Kenney, the superintendent of the road, with reference to a plan of operation which I proposed, and which was considered would result in obtaining the information so much to be desired.

I resolved to locate my men at the various towns along the road, selecting such places where, it was believed, disaffection existed. With a view, therefore, of acquiring the facts necessary for an intelligent prosecution of the inquiry, I took passage on one of the trains of the road, intending to see for myself how affairs stood, and to distribute my men in such a manner as to me seemed best.

At the city of Wilmington, in Delaware, I found evidences of a great political excitement, but nothing that indicated a hostile disposition or which led me to believe that any danger was to be apprehended at this place. Nothing that savoured of organisation was apparent, and I was therefore compelled to look further for the existence of any antagonism to the rail road or any desire to prevent the running of their trains.

At Perryville I found the same excitable condition of affairs, but nothing of a more aggressive character than at Wilmington. Men indulged in fierce arguments, in which both sides were forcibly represented, but aside from this I discovered no cause for apprehension, and no occasion for active detective work as yet.

At Havre de Grace, however, the lines were more clearly drawn and the popular feeling much more bitter. It was at this point that the boats which carried the trains crossed the Susquehanna river, and where serious damage might be done to the company, should the ferries be destroyed. I therefore left one man at this place, with instructions to become acquainted with such men as he might, on observation, consider suspicious, and to endeavour to obtain from them, by association, a knowledge of their intentions.

At Perrymansville, in Maryland, the feeling was considerably more intense. Under the influence of bad men the secession movement had gained many supporters and sympathizers. Loud threats were uttered against the railroad company, and it was boastfully asserted that 'no d—d abolitionist should be allowed to pass through the town alive.'

I have always found it a truism that 'a barking dog never bites', and although I had but little fear that these blatant talkers would perform any dangerous deeds, I considered it best to be fully posted as to their movements, in order to prevent a catastrophe, if possible.

I accordingly directed Timothy Webster, a daring and discreet man upon my force, to locate himself at this point, and to carefully note everything that transpired which had any relation to attempted violence or a disposition to resort to aggressive measures.

As I neared the city of Baltimore the opposition to the government and the sympathy with secession was manifestly more intense. At Magnolia, particularly, I observed a very dangerous feeling, and among men of all classes the general sentiment was in favour of resistance and force. Another operative, John Seaford, was accordingly left at this place, with instructions similar to those which had been given to the others.

I then proceeded on to Baltimore, and there I found the greatest amount of excitement that I had yet experienced. I took quarters at the Howard House, and proceeded to inquire closely and carefully into the political situation. I soon found that the fears of the railroad officials were not wholly without foundation. The opposition to Mr Lincoln's inauguration was most violent and bitter, and a few days' sojourn in this city convinced me that great danger was to be apprehended, and that the sentiment of disunion was far more widespread and deeply rooted than I had before imagined.

The police force of the city was under the control of Marshal George P. Kane, and was almost entirely composed of men with disunion proclivities. Their leader was pronouncedly in favour of secession, and by his orders the broadest license was given to disorderly persons and to the dissemination of insurrectionary information. This individual was subsequently arrested and, after a brief sojourn in Fort McHenry, fled in 1863 to the more congenial associations of Richmond.

From the knowledge I gained of the situation in Baltimore, I resolved to establish my headquarters in that city. I accordingly engaged a building situated on South Street, and in a position where I could receive prompt reports from all quarters of the metropolis. I also sent for an additional force of whom I distributed among the people of all grades and conditions of life. The building I had selected was admirably adapted for my purpose, and was so constructed that entrance could be gained to it from all four sides, through alleyways that led in from neighbouring streets.

Day by day, the reports of my men contained many important revelations of the designs of the opposition, and as a matter of additional precaution, I advised Mr Felton to employ a small number of men to guard the various bridges and ferries, who could be warned in time to resist attack should such be made.

The chief opposition seemed to be to the inauguration of President Lincoln, and the plan of the conspirators was to excite and exasperate the popular feeling against the President-elect to the utmost, and so successfully had this been done that a majority of the wealthier classes, with few exceptions, those in office and the mob element in general, were in full accord in their desire to prevent the inauguration from taking place.

On the eleventh day of February, Mr Lincoln, with a few of his personal friends, left his quiet home in Springfield to enter upon that tempestuous political career which eventually carried him to a martyr's grave. Among the party who accompanied the President were Norman B. Judd Esq., Col. Ward H. Lamon, Judge Davis, Col. Sumner, a brave and impetuous officer, Major Hunter, Capt. John Pope, Col. Ellsworth, whose heroic death took place shortly afterwards, and John G. Nicolay, the President's private secretary.

As the President was about leaving his home, the people turned out *en masse* to bid him farewell, and to them Mr Lincoln addressed the following pathetic words of parting:

'My Friends: No one who has never been placed in a like position can understand my feelings at this hour, nor the oppressive sadness I feel at this parting. For more than a quarter of a century I have lived among you, and during all that time I have received nothing but kindness at your hands. Here I have lived from youth until now I am an old man; here the most sacred ties of earth were assumed; here all my children were born, and here one of them lies buried. To you, dear friends, I owe all that I have, and all that I am. All the strange checkered past seems now to crowd upon my mind. Today I leave you. I go to assume a task more difficult than that which devolved upon Washington. Unless the great God who assisted him shall be with me and aid me, I must fail; but if the same Omniscient Mind and Almighty Arm that directed and protected him shall guide and support me, I shall not fail, I shall succeed. Let us all pray that the God of our fathers may not forsake us now. To Him I commend you all. Permit me to ask that with equal sincerity and faith you will invoke His wisdom and guidance for me. With these few words I must leave you, for how long I know not Friends, one and all, I must bid you an affectionate farewell.'

How touchingly simple and earnest seem these words. A strange and almost weird presentiment of grief and suffering give his utterances a pathos that becomes profoundly impressive when linked with subsequent events. How prophetic too, full of tears and fraught with the prescience of a future terrible and bloody war, they bear yet an echo like that of the voice that sounded in the ear of Halleck's dying hero, for surely in their tones are heard the thanks of millions yet to come. How more than prophetic they seemed when, four years later, 'a funeral train, covered with the emblems of splendid mourning, rolled into the same city, bearing a corpse whose obsequies were being celebrated in every part of the civilised world.

From Springfield the passage was a perfect continuous ovation. Cities and towns, villages and hamlets, vied with each other in testifying their devotion to the Union and their determination to uphold the chief magistrate in the great trial before him. Immense crowds surrounded the stations at which the special train halted, and in the cities of Indianapolis, Cincinnati, Columbus, Pittsburgh, Cleveland, Erie, Buffalo, Albany, New York, Trenton, Newark, Philadelphia and Harrisburg, public demonstrations of an imposing character were given in his honour, and vast concourses of people assembled to greet him. Everywhere he was received and honoured as the chief of a free people, and in reply to complimentary addresses which he day by day received, the President endeavoured to utter cheering words, and indicated a disbelief in any bloody issue of our domestic complications.

On the day prior to the departure of Mr Lincoln from his home, I received a letter from the master mechanic of the railroad, of which the following is an extract:

> 'I am informed that a son of a distinguished citizen of Maryland said that he had taken an oath with others to assassinate Mr Lincoln before he gets to Washington, and they may attempt to do it while he is passing over our road. I think you had better look after this man, if possible. This information is perfectly reliable. I have nothing more to say at this time, but will try to see you in a few days.'

This communication was confirmatory of reports of an indefinite character which had reached me prior to this, and the information was far too important to be disregarded. I determined therefore, to probe the matter to the bottom, and obtaining the authority of Mr Felton for such action, I immediately set about the discovery of the existence of the conspiracy and the intention of its organisation, and then, if coolness, courage and skill could save the life of Mr Lincoln, and prevent the revolution which would inevitably follow his violent death, I felt sure of accomplishing it.

My plans were soon perfected, and they were to have several of my men, together with myself, announced as residents of Charleston and New Orleans, and by assuming to be secessionists of the most ultra type, to secure entrance into their secret societies and military organisations, and thus become possessed of their secret designs. In looking over the qualifications of the members of my corps I found two men admirably adapted to the object I had in view. They were both young and both fully able to assume and successfully carry out the character of a hot-blooded, fiery secessionist.

One of these men, whom I shall call Joseph Howard, was a young man of fine personal appearance, and of insinuating manners. He was of French descent, and in his youth had been carefully educated for a Jesuit priest, but finding the vocation distasteful to him, he had abandoned it. Added to his collegiate studies, he possessed the advantage of extensive foreign travel, and the ability to speak, with great facility, several foreign languages. He had a thorough knowledge of the South, its localities, prejudices, customs and leading men, which had been derived from several years residence in New Orleans and other Southern cities, and was gifted with the power of adaptation to persons whom they wish to influence, so popularly attributed to the Jesuits.

Howard was instructed to assume the character of an extreme secessionist, to obtain quarters at one of the first-class hotels, and register his name, with residence at New Orleans. This was done because he was well acquainted with the city, having resided there for a long time, and was consequently enabled to talk familiarly of prominent individuals of that city whom he had met.

The other man whom I selected for this important work was Timothy Webster. He was a man of great physical strength and endurance, skilled in all athletic sports, and a good shot. Possessed of a strong will and a courage that knew no fear, he was the very man to operate upon the middle and lower classes who composed the disunion element.

His subsequent career as a Union spy, one of the most perilous and thankless positions, and his ignominious death at Richmond, at the hands of the rebels, have passed into history, but no historian will ever relate the thousand perils through which he passed in the service of his country; of his boldness and ingenuity in acquiring information that was of incalculable value to the Union officers, nor of his wonderful fertility of invention, which frequently enabled him to escape from dangers which would have appalled a less brave or less devoted man. Arrested at last, he was condemned as a spy, and on the thirtieth day of April, 1862, he was executed in the City of Richmond, by order of Jefferson Davis. Even then he would have succeeded in effecting a well-devised plan of escape, had he not been rendered incapable of movement by reason of a prostrating sickness. His name is unknown to fame, but fewer hearts beat truer to the Union, and fewer arms performed more devoted service in its cause, and a record of his daring and romantic adventures as a Union spy, would certainly equal, if not surpass, those of the Harvey Birch of Cooper.

It was not long before I received undoubted evidence of the existence of a systematized organisation whose avowed object was to assist the rebellious States, but which was in reality formed to compass the death of the President, and thus accomplish the separation of the States. I learned also that a branch of this conspiracy existed at Perrymansville, under the guise of a company of cavalry, who met frequently and drilled regularly. Leaving Harwood to operate in Baltimore with the others, I dispatched Timothy Webster back to Perrymansville, and in twenty-four hours thereafter he had enrolled himself as a member of the company, and was recognised as a hail fellow among his rebel associates.

Every day reports would be brought to me from the numerous men I had detailed along the line of the railroad, and regularly on alternate days I would make the journey from Baltimore to Philadelphia for consultation with the officers of the company.

At every visit which I made to the suspected localities, I could not fail to notice an increase in the excitement and the indications of a disposition to open revolt became more evident. Everywhere the ruling principle seemed to be opposition to the new administration and a decided inclination to aid the Confederacy. As the daily papers, which chronicled the events which occurred upon the journey of Mr Lincoln towards Washington, or the desperate movements of the Southern ringleaders, were perused by the people, or were read aloud in tavern or store, they would be greeted by alternate expressions of hate and malignity for the abolitionist and wild cheers for the rebellion.

This feeling, too, was largely increased by the visits which prominent villagers would make to Baltimore, and who, upon their return, would relate marvellous stories of what they had seen and heard of the courage, the unity and the determination of the Southern people. Everything calculated to inflame the popular mind was seized upon, and the wonderful spirit of invention which these men evinced was simply astonishing. As a consequence, the ignorant residents of these villages and towns, having no authoritative information of their own, relied implicitly upon the exaggerated statements and untruthful reports of their leaders, and were kept in a condition of excitement that made them ready tools of their unscrupulous and better-informed managers. As far as could be learned, however, no definite plan of action had been arranged, and no public outbreak had as yet occurred

Barnum's Hotel, in Baltimore, appeared to be the favourite resort of the Southern element. The visitors from all portions of the South located at this house and in the evenings the corridors and parlours would be thronged by the tall, lank forms of the long-haired gentlemen who represented the aristocracy of the slaveholding interests. Their conversations were loud and unrestrained, and any one bold enough or sufficiently indiscreet to venture an opinion contrary to the righteousness of their cause, would soon find himself in an unenviable position and frequently the subject of violence.

As this hotel was so largely patronized by the so called 'Fire-eaters', I instructed Howard to go there in order to secure quarters and to ingratiate himself with these extremists. It was not long after this that, joining a company of gentlemen who were loudly declaiming against the ruling powers of the country, he entered into their discussion, and by blatant expressions of the most rebellious nature, he was warmly welcomed by the coterie and instantly made one of their number.

Hailing as he did from New Orleans, his residence was a ready passport to their favour and confidence, and his fine personal appearance, gentlemanly address and the fervour of his utterances soon won the favour of those with whom he associated. To a general inquiry he stated that private affairs of a financial nature required his presence in Baltimore, but as his acquaintance with the trustworthy emissaries of rebeldom increased, he quietly insinuated that affairs of a national character were far more dear to him than individual interests or private concerns.

By continued intercourse with these men, he greatly increased the circle of his acquaintances, and soon became a welcome guest at the residences of many of the first families of that refined and aristocratic city. Here his accomplishments appeared to the best advantage. His romantic disposition and the ease of his manner captivated many of the susceptible hearts of the beautiful Baltimore belles, whose eyes grew brighter in his presence, and who listened enraptured to the poetic utterances which were whispered into their ears under the witching spell of music and moonlit nature.

He gradually neared the circle of which Marshal George P. Kane appeared to be the leader, and in a short time he had succeeded in entirely winning his confidence, and from this gentleman Howard acquired many important items of information. The entire police force of the city officers and men were in full sympathy with the rebellion, and it became apparent to him that a strict watch was kept over every man who expressed Northern opinions, or who was not identified with the cause which they had espoused.

To all of these arrangements Howard signified his hearty endorsement, and by every means in his power he sought to convince the leaders of his full sympathy with their efforts and his resolve to take a leading part in the struggle that seemed to be impending.

Accepting the invitation of Mr Kane, he one evening accompanied that gentleman to a meeting of one of the secret societies that then existed, the first one he had succeeded in gaining entrance to. Arriving at the place of assembly, he was surprised at the many familiar faces which greeted him. Men whose aristocratic doors had opened to his entrance and whose social positions were unquestioned; young men who traced their lineage through several generations, and whose wealth and intelligence gave them a social status of no ordinary character, were found in full accord and upon perfect equality with tradesmen, artificers, and even with those whose vocation was decidedly doubtful, and some of whom had heard the key of a prison lock turned upon them for offences committed in days gone by.

The leader and President of this society was a Captain Fernandina, who was known as one of the most active of the conspirators. This individual at one time occupied the exalted position of a barber at Barnum's Hotel, but treason and conspiracy had elevated him to the station of a military captain whose orders were to be obeyed, and a leader whose mandates compelled respect. He was an Italian or of Italian descent, and having lived in the South for a number of years he was thoroughly impressed with the idea of Southern wrongs, and that the election of Mr Lincoln was an outrage which must not be tamely submitted to by the high-toned and chivalrous people of the South.

He was an enthusiast and fanatic, a dangerous man in any crisis, and particularly so in the one now impending, which threatened a civil war and all its direful consequences. Educated with Italian ideas and possessed of the temperament of his people, he openly justified the use of the stiletto, and fiercely advocated assassination as the means of preventing the President-elect from taking his seat in the executive chair. He was also the captain of a military company which drilled regularly and whose members were believed to fully indorse the views of their chief.

At this meeting Fernandina delivered an address which, for its treasonable nature and its violent opposition to all laws, human or divine, has scarcely a parallel. He boldly advocated the doctrine of State rights; he fiercely denounced the party who had succeeded in obtaining power; he inveighed in violent language against the policy of the so-called abolitionists, and his arraignment of Mr Lincoln was most vile and repulsive. As these words fell from his lips the excitement became intense. Faces were eagerly turned towards him, eyes glistened with the fires of hate, and hands were clenched as though each one present was imbued with the same feelings which animated their sanguinary leader.

As he proceeded, overcome by the violence of his emotions, he drew from his breast a long, glittering knife, and waving it aloft, exclaimed:

'This hireling Lincoln shall never, never be President. My life is of no consequence in a cause like this, and I am willing to give it for his. As Orsini gave his life for Italy, I am ready to die for the rights of the South and to crush out the abolitionist.'

As he stood before them, his black eyes flashing with excitement, his sallow face pale and colourless and his long hair brushed fiercely back from his low forehead, he seemed a fitting representative of so desperate a cause, and his influence over the assemblage was wonderful to behold. Loud cheers and wild clapping of hands greeted his utterances, and all seemed in perfect accord with his declared intentions.

There could be no mistaking the fact, that the object of these men was dangerous, and that they had fully determined to oppose and prevent the inauguration of Mr Lincoln, but the exact plan of operation had not as yet been agreed upon.

Upon these facts being conveyed to me by Howard on the following morning, I resolved to interview this desperate leader of the conspiracy myself, and endeavour to learn from him further particulars of their movements and designs.

In the immediate vicinity of Barnum's Hotel at that time there was a famous restaurant, popularly known as 'Guy's', and this place was much frequented by the secessionists who were in the city. Fernandina spent much of his time there, either in drinking or in consultation with his numerous political friends, who all seemed to regard him as an important personage, and one who was eventually to perform giant service in the cause.

Howard having effected an introduction to Fernandina, and convinced him of his devotion to the interests of the South, I experienced no difficulty in obtaining the desired interview. About three o'clock on the following afternoon Howard and myself carelessly entered the saloon, and were gratified to perceive that Fernandina was also there, accompanied by several members of the military company which he commanded. Walking directly up to these gentle men, Howard introduced me as a resident of Georgia, who was an earnest worker in the cause of secession, and whose sympathy and discretion could be implicitly relied upon.

Fernandina cordially grasped my hand, and we all retired to a private saloon, where, after ordering the necessary drinks and cigars, the conversation became general and to me, absorbingly interesting.

The question of assassinating the President was freely discussed, and Captain Fernandina expressed himself vehemently in its favour.

Someone in the party remarked:

'Are there no other means of saving the South except by assassination?'

'No,' replied Fernandina; 'as well might you attempt to move the Washington Monument yonder with your breath, as to change our purpose. He must die and die he shall. And,' he continued, turning to Captain Trichot, a fellow-conspirator who stood near, 'if necessary, we will die together.'

'There seems to be no other way,' interposed Howard, 'and while bloodshed is to be regretted, it will be done in a noble cause.'

Fernandina gazed approvingly at Howard, and then added: 'Yes, the cause is a noble one, and on that day every captain will prove himself a hero. With the first shot the chief traitor, Lincoln, will die, then all Maryland will be with us, and the South will be for ever free.'

'But,' said I, 'have all the plans been matured, and are there no fears of failure? A misstep in so important a direction would be fatal to the South and ought to be well considered.'

'Our plans are fully arranged,' answered the Captain, 'and they cannot fail, and,' he added, with a wicked gleam in his eyes, 'if I alone must strike the blow, I shall not hesitate or shrink from the task. Lincoln shall certainly not depart from this city alive.'

'Yes,' added Captain Trichot, 'it is determined that this G—d d—d Lincoln shall never pass through here alive, and no d—d abolitionist shall ever set foot upon Southern soil except to find a grave.'

'But about the authorities,' I asked. 'Is there no danger to be apprehended from them?'

'Oh no,' said the Captain, assuringly. 'They are all with us. I have seen Col. Kane, the Chief Marshal of Police, and he is all right. In a week from today the North shall want another President, for Lincoln will be a corpse.'

All the company gave approving responses to these threats, with but one exception, and he remained silent, with a doubtful, troubled expression upon his face. This young man was one of the fast 'bloods' of the city, who proudly wore upon his breast a gold Palmetto badge, and who was a Lieutenant in the Palmetto Guards, a secret military organisation of Baltimore, and I determined to select this man for the purpose of obtaining the information I so much desired; and as the company shortly afterwards broke up, Howard and myself accompanied Lieutenant Hill from the saloon.

Hill soon proved a pliant tool in our hands. Being of a weak nature and having been reared in the lap of luxury, he had entered into this movement more from a temporary burst of enthusiasm and because it was fashionable, than from any other cause. Now that matters began to assume such a warlike attitude, he was inclined to hesitate before the affair had gone too far, but still he seemed to be enamoured with the glory of the undertaking.

By my directions, Howard, the ardent secessionist from Louisiana, and Hill, of the Palmetto Guards, became bosom friends and inseparable companions. They drank together, and visited theatres and places of amusement in each other's company.

By reason of his high social position, Hill was enabled to introduce his friend to the leading families and into the most aristocratic clubs and societies of which the city boasted, and Howard made many valuable acquaintances through the influence of this rebellious scion of Baltimore aristocracy. Finally the young man was induced to open to his companion the secrets of the plot to assassinate the President. It was evident, however, that Hill was playing his part in the conspiracy with great reluctance, and one day he said to Howard: 'What a pity it is that this glorious Union must be destroyed all on account of that monster Lincoln.'

From Hill it was learned that the plans of the conspirators were first to excite and exasperate the popular feeling against Mr Lincoln to the utmost, and thus far this had been successfully accomplished. From the published programme Mr Lincoln was to reach Baltimore from Harrisburg by the Northern Central Railroad on the twenty-third day of February, now but a few days distant. He would, therefore, reach the city about the middle of the day. A vast crowd would meet him at the Calvert street depot, at which point it was expected that he would enter an open carriage and ride nearly half a mile to the Washington depot. Here it was arranged that but a small force of policemen should be stationed, and as the President arrived a disturbance would be created which would attract the attention of these guardians of the peace, and this accomplished, it would be an easy task for a determined man to shoot the President and, aided by his companions, succeed in making his escape.

Agents of the conspirators had been dispatched to all the principal Northern cities, to watch the movements of the presidential party, and ready to telegraph to Baltimore any change of route or delay in arrival. A cipher had been agreed upon between them, so that the conspirators could communicate with each other without the possibility of detection, and everything seemed to be satisfactorily arranged except to depute one of their number to commit the fatal deed. This was to be determined by ballot, and as yet no one knew upon whom might devolve the bloody task.

Meanwhile, the idea of assassination was preying heavily upon the mind of the Lieutenant of the Palmetto Guards; he grew sad and melancholy, and plunged still deeper into dissipation. Howard had now become a necessity to him and they were scarcely ever separated. Under the influence of the master spirit, the disposition of Hill underwent wonderful changes. At times, he would be thoughtful and morose, and then would suddenly break out into enthusiastic rhapsodies. His sleep became tormented with dreams in which he saw himself the martyr to a glorious cause and the saviour of his country.

At such times he would address himself to Howard, in the most extravagant language.

'I am destined to die,' said he one day, 'shrouded with glory. I shall immortalize myself by plunging a knife into Lincoln's heart.'

Howard endeavoured to calm his transports, but he exclaimed: 'Rome had her Brutus, why should not we? I swear to you, Howard, if it falls to me I will kill Lincoln before he reaches the Washington Depot, not that I love Lincoln less, but my country more.'

As the day drew nearer for the arrival of the President, he became more nervous and excited, and would more frequently indulge in extravagant expressions, which would have been regarded as absurd, but for the fact that he was but one of a large number of fanatics, who seriously entertained the same ideas of murder, and his expressions but the reflex of others, more determined.

Timothy Webster was still at Perrymansville, and by this time had fully identified himself with the rebel cause, and the company of cavalry of which he was a member. On several occasions he had given undoubted indications of his loyalty and devotion to the South, and was generally looked upon as a man who could be trusted. He became quite intimate with the officers of the company, and succeeded in gaining their entire confidence. As yet, however, he had learned but little of the important movement which we believed was in contemplation, as all conversations upon that subject appeared to be between the officers of the company, at their secret meetings, to which he had not been able as yet to gain an entrance.

At length one morning, after the usual daily drill, and when the company had been dismissed, the Captain addressed Webster and requested him to be present at his house that evening, as he desired to consult with him upon important affairs, at the same time cautioning him to say nothing to any one concerning the matter.

Promptly at the time appointed Webster presented himself at the residence of the Captain, and was ushered into a room upon the upper floor, where there were several men already assembled. The curtains had been drawn close, and heavy quilts had been hung over the windows, which effectually prevented any one from the outside from discovering a light in the room. On his entrance he was introduced to the gentlemen present, three of whom were unknown to him, who were members of the secret league from Baltimore, and who were evidently impressed with the solemnity and importance of their undertaking. They greeted Webster cordially, however, and made room for him at the table around which they were sitting.

A few minutes satisfied Webster as to the nature of the meeting, and that it was a conclave of the conspirators, who had met to discuss a plan of action. Intensely eager as he was to acquire all possible in formation, he was obliged to restrain his impetuosity and to listen calmly to the developments that were made. From what transpired that evening there could be no doubt of the desperation of the men engaged in the conspiracy, or of the widespread interest which was taken in their movements.

The plans for the assassination of the President had been fully matured, and only needed the selection of the person to perform the deed, in order to carry them into effect. In the meantime, however, other important measures required attention and consideration. If the affair stopped simply with the assassination of the President, but little, if any, good would be accomplished. The North would rise as one man to avenge the death of their leader, and they would only hasten a disaster they were anxious to avoid. It was necessary, therefore, that the work should be thoroughly done, and the plan suggested was as follows: as soon as the deed had been accomplished in Baltimore, the news was to be telegraphed along the line of the road, and immediately upon the reception of this intelligence the telegraph wires were to be cut, the railroad bridges destroyed and the tracks torn up, in order to prevent for some time any information being conveyed to the cities of the North, or the passage of any Northern men towards the capital.

Wild as the scheme was, it found instant favour with the reckless men assembled together, and all signified their hearty assent to the propositions and offered their aid in successfully carrying them out. Among the most earnest in their protestations was Timothy Webster and as he announced his intention to perform his duty in the affair he was warmly congratulated.

Matters were evidently getting warm, and but little time was left for action.

I had already written to Mr Norman B. Judd as the party reached Cincinnati, informing him that I had reason to believe that there was a plot on foot to murder the President on his passage through Baltimore, and promising to advise him further as the party progressed eastward.

This information Mr Judd did not divulge to any one, fearing to occasion undue anxiety or unnecessary alarm, and knowing that I was upon the ground and could be depended upon to act at the proper time.

When the party reached Buffalo another note from me awaited Mr Judd, informing him of the accumulation of evidence, but conveying no particulars. The party were now journeying towards New York city, and I determined to learn all that there was to learn before many hours.

Previous to this, in addition to the men engaged in Baltimore, I had sent for Mrs Kate Warne, the lady superintendent of my agency. This lady had arrived several days before, and had already made remarkable progress in cultivating the acquaintance of the wives and daughters of the conspirators.

Mrs Warne was eminently fitted for this task. Of rather a commanding person, with clear-cut, expressive features, and with an ease of manner that was quite captivating at times, she was calculated to make a favourable impression at once. She was of Northern birth, but in order to vouch for her Southern opinions, she represented herself as from Montgomery, Alabama, a locality with which she was perfectly familiar, from her connection with the detection of the robbery of the Adams Express Company, at that place. Her experience in that case, which is fully detailed in 'The Expressman and the Detective', fully qualified her for the task of representing herself as a resident of the South.

She was a brilliant conversationalist when so disposed, and could be quite vivacious, but she also understood that rarer quality in womankind, the art of being silent.

The information she received was invaluable, but as yet the meetings of the chief conspirators had not been entered. Mrs Warne displayed upon her breast, as did many of the ladies of Baltimore, the black and white cockade, which had been temporarily adopted as the emblem of secession, and many hints were dropped in her presence which found their way to my ears, and were of great benefit to me.

As I have said, the Presidential party were in Buffalo, and I had resolved upon prompt and decisive measures to discover the inward workings of the conspirators. Accordingly I obtained an interview with Howard, and gave him such instructions as I deemed necessary under the circumstances. He was to insist upon Hill taking him to the meeting at which the ballots were to be drawn, and where he, too, would have an opportunity to immortalize himself, and then, that being accomplished, the rest, would be easy and all further danger would be over.

Accordingly, that day Howard broached the matter to Hill in a manner which convinced him of his earnestness, and the young Lieutenant promised his utmost efforts to secure his admission. At five o'clock in the afternoon they again met, and Hill joyfully informed his companion that his request had been granted, and that, upon his vouching for the fidelity of his friend, he had succeeded in obtaining permission for him to enter their society.

That evening Howard accompanied his friend Hill to the rendezvous of the league, and as they entered the darkened chamber, they found many of the conspirators already assembled. The members were strangely silent, and an ominous awe seemed to pervade the entire assembly. About twenty men comprised the number, but many entered afterward. After a few preliminary movements, Howard was conducted to the station of the President of the assembly and duly sworn, the members gathering around him in a circle as this was being done.

Having passed through the required formula, Howard was warmly taken by the hand by his associates, many of whom he had met in the polite circles of society. After quiet had been restored, the President, who was none other than Captain Fernandina, arose, and in a dramatic manner detailed the particulars of the plot.

It had been fully determined that the assassination should take place at the Calvert Street depot. A vast crowd of secessionists were to assemble at that place to await the arrival of the train with Mr Lincoln. They would appear early and fill the narrow streets and passages immediately surrounding it. No attempt at secrecy was made of the fact that the Marshal of Police was conversant with their plans, and that he would detail but a small force of police men to attend the arrival, and nominally clear and protect a passage for Mr Lincoln and his suite. Nor was the fact disguised that these policemen were in active sympathy with the movement. George P. Kane's animus was fully shown when he was subsequently arrested by General Banks, and afterwards became an officer in the rebel army.

When the train entered the depot, and Mr Lincoln attempted to pass through the narrow passage leading to the streets, a party already delegated were to engage in a conflict on the outside, and then the policemen were to rush away to quell the disturbance. At this moment, the police being entirely withdrawn, Mr Lincoln would find himself surrounded by a dense, excited and hostile crowd, all hustling and jamming against him, and then the fatal blow was to be struck.

A swift steamer was to be stationed in Chesapeake Bay, with a boat awaiting upon the shore, ready to take the assassin on board as soon as the deed was done, and convey him to a Southern port, where he would be received with acclamations of joy and honoured as a hero.

The question to be decided this evening was: Who should do the deed? Who should assume the task of liberating the nation of the foul presence of the abolitionist leader? For this purpose the meeting had been called tonight, and tonight the important decision was to be reached.

It was finally determined that ballots should be prepared and placed in a box arranged for that purpose, and that the person who drew a red ballot should perform the duty of assassination.

In order that none should know who drew the fatal ballot, except he who did so, the room was rendered still darker, and every one was pledged to secrecy as to the colour of the ballot he drew. The leaders, however, had determined that their plans should not fail, and doubting the courage of some of their number, instead of placing but one red ballot in the box, they placed eight of the designated colour, and these eight ballots were drawn each man who drew them believing that upon him, his courage, strength and devotion, depended the cause of the South, each supposing that he alone was charged with the execution of the deed.

After the ballots had been drawn the President again addressed the assembly. He violently assailed the enemies of the South, and in glowing words pointed out the glory that awaited the man who would prove himself the hero upon this great occasion, and finally, amid much restrained enthusiasm, the meeting adjourned, and their duties had thus far been accomplished.

My time for action had now arrived; my plans had been perfected and I resolved to act at once. Taking Mrs Warne with me I reached New York city on the same day that the presidential party arrived there, and leaving Mrs Warne to perfect arrangements, I proceeded at once to Philadelphia. That evening Mrs Warne repaired to the Astor House and requested an interview with Mr Judd. Her request being granted, Mrs Warne informed that gentleman that, fearing to trust the mail in so important a matter, she had been delegated by me to arrange for a personal interview, at which all the proofs relating to the conspiracy could be submitted to him. It was suggested that immediately after the arrival of the party in Philadelphia, I should inform Mr Judd of my plans for an interview, and that he would be governed accordingly.

While they were conversing, Col. E. S. Sandford, President of the American Telegraph Company called, and was introduced by Mrs Warne to Mr Judd. This gentleman had been made fully acquainted with what I had learned, and had promised all the assistance within his power, and he accordingly tendered to Mr Judd his own personal service and the unlimited use of the telegraph lines under his control, for any communications he might desire to make.

On arriving at Philadelphia, I proceeded directly to the office of Mr Felton, and acquainted him with all the information I had received, of the designs of the conspirators with regard to Mr Lincoln, and of their intention to destroy the railroad should their plot be successful. The situation was truly alarming, and cautious measures were absolutely necessary. It was therefore resolved to obtain an interview with Mr Lincoln, submit the facts to him, and be governed by his suggestions, whatever they might be.

This interview took place on the 20th day of February, and Mr Lincoln was expected to arrive on the following day. Great preparations had been made for his reception, and the military, of which Philadelphia was justly proud, were to escort the President-elect from the depot to the Continental Hotel, where quarters had been engaged for him, and where he would receive the congratulations of the people.

The twenty-first dawned bright and sunny, and the streets were alive with the eager populace, all anxious to do honour to the new President, and to witness the scenes attendant upon his reception. In due time the train containing the party arrived, and after an informal welcome they took carriages and, escorted by the troops, the procession took up the line of march for the hotel. Vast crowds lined the sidewalks and the enthusiasm of the people was unbounded. The President graciously acknowledged their courtesies as he passed along. On each side of the carriage in which Mr Lincoln was seated, accompanied by Mr Judd, was a file of policemen, whose duty it was to prevent the mass of people from pressing too closely to the vehicle. As the procession reached the corner of Broad and Chestnut streets, a young man approached the file of policemen and endeavoured to attract the attention of the occupants of the carriage. Finding this impossible, he boldly plunged through the ranks of the officers and coming to the side of the carriage, he handed to Mr Judd a slip of paper, on which was written:

St Louis Hotel, ask for J. H. Hutchinson

This young man was Mr George H. Burns, an attaché of the American Telegraph Company and confidential agent of E. S. Sandford Esq., who acted as my messenger, and who afterwards distinguished himself for his courage and daring in the rebellion. It is needless to add that J. H. Hutchinson was the name I had assumed in registering at the hotel, in order to avoid any suspicion or curiosity in case any emissary of the conspirators should ascertain my real name and thus be warned of the discovery of their scheme.

Shortly after the arrival of Mr Lincoln at the Continental, Mr Judd was announced at the St Louis Hotel as desiring to see me. Mr Felton was with me at the time, and in a few minutes Mr Judd made his appearance. More than an hour was occupied in going over the proofs which I produced of the existence of the conspiracy, at the end of which time Mr Judd expressed himself fully convinced that the plot was a reality, and that prompt measures were required to secure the safety of the President.

'My advice is,' said I, after I had succeeded in convincing Mr Judd that my information was reliable, 'that Mr Lincoln shall proceed to Washington this evening by the eleven o'clock train, and then once safe at the capital, General Scott and his soldiery will afford him ample protection.'

'I fear very much that Mr Lincoln will not accede to this,' replied Mr Judd, 'but as the President is an old acquaintance and friend of yours and has had occasion before this to test your reliability and prudence, suppose you accompany me to the Continental Hotel, and we can then lay this information before him in person and abide by his decision.' This idea was at once adopted and we proceeded to the hotel. Here we found the entrances blocked up by a surging multitude which effectually prevented our admission, and we were obliged to enter by the rear of the building through a door used by the servants.

On reaching the room occupied by Mr Judd that gentleman summoned Mr Nicolay, the President's private secretary, and dispatched him with a note requesting the presence of Mr Lincoln upon a matter of urgent importance.

The President at that time was in one of the large parlours surrounded by a number of ladies and gentlemen, all eager to extend to him the hospitalities of the city and to express their good wishes for the success of his administration. Upon receiving the message, however, he at once excused himself, and forcing his way through the crowd came directly to us.

Up to this time Mr Lincoln had been kept to entire ignorance of any threatened danger, and as he listened to the facts that were now presented to him a shade of sadness fell upon his face. He seemed loth to credit the statement, and could scarce believe it possible that such a conspiracy could exist. Slowly he went over the points presented, questioning me minutely the while, but at length finding it impossible to discredit the truthfulness of what I stated to him, he yielded a reluctant credence to the facts.

After he had been fully made acquainted with the startling disclosures, Mr Judd submitted to him the plan proposed by me, that he should leave Philadelphia for Washington that evening.

'But,' added Mr Judd, 'the proofs that have just been laid before you cannot be published, as it still involves the lives of several devoted men now on Mr Pinkerton's force, especially that of Timothy Webster, who is now serving in a rebel cavalry company under drill at Perrymansville in Maryland.'

Mr Lincoln at once acknowledged the correctness of this view, but appeared at a loss as to what course to pursue.

'You will therefore perceive,' continued Mr Judd, 'that if you follow the course suggested, that of proceeding to Washington tonight, you will necessarily be subjected to the scoffs and sneers of your enemies, and the disapproval of your friends who cannot be made to believe in the existence of so desperate a plot.'

'I fully appreciate these suggestions,' replied Mr Lincoln, 'and I can stand anything that is necessary, but,' he added rising to his feet, 'I cannot go tonight. I have promised to raise the flag over Independence Hall tomorrow morning, and to visit the legislature at Harrisburg in the afternoon, beyond that I have no engagements. Any plan that may be adopted that will enable me to fulfill these promises I will accede to, and you can inform me what is concluded upon tomorrow.'

Saying which Mr Lincoln left the room and joined the people in the parlour. During the entire interview, he had not evinced the slightest evidence of agitation or fear. Calm and self-possessed, his only sentiments appeared to be those of profound regret, that the Southern sympathizers could be so far led away by the excitement of the hour, as to consider his death a necessity for the furtherance of their cause.

From his manner, it was deemed useless to attempt to induce him to alter his mind, and after a few minutes further conversation, which was participated in by Mr Sandford, who had entered the room, I left for the purpose of finding Thomas A. Scott Esq., the Vice-President of the Pennsylvania Central Railroad, in order to make arrangements for the carrying out of a plan which had occurred to me, and which would enable Mr Lincoln to fulfill his engagements.

I was unable, however, to find Mr Scott, but succeeded in reaching Mr G. C. Franciscus, the general manager of the road, and at twelve o'clock that night, in company with that gentleman and Mr Sandford, we called again upon Mr Judd.

At this meeting a full discussion of the entire matter was had between us, and after all possible contingencies had been considered, the following programme was agreed upon.

After the formal reception at Harrisburg had taken place, a special train, consisting of a baggage car and one passenger coach, should leave there at six o'clock pm to carry Mr Lincoln and one companion back to Philadelphia; this train was to be under the immediate control of Mr Franciscus and Mr Enoch Lewis, the general superintendent. In order to avoid the possibility of accident, the track was to be cleared of everything between Harrisburg and Philadelphia from half-past five o'clock until after the passage of the special train. Mr Felton was to detain the eleven o'clock pm Baltimore train until the arrival of the special train from Harrisburg, Mrs Warne in the meantime engaging berths in the sleeping-car bound for Baltimore.

I was to remain in Philadelphia in order that no accident might occur in conveying the President from one depot to another, and Mr Judd was to manage the affair at Harrisburg. Everything that could be suggested in relation to this matter was fully considered, and having at length perfected our plans, the party separated at half-past four o'clock in the morning, fully prepared to carry out the programme agreed upon.

At six o'clock on the morning of the 22nd, a vast concourse of people assembled in front of Independence Hall on Chestnut Street, and at precisely the hour appointed Mr Lincoln made his appearance. With his own hands he drew to the top of the staff surmounting the edifice a beautiful new American flag, and as its stripes and stars floated out gracefully to the breeze, the air was rent with the shouts of the multitude and the music of the band.

Mr Lincoln's speech upon this occasion was the most impressive and characteristic of any which he had delivered upon his journey to the capital, while a tinge of sadness pervaded his remarks, never noticed before, and which were occasioned no doubt by the revelations of the preceding night. He gave a most eloquent expression to the emotions and associations which were suggested by the day and by the historic old hall where he then stood. He declared that all his political sentiments were drawn from the inspired utterances of those who had sat within the walls of that ancient edifice.

He alluded most feelingly to the dangers and toils and sufferings of those who had adopted and made good the Declaration of Independence, a declaration which gave promise that 'in due time the weight would be lifted from the shoulders of all men'. Conscious of the dangers that threatened his country, and feeling also that those dangers originated in opposition to the principles enunciated in the Declaration of Independence, knowing that his own life was even then threatened because of his devotion to liberty, and that his way to the national capital was beset by assassins, he did not hesitate to declare boldly and fearlessly that he would rather be assassinated on the spot than surrender those principles so dear to him.

After these proceedings, Mr Lincoln was driven back to the Continental Hotel, and sending for Mr Judd, he introduced him to Mr Frederick H. Seward, a son of the late William H. Seward, who was in the room with the President. Mr Lincoln then informed Mr Judd that Mr Seward had been sent from Washington by his father and General Scott to warn him of the danger of passing through Baltimore, and to urge him to come direct to Washington.

From whom this information was originally obtained did not appear, but the facts were deemed of sufficient moment to be brought to the ears of the President, and hence Mr Seward's visit to Philadelphia. Mr Lincoln evinced no further hesitancy in the matter, and signified his readiness to do whatever was required of him. Mr Judd then directed Mr Seward to inform his father that all had been arranged, and that, so far as human foresight could predict, Mr Lincoln would be in Washington before the evening of the following day, and cautioned him to preserve the utmost secrecy in regard to the matter. No particulars were given and none were asked.

At the time appointed Mr Lincoln started for Harrisburg, and I busied myself with the preparations that were necessary to successfully carry our plans into operation. From reports which I received from Baltimore, the excitement in that city had grown more intense, and the arrival of the President was awaited with the most feverish impatience. The common and accepted belief was that Mr Lincoln would journey from Harrisburg to Baltimore over the Northern Central Railroad, and the plans of the conspirators were arranged accordingly.

It became a matter of the utmost importance, therefore, that no intimation of our movements should reach that city. I had no doubt but that trusty agents of the conspirators were following the presidential party, and after the absence of Mr Lincoln had been discovered, the telegraph would be put into active operation to apprise the movers of this scheme of the change that had been made. To effectually prevent this I determined that the telegraph wires which connected Harrisburg with her neighbouring cities should be so 'fixed' as to render communication impossible.

To arrange this matter Capt. Burns was sent to the office of the American Telegraph Company, and obtaining from Mr H. H. Thayer, the manager of the company, a competent and trustworthy man for the purpose, departed for Harrisburg, in order to carry out the proposed measures. Mr Thayer, in the meantime, was to remain in the office during the night, in order to intercept any dispatches that might be sent over the wires from any point between Harrisburg and Baltimore, and to immediately deliver any messages that might be sent to me.

Mr W. P. Westervelt, the superintendent, and Mr Andrew Wynne, the line-man of the telegraph company, were delegated to Harrisburg to 'fix' the wires leading from that place in such a manner as to prevent any communication from passing over them, and to report to Capt. Burns upon their arrival.

After the train containing Mr Lincoln and his party had left Philadelphia, Mr Judd sought the first favourable opportunity of conversing with Mr Lincoln alone, and fully detailed to him the plan that had been agreed upon, all of which met with the hearty approval of the President, who signified a cheerful willingness to adapt himself to the novel circumstances.

It was evident, from the manner of several of the gentlemen of the party, that they suspected something was transpiring of which they had not been advised, but they all very judiciously refrained from asking any questions. Mr Judd, however, who felt the responsibility of his position, finally suggested to Mr Lincoln the propriety and advisability of informing them of what had taken place, and of consulting with them upon the proper carrying out of the contemplated journey. To this Mr Lincoln yielded a ready assent, adding, with an amused smile: 'I suppose they will laugh at us, Judd. but I think you had better get them together'.

It was therefore arranged that after the reception at the State House had taken place, and before they sat down to dinner, the matter should be fully laid before the following gentlemen of the party: Judge David Davis, Col. Sumner, Major David Hunter, Capt. John Pope and Ward H. Lamon Esq.

Mr Lincoln arrived at Harrisburg at noon, and was introduced to the people from the balcony of the Jones House, where an address was delivered by Gov. Andrew G. Curtin, whose fame became widespread during the dark days of the rebellion that followed, as the ' War Governor of Pennsylvania.' From the hotel the party proceeded to the House of Representatives, where he was welcomed by the Speaker, to which he replied in a few well-chosen words.

After a short time spent in congratulations and hand-shaking they returned to the hotel, and the gentlemen who have been previously named were invited (in company with the Governor) to confer with the President in the parlour. At this meeting the information of the discovery of the plot to assassinate the President was laid before them, and also the details of the proposed journey to Washington. After the matter had been fully explained, a great diversity of opinion manifested itself among the gentlemen present, and some warm discussion was indulged in. Finally, Judge Davis, who had expressed no opinion upon the subject as yet, addressed the President, saying: 'Well, Mr Lincoln, what is your own judgment upon this matter?'

'I have thought over this matter considerably since I went over the ground with Mr Pinkerton last night,' answered Mr Lincoln, 'and the appearance of Mr Frederick Seward, with warning from another source, confirms my belief in Mr Pinkerton's statement; therefore, unless there are some other reasons than a fear of ridicule, I am disposed to carry out Mr Judd's plan.'

Judge Davis turned to the others and said: 'That settles the matter, gentlemen.'

'So be it,' exclaimed Col. Sumner. 'It is against my judgment, but I have undertaken to go to Washington with Mr Lincoln, and I shall do it.'

Mr Judd endeavoured in vain to convince the gallant old soldier that every additional person only added to the risk, but the fiery spirit of the veteran was aroused and debate was useless.

Having arranged the matter thus satisfactorily the party, at about four o'clock in the afternoon, repaired to the dining-room for dinner.

All the preliminaries had now been successfully arranged. The special train, ostensibly to take the officers of the railroad company back to Philadelphia, was waiting upon a side track just outside of the town. The telegraph operators had performed their work admirably. Walking out of the city nearly two miles, Mr Wynne climbed the poles, and placing fine copper ground wires upon the regular lines, the city was soon entirely isolated from her neighbours. No message could possibly be sent from Harrisburg, and the capital of Pennsylvania was cut off temporarily from the rest of the world.

The preparations in Philadelphia had also been fully made. Mrs Warne had succeeded in engaging the rear half of a sleeping-car for the accommodation of her invalid brother, and that portion of the car was to be entirely separated from the rest by a curtain, so arranged that no one in the forward part of the car would be aware of the occupants of the same coach.

In order to detain the Baltimore train until the arrival of Mr Lincoln, the conductor was directed not to start his train until he received personal instructions to that effect from Mr H. F. Kinney, the superintendent, who would hand him an important parcel, which President Felton desired should be delivered early on the following morning to Mr E. J. Allen at Willard's Hotel, in Washington. (E. J. Allen was the *nom-de-plume* I generally used when on detective operations.)

At a quarter to six o'clock everything was in readiness. A carriage was in waiting at the side entrance of the hotel, and the entire party were still at the table. A message was delivered to the President by Mr Nicolay, and upon receiving it he immediately arose and, accompanied by Mr Curtin, Mr Lamon and Mr Judd, he left the dining-room. Mr Lincoln exchanged his dinner dress for a travelling suit, and soon returned with a shawl upon his arm and a soft felt hat protruding from his coat pocket.

The halls, stairways and pavement were filled with a mass of people who, seeing the President in company with the Governor, at once imagined that they were going to the executive mansion, where a reception was to be held in the evening.

Mr Judd whispered to Mr Lamon to proceed in advance, adding: 'As soon as Mr Lincoln is in the carriage, drive off.'

As the party, consisting of Mr Lincoln, Governor Curtin, and Mr Lamon entered the carriage, Col. Sumner attempted to follow them, but Mr Judd gently put his hand upon the old gentleman's shoulder, and as he turned quickly around to inquire what was wanted, the carriage was driven rapidly away.

Thus far everything had passed off admirably, and in a short time Mr Lincoln was upon the special train, accompanied only by Mr Lamon and the railroad officials, and speeding along toward Philadelphia.

Without accident the party arrived at the Quaker City shortly after ten o'clock, where I was waiting with a carriage, in company with Mr Kinney. Without a word, Mr Lincoln, Mr Lamon and myself entered the vehicle, while Mr Kinney seated himself alongside of the driver, and we proceeded directly to the depot of the Philadelphia, Wilmington and Baltimore Railroad.

Driving up to the sidewalk on Carpenter street, and in the shadow of a tall fence, the carriage was stopped and the party alighted. As we approached the train Mrs Warne came forward and, familiarly greeting the President as her brother, we entered the sleeping-car by the rear door without unnecessary delay, and without anyone being aware of the distinguished passenger who had arrived.

A carefully enclosed package, which resembled a formidable official document, but which contained only some neatly folded daily papers, was placed in the hands of the unsuspecting conductor; the whistle sounded, and soon the train was in motion, whirling on towards the capital of the nation.

So carefully had all our movements been conducted, that no one in Philadelphia saw Mr Lincoln enter the car, and no one on the train, except his own immediate party, not even the conductor, knew of his presence, and the President, feeling fatigued from the labours and the journeys of the day, at once retired to his berth.

In order to prevent the possibility of accident, I had arranged with my men a series of signals along the road. It was barely possible that the work of destroying the railroad might be attempted by some reckless individuals, or that a suspicion of our movements might be entertained by the conspirators, and therefore, the utmost caution must be observed.

As the train approached Havre de Grace, I went to the rear platform of the car, and as the train passed on a bright light flashed suddenly upon my gaze and was as quickly extinguished, and then I knew that thus far all was well.

From this point all the way to Baltimore, at every bridge-crossing these lights flashed, and their rays carried the comforting assurance 'All's Well!'

We reached Baltimore at about half-past three o'clock in the morning, and as the train rumbled into the depot an officer of the road entered the car and whispered in my ear the welcome words 'All's Well!'

The city was in profound repose as we passed through. Darkness and silence reigned over all. Perhaps, at this moment, however, the reckless conspirators were astir perfecting their plans for a tragedy as infamous as any which has ever disgraced a free country; perhaps even now the holders of the red ballots were nerving themselves for their part in the dreadful work, or were tossing restlessly upon sleepless couches.

Be that as it may, our presence in Baltimore was entirely unsuspected, and as the sleeping-car in which we were, was drawn by horses through the streets from the Philadelphia, Wilmington and Baltimore depot, until we reached the Washington station, no sign of life was apparent in the great slumbering city. At the depot, however, a number of people were gathered, awaiting the arrival and departure of the various trains, and here the usual bustle and activity were manifested.

We were compelled to remain here fully two hours, owing to the detention of the train from the West, and during that time Mr Lincoln remained quietly in his berth, joking with rare good humour with those around him.

Ever and anon some snatches of rebel harmony would reach our ears, as they were rather discordantly sung by the waiting passengers in and around the depot; 'My Maryland' and 'Dixie' appeared to be the favourites, and once, after an intoxicated individual had roared through one stanza of the latter song, Mr Lincoln turned quietly and rather sadly to me and said: 'No doubt there will be a great time in Dixie by and by'.

How prophetic his words were, the succeeding years too fully proved.

At length the train arrived and we proceeded on our way, arriving in Washington about six o'clock in the morning. Mr Lincoln wrapped his travelling shawl about his shoulders, and in company with Mr Lamon, started to leave the car. I followed close behind, and on the platform found two of my men awaiting our arrival. A great many people were gathered about the depot, but Mr Lincoln entirely escaped recognition, until as we were about leaving the depot, Mr Washburne, of Illinois, came up and cordially shook him by the hand.

The surprise of this gentleman was unbounded, and many of those standing around, observing his movements, and the tall form of Mr Lincoln exciting curiosity, I feared that danger might result in case he was recognised at this time. I accordingly went up to them hurriedly, and pressing between them whispered rather loudly: 'No talking here!'

Mr Washburne gazed inquiringly at me, and was about to resent my interference, when Mr Lincoln interposed: 'That is Mr Pinkerton, and everything is all right.'

Thus satisfied, Mr Washburne quickly led the way to a carriage in waiting outside, where we met Mr Seward, who warmly greeted the President, and then the party were rapidly driven down Pennsylvania Avenue to Willard's Hotel, I following closely behind them with my men, in another vehicle.

On his arrival at the hotel, Mr Lincoln was warmly greeted by his friends, who were rejoiced at his safe arrival, and leaving him in the hands of those whose fealty was undoubted, I withdrew, and engaged temporary quarters at another hotel.

During the forenoon I received a note from Mr Lincoln requesting an interview, and received his warm expressions of thankfulness for the part I had performed in securing his safety, after which, finding that my object had been fully accomplished, I took the train and returned to Baltimore.

After the Civil War, Pinkerton took over again the direction of his agency from George Bangs and Francis Warner who had managed it during the Rebellion, and had in the process opened offices in New York and Philadelphia.

Pinkerton's sons joined—the elder, William, was happiest out on the chase (as the next tale shows) while Robert's talents were in administration—he established the card-file system that served as the model for law enforcement bodies since.

This 1868 yarn of the Old West concerns William Allen Pinkerton as the protagonist detective, and how he deals with the dashing, handsome Captain Harry. (Could you seriously believe Wyatt Earp or Pat Garrett saying 'I say, gentlemen, that won't do. You must stand back!')

Pinkerton gives a humorous and remarkably detailed description of the Texas floods, stage negro dialogue, the character of stagecoach drivers and stagecoach robbers, the Klu Klux Klan, the chivalric ethics of a saloon gun-fight and other colour which is all the more remarkable for him not being there to experience it. He also takes pains to remind his readers, once again, that he is conversant with the works of Dickens and Longfellow.

⊰ A Detective's Hard Life ⊱

Every person who may have survived the experience has undoubtedly a lively recollection of the wild groups of people which the building of the Union and Central Pacific Railroads brought together from all directions, and from all causes.

There were millions upon millions of dollars to be expended; and as the points of construction neared each other, and the twin bands of iron crept along the earth's surface like two huge serpents, spanning mighty rivers, penetrating vast mountains, and trailing through majestic forests, creeping slowly but surely towards each other, there was always the greatest dread at the most advanced points which, like the heads of serpents, always contained danger and death; and the vast cities of a day that then sprang into existence, and melted away like school children's snow-houses, were the points where such wild scenes were enacted as will probably never again occur in the history of railroad building.

Everything contributed to make these places typical of Babelic confusion, or pandemoniac contention. Foreigners were told of the exhaustless work, and the exhaustless wealth, of this new country which was being so rapidly developed, and they came; brave men, who had been on the wrong side during the late irritation, and who had lost all, having staked all on the result of the war, saw a possible opportunity of retrieving their fortunes rapidly, and they came; the big-headed youth of the village whose smattering of books at the academy, or the seminary, so had enlarged his brain and contracted his sense so that he was too good for the common duties and everyday drudgeries which, with patience, lead to success, learned of the glory and grandeur of that new land, and he came; the speculating shirk and the peculating clerk came; the almond-eyed sons of the Orient in herds—herds of quick-witted, patient, plodding beings who could be beaten, starved, even murdered came; the forger, the bruiser, the counterfeiter, the gambler, the garroter, the prostitute, the robber, and the murderer, each and every, came. There was adventure for the adventurous, gold for the thief, waiting throats for the murderer; while the few respectable people quickly became discouraged, and fell into the general looseness of habits that the loose life engendered, and gradually grew reckless as the most reckless, or quickly acquiesced in the wild orgies or startling crimes which were of common occurrence. In fact, as in the human system, when any portion of it becomes diseased and all the poison in the blood flows to it, further corrupting and diseasing it until arrested by a gradual purification of the whole body, or by some severe treatment, so from every portion of the country flowed these streams of morally corrupt people, until nearly every town west of Missouri, or east of the mountains, along these lines, became a terror to honest people, and continued so until an irresistible conflict compelled a moral revulsion, sometimes so sweeping and violent as to cause an application of that unwritten, though often exceedingly just law, the execution of which leaves offenders dangling to limbs of trees, lamp-posts, and other convenient points of suspension.

As a rule, in these places every man, whatever his business and condition, was thoroughly armed, the question of self-defence being a paramount one, from the fact that laws which governed older communities were completely a dead letter; and the law of might, in a few instances made somewhat respectable by a faint outline of ruffianly honour, alone prevailed, until advancing civilisation and altered conditions brought about a better state of society. So that in these reckless crowds which pushed after the constantly changing termini of the approaching roads, any instrument of bloodshed was considered valuable, and stores where arms and ammunition could be secured did quite as large a trade as those devoted to any other branch of business. While so outrageous was the price extorted for these instruments of aggression or defence, that they have often been known to sell for their weight in gold; and just as during the war, the army was followed by enterprising traders who turned many an honest penny trafficking at the heels of the weary soldiers, so the same class of people were not slow to take advantage of such opportunities for gigantic profits which, though often lessened by the many risks run in such trading, were still heavy enough to prove peculiarly attractive.

As a consequence, there were many firms engaged in this particular business, but probably the heaviest was that of Kuhn Brothers, who were reported to be worth upwards of one hundred thousand dollars, which had principally been made along the line of the road, and who, with headquarters at Cheyenne, had established various 'stores' at different points as the Union Pacific was pushed on, always keeping the largest stock at the most advanced point, and withdrawing stocks from the paper cities which had been left behind, though only in those towns which had not been altogether destroyed by the periodical exodus occasioned by each change of terminus.

For this reason, the firms were obliged to entrust their business to the honesty of many different employees, who were subject to the vitiating influences and temptations, which were unusual and severe under the circumstances already mentioned, while the distances between the points, and the scarcity of secure means of safely keeping the large sums of money which would occasionally unavoidably accrue at certain points, left Kuhn Brothers, in many instances, really dependent on those dependent on them.

In this condition of affairs, and after a slight defalcation had occurred at one of their smaller stores in the spring of 1867, the firm were seeking a man whom they could place in actual charge of one or two of their establishments at the larger towns, and give a sort of general supervision over the others, when the senior member of the firm, being in Laramie, casually met a young gentleman, who happened to be able to do him so great a favour that the incident led to a close friendship and ultimate business relations, eventually resulting in this narrative of facts.

It was a pleasant May evening, and Mr Kuhn had decided to returned to Cheyenne in order to secure a proper man for the superintendency nearer home. He was to have left Laramie for the East at a late hour of the evening and, being at a loss how to pass the intervening time, strolled out from the hotel with no particular destination in view, and his mind fully occupied with the cares of his business, only occasionally noticing some peculiarity or strange sight more than usually striking among the thousands of weird things, to which his frontier business had compelled him to become accustomed, when suddenly he found himself in front of a mammoth dance-house, and yielding to a momentary impulse of curiosity, turned into the place with the stream of gamblers, adventurers, greasers and, in fact, everybody respectable or otherwise who, so far from civilisation, found such a place peculiarly attractive.

The dance-house was a sort of hell's bazaar, if the term may be allowed, and it is certainly the one most befitting it and was really no 'house' at all, being merely a very large board enclosure covered with a gigantic tent or series of tents, bedecked with flags and gaudy streamers. The entrance fee to this elegant place of amusement was one dollar, and you had only paid an initiatory fee when you had gained admission.

On either side as you entered were immense bars, built of the roughest of boards, where every kind of liquid poison was dispensed at the moderate sum of twenty-five cents a drink, five-cent cigars selling at the same price, and the united efforts of a half-dozen murderous-

77

looking bartenders at each side were required to assuage the thirst of the quite as murderous-looking crowd that swayed back and forth within the space evidently prepared for that purpose. Beyond this point, and to either side, as also down the centre for some distance, could be found almost every known game of chance, dealt, of course, 'by the house', while surrounding the lay-outs were every description of men crazed with drink; hushed with success, or deathly pale from sudden ruin. While everywhere the revolver or the Bowie intimated with what terrible swiftness and certainty any trifling dispute, rankling grudge, or violent insult would be settled, one way or the other, and to be marked by the mere pitching of an inanimate form into the street!

After these attractions came a stout partition which had evidently been found necessary, for beyond it there was the strikingly strange heaven of a mushroom city, a vast department where there were music and women; and it seemed that the 'management' of this grand robbers' roost had shrewdly calculated on the fact that if a poor fool had not been swindled out of every dollar he might have had before he reached this point, those two elements, all powerful for good or evil the world over, would wring the last penny from him.

Here was another but a finer bar, where more time was taken to prepare a drink and drug a man with some show of artistic excellence, and where a half dollar was changed for a single measure of poison; women, shrewd, devilish women who could shoot or cut, if occasion required, with the nicety and effect of a man, 'steering' every person giving token of having money in his possession to the more genteelly gotten up 'lay-outs', and acting in the same capacity, only with far more successful results, as the ordinary 'ropers-in' of any large city. A wild, discordant orchestra that would have been hooted out of the lowest of the 'varieties' east of the Missouri; but in this place, and to these ears, so long unused to the music of the far-away homes beyond the Mississippi, producing the very perfection of enchanting harmonies; but above all, and the crowning attraction before which every other thing paled and dwindled to insignificance, a score of abandoned women, dancing and ogling with every manner of man, robbing them while embracing, cheering and drinking with them, and in every way bedevilling them; the whole forming a scene viler than imagination

78

or the pen of man can conceive or picture; a grouping of wild orgies and terrible debaucheries, such as would put Lucifer to a blush, and compel a revolution in the lowest depths of Hades.

Kuhn had strolled through the place, and now, out of compliment to general custom, purchased a cigar and was just turning to depart, when he suddenly found himself being hustled back and forth among several hard-looking fellows, who, evidently knowing his business, and surmising that he carried large sums of money upon his person, had determined to provoke him to resistance; when there would, according to the social codes then in existence at Laramie, have been a just cause for either robbing and beating him, or murdering him outright and robbing him afterwards; when a tall, finely-formed man suddenly stepped into the crowd, and in a very decided tone of voice said:

'I say, gentlemen, that won't do. You must stand back!'

Then taking the terror-stricken ammunition dealer by the coat collar with his left hand, but keeping his right hand free for quick use and certain work, if necessary, he trotted him through the now excited throng and out into the open air, hastily telling him to 'cut for the hotel' which were quite unnecessary instructions, as he made for that point at as lively a gait as his rather dumpy legs could carry him.

The person who had thus prevented the merchant's being robbed, and had also possibly saved his life, was a tall, comely young man of about twenty-eight years of age, and with a complexion as fair as a woman's, pleasant, though determined, blue eyes, and a long, reddish, luxuriant beard, all of which, with a decidedly military cut to his gray, woollen garments, and long fair hair falling upon his shoulders, the whole crowned, or rather slouched over, by a white hat of extraordinary width of brim, gave him the appearance of an ex-Confederate officer. A right good fellow, as the term goes, perfectly capable of caring for himself wherever his fortune, or misfortune, might lead him, which proved the case as he turned and confronted the desperadoes, who had immediately followed him in a threatening manner, and whom he stood ready to receive with a navy revolver half as long as his arm, mysteriously whipped from some hiding-place, in each steady hand.

A critical examination of the man as he stood there, and a very casual survey of him, for that matter, would have instantly suggested the fact to an ordinary observer that a very cool man at the rear ends of two navy revolvers huge enough to have been mounted for light-artillery service, was something well calculated to check the mounting ambition on the part of most anybody to punish him for the character of the interference shown. The leader of the gang contented himself with remarking, 'See here, Captain Harry, if it wasn't you, there'd be a reck'ning here; lively, too, I'm tellin' ye!'

'Well, but it is me and so there won't be any reck'ning. Will there, now, eh?'

The ruffians made no answer, but sullenly returned to the dance-house, when Captain Harry, as he had been called, rammed the two huge revolvers into his boot legs, which action displayed a smaller weapon of the same kind upon each hip; after which he nodded a pleasant 'good-night' to the bystanders, and walked away leisurely in the direction Mr Kuhn had taken, pleasantly whistling 'The Bonnie Blue Flag' or 'The Star Spangled Banner' as best suited him.

The moment that Mr Kuhn's protector appeared at the hotel, the former gentleman expressed his liveliest thanks for the opportune as-sistance he had been rendered, and introduced himself to the Captain, who already knew of him, and who in return gave his name as 'Harry G. Taylor, the man from somewhere', as he himself expressed it with a pleasant laugh.

It was easy to be seen that there was a stroke of business in Mr Kuhn's eye, which his escape from the dance-house had suggested, as he told Taylor that he had intended to return to Cheyenne that night; but he further stated that as he had so unexpectedly been befriended, he should certainly be obliged to remain another day in order to se-cure a further acquaintance with the man to whom he already owed so much.

Mr Kuhn then produced some choice cigars, and the gentlemen secured a retired place upon the hotel-porch, at once entering into a general conversation which, from the merchant's evident unusual cu-riosity, and Taylor's quite as evident good-humoured, devil-may-care disposition, caused it to drift into the Captain's account of himself.

He told Mr Kuhn that his family resided at that time in Philadelphia, where they had moved after his father had failed in business at Raleigh, NC, but had taken so honourable a name with him to the former city that he had been able to retrieve his fortunes to some extent. The Captain was born at Raleigh, and had received his education in the South and, being unable to share in his father's regard for the North, even as a portion of the country best adapted for doing business, sought out some of his old college friends in Louisville, Atlanta, and New Orleans, who had been able to secure him a fine business position at Atlanta, where by care and economy in 1860, though but a mere boy yet, he had accumulated property that would have satisfied many a man twenty years his senior.

Being impulsive and a warm admirer of Southern institutions, he was one of the first men to join the Confederate army at Atlanta, and fought in a Georgia regiment under Johnson and Hood during the entire war, at Jonesville and Rough-and-Ready Station seeing the smoke ascend above the ruins of the once beautiful city, and realising that the most of his earthly possessions had disappeared when the flames died away.

Having been promoted to a captaincy, he had fought as bravely as he could against the 'blue-coats', like a man, acknowledging their bravery as well as that of his comrades; and at the close of the war, which of course terminated disadvantageous to his interests, he had sold his lots at Atlanta for what ever he could get for them, and with thousands of others in like circumstances, had come West and taken his chances at retrieving his fortunes.

This was told in a frank, straightforward way, which seemed to completely captivate Mr Kuhn, for he at once spoke to Taylor concerning his business in Laramie, and bluntly asked him, in the event of mutual and satisfactory references being exchanged, whether he would accept the engagement as superintendent of his business over that portion of the road, and take actual charge of the store in that place, and the one about to be established at Benton City.

The result of the evening's interview was the engagement of Taylor by the firm at a large salary; his immediately taking supervision of the business without bonds or any security whatever. For a time his management and habits were so able and irreproachable that, with the gratitude for his protection of Mr Kuhn at Laramie still fresh and sincere, the firm felt that they had been most fortunate in their selection of an utter stranger, and were in every way gratified with the turn events had taken.

During the early morning of a blustering December day of the same year, I was quite annoyed by the persistence of a gentleman to see me, on what he insisted, in the business office of my Chicago agency, on terming 'important business'.

It was not later than half-past eight o'clock; and, as I have made it a life-long practice to get at business at an early hour, get ahead of it, and keep ahead of it during the day, I was elbow-deep in the mass of letters, telegrams, and communications of a different nature which, in my business, invariably accumulates during the night, and felt anxious to wade through it before taking up any other matter.

The gentleman, who gave the name of Kuhn, seemed very anxious to see me, however he let drop the statements that he greatly desired to take the morning train for Cheyenne, where he resided; might not be able to be in Chicago again for some time; felt very desirous of seeing me personally; and would require but a few moments to explain his business, which he agreed to make explicit; I concluded to drop everything else and see him. On being ushered into my private apartments, he at once hastily gave me an outline of the facts related in the previous chapter, adding a new series of incidents which occasioned his visit, and to the effect that the firm had made the necessary arrangements for increasing their business under their new superintendent, having added largely to their stock at Laramie, and placed about twenty thousand dollars' worth of goods at Benton City.

According to the agreement, he was required to forward money whenever the sales had reached a stated sum at each point, and was given authority to take charge of goods or money on hand at any of the less important stations, when convinced that things were being run loosely, or whenever it in any way appeared for the interests of the firm for him to do so.

It will be seen that under this arrangement, which was in every respect injudicious, no security having been given by Taylor, he immediately became possessed of great responsibility, as well as power; but appeared to appreciate the unusual confidence reposed in him, and conducted the business of Kuhn Brothers with unusual profit to them and credit to himself. Matters progressed in this way for some time, when suddenly, on about the first of October, the firm at Cheyenne began to receive dispatches from different employees along the road, inquiring when Taylor was to return from Cheyenne, and intimating that business was greatly suffering from his absence. The members of the firm were astonished. They knew nothing of Taylor's being in Cheyenne. On the contrary, their last advices from him were to the effect that he should be at their city on the tenth of that month, with large collections; and the announcement was accompanied with glowing accounts of the prosperity of their business under his careful management.

After the startling intelligence of Taylor's unaccountable absence, a member of the firm immediately left for Laramie, Benton City, and other points, to ascertain the true condition of affairs, still unable to believe that the handsome, chivalrous captain had wronged them, and that everything would be found right upon examination of matters, which was immediately and searchingly entered upon; but the first glance at affairs showed conclusively that they had been swindled, and it was soon discovered that he had gathered together at the stores under his own charge, and at different points along the line, under various pretexts, fully fourteen thousand dollars, and had been given two weeks in which to escape.

Mr Kuhn did not desire to give the case into my hands on that morning; but explained that he had returned from a fruitless trip to Philadelphia in search of his former superintendent, and had been advised by a telegram from his brothers to lay the case before me and request my advice about the matter; at the same time securing information about the probable pecuniary outlay necessary for further prosecution of the search, and such other items of information as would enable him to counsel with the remainder of the firm concerning the case, and be able to give the case into my hands, should they decide to do so, without further delay.

This was given to him and I, in turn, secured from Mr Kuhn all the information possible concerning Taylor, which was scant indeed, as they had seen very little of him, could give but a very general description of the man, and here they had injudiciously given him over two weeks' start, during which time he might have safely got to the other side of the world.

Only one item of information had been developed by which a clue to his whereabouts could by any possibility be imagined. He had often spoken to Mr Kuhn in the most glowing terms of life in both Texas and Mexico. He had passed, so he had said, a portion of a year in that part of America, since the close of the war, and in connection with the subject, he had stated that he should have remained there had he been supplied with sufficient capital to have enabled him to begin business.

This was all; and I dismissed the swindled merchant with little encouragement as to the result of a chase for a thief who had got so much the advantage, or rather, intimated to him that though I had no doubts of being able to eventually catch him, it would be rather a poor investment for the firm to expend the amount of money which might be necessary to effect his capture, unless in looking into the matter further, I should be able to see opportunities for securing much better knowledge as to his present whereabouts, or clues which could be made to lead to them.

With this not very cheering assurance, Mr Kuhn returned to Cheyenne.

Not hearing from the firm for several days, I finally dismissed the matter entirely from mind, but on arriving at the agency one morning, I received instructions from the Cheyenne firm to proceed in the matter, and with all expedition possible endeavour to cage the flown bird for them.

I at once detailed William A. Pinkerton, my eldest son, and at present Assistant Superintendent of my Chicago agency, to proceed to Cheyenne and look over the ground thoroughly there, and also, if necessary, to proceed along the line of the Union Pacific and, after ascertaining who were Taylor's friends and companions, work up a trail through them, which would eventually bring him down.

The latter course was not necessary to be followed however, as on arriving at Cheyenne, with some little information gleaned from the firm, he was able to ascertain that a young lawyer there named

La Grange, also originally from the South, had been a quite intimate friend of Taylor's; so much so in fact, that La Grange had for the last six months regularly corresponded with the Captain's sister, who had been described to him as not only an exceedingly beautiful woman, but as also a lady possessed of unusual accomplishments and amiability.

My son 'cultivated' La Grange largely, but could secure but little information through him. He seemed to know nothing further concerning either Taylor or his family, save that he had incidentally met him along the line of the Union Pacific. They had naturally taken a sort of liking to each other, and in that way became friends in much the same manner that most friendships were made in that country. He further recollected that he had always directed his letters to a certain post-office box, instead of to a street number, but seemed perfectly mystified concerning the action of the brother. He had just returned from a three months' absence in Kentucky, and it was the first intimation he had had of the Captain's crime. La Grange also said that as he had been very busy, he had not written to Miss Lizzie (evidently referring to the sister), nor had he received any communication from her during that time. He had had a photograph of Harry, taken in full-dress uniform while stationed at Atlanta, which had been copied in Philadelphia, but a thorough search among his papers failed to reveal it.

This was all that my son could secure, as La Grange, evidently suspecting that, in his surprise at Taylor's crime, he might say something to compromise himself and endanger Taylor or wound his beautiful sister, to whom he seemed greatly attached, positively refused to have anything further to say concerning the matter. With what information he had, William returned to the hotel in a brown study, determined to take time to exhaust the material at Cheyenne before proceeding on the proposed trip along the Union Pacific.

After summing up and arranging the points he had got hold of, he telegraphed me fully, adding his own impression that Taylor was in Texas, but expressing a doubt as to whether he had better proceed along the Union Pacific for more information, or go on to Philadelphia at once, and in some way secure information of the family as to their son's whereabouts.

On the receipt of this telegram, which arrived in Chicago about noon, I at once resolved upon a little strategy, being myself satisfied that Taylor had proceeded, via St Louis and New Orleans into either Texas or Mexico, and was then engaged under his own or an assumed name, in some business agreeable to his taste, as formerly explained to Mr Kuhn, and immediately telegraphed to my son: 'Keep La Grange busied all day so he cannot write, or mail letters. Study La Grange's language and modes of expression. Get La Grange's and Taylor's handwriting, signatures, and Miss Taylor's address, and come next train.'

Agreeable to these instructions, he secured several letters from Taylor to Kuhn Brothers concerning business matters, with the last one containing the announcement that, he would be in Cheyenne on the tenth of October with collections; and immediately sent by a messenger a courteous note to La Grange, desiring an outline of Taylor's life so far as he might feel justified in giving it, and requesting an answer, which was politely but firmly given in the negative over Adolph La Grange's own signature, which completed a portion of his work neatly.

The balance was more difficult. He ordered a sleigh, and after settling his hotel bill, but reserving his room for the night, at once drove to La Grange's office, where he in person thanked him for his courteous letter, even if he did not feel justified in giving him the information desired. A little complimentary conversation ensued, during which time my son's quick eyes noticed in the lawyer's waste-basket an envelope evidently discarded on account of its soiled appearance, addressed to 'Miss Lizzie Taylor, Post-office Box, Philadelphia', which on the first opportunity he appropriated. The next move was to prevent La Grange's mailing any letter, as it was evident he had written several, including one to Taylor's sister, which were only waiting to be mailed.

Seeing that he had made a pleasant impression upon La Grange, who appreciated the courtesy of the call under the circumstances, and informing him that he had decided to make no further inquiries there, but was to proceed west on the following morning, he prevailed upon him to take a ride in his company about the city and its environs. In leaving his office, La Grange hesitated a moment as if deciding the propriety of taking the letters with him, or returning for them after the sleigh-ride; but evidently decided to do the latter, as he left them, much to my son's relief.

The drive was prolonged as much as possible, and the outlying forts visited where, having letters of introduction from myself to several army-officers stationed there, both he and his companion were so hospitably treated that the afternoon slipped away quickly and the two returned to town evidently in high spirits. La Grange felt compelled to reciprocate as far as in his power, and billiards, with frequent drinks for the lawyer and a liberal supply of water for the detective, were in order until within a half hour of the eastern bound train time, when La Grange succumbed to an accumulation of good-fellowship, and on his own suggestion, as he 'wash a rising y'n'g 'torny y'know!' accepted the hospitalities of my son's room, at the Rawlins House, where he left him sweetly sleeping at a rate which would prevent the mailing of the letters he had left locked in his office for at least two days to come; 'rising young attorneys', as a rule, sober off in a carefully graduated diminishing scale of excesses of quite similar construction to the original.

On the arrival of my son in Chicago, I immediately caused to be written a letter addressed to Miss Lizzie Taylor, at her post-office box in Philadelphia, of which the following is a copy:

SHERMAN HOUSE, CHICAGO, Jan. 1868.

MISS TAYLOR,

MY DEAR FRIEND: You know of my intended absence from Cheyenne in the South. During that trip, I really never had the time when I could write you so fully as I desired, and even now I am only able to send you a few words. I am on route to Washington on business, and have now to ask you to send the street and number of your father's house, even if it is not a magnificent one, as you have told me, to my address, at the Girard House in your city on receipt of this, as I shall be in Washington but one day, and would wish to see both you and your people without delay. I not only greatly wish to see you for selfish reasons, which our long and pleasant correspondence will suggest to you as both reasonable and natural, but there are other good reasons, which you all will readily understand when I tell you that I met him accidentally just before my return to Cheyenne, and that I have a communication of a personal nature to deliver. While not upholding him in the step he has taken, I cannot forget that I am his friend, and he your brother.

In great haste,

Your true friend,

ADOLPH LA G.

P. S. I leave here for the East this morning. Please answer on immediate receipt.
A. L.

This was posted on the eastern-bound train not an hour after my son's arrival from the West; and another note was written upon the back of an envelope which had passed through the mail, and had got a very much used appearance, and ran thus:

FATHER OF LIZZIE:

Treat Adolph well, you can trust him. Give him one of the 'photos' taken at Atlanta in my full-dress uniform; keep one other of the same for yourselves; but destroy all the rest. Have been so hurried and worried that I don't remember whether I have said anything about photographs before. But this is a matter of imperative necessity. Adolph will explain how he met me.
Goodbye,

H

It was impossible to detect any difference between this handwriting and that of Captain Taylor's in his business correspondence to Kuhn Brothers; and, armed with this document, with the assistance of the epistolary self-introduction which had preceded it, I directed my son to leave for Philadelphia that evening, secure admission to Taylor's residence and the family's confidence, agreeable to the appointment made by mail, and thus not only secure the man's photograph, but other information that would be definite.

On arrival at Philadelphia, he secured the services of an operative from my agency in that city, to follow any member of the Taylor family who might call for the letter, to their residence, in the event of an answer not being received at his hotel in due time from the one assumed to have been sent from the hotel in Chicago from La Grange, who found Taylor's home, an unpretentious house on Locust street, while my son remained at the hotel, fully expecting the coveted invitation to visit the Captain's beautiful sister, which arrived at his hotel only a half day after he did, and strongly urged him to call at his convenience.

He was satisfied from this that our theory regarding his being in Texas, or Mexico, was correct; that the family had not the slightest suspicion of his identity, and that, wherever Captain Taylor might be, communication with his people had been very infrequent, and that, with what he would be able to invent after being received at Taylor's house, he could secure at least sufficient information to put him upon his son's trail. Not desiring to play upon their feelings and friendship as another person any longer than necessary, however, he sent word by a messenger, not daring to trust his own handwriting, that he would call that evening, though necessarily at a late hour and, accordingly, that evening, about nine o'clock, found him at the door of a pleasant Locust street cottage, ringing for admission.

A tall, handsome young woman greeted him at the door, and accordingly bade him enter, saying pleasantly, as she ushered him into the cosy little parlour, that she was Miss Lizzie Taylor, and presumed he was Mr La Grange, with whom she had had so long and so pleasant a correspondence; and of whom 'poor Harry', as she said with a shade of sadness and tenderness in her voice, had so often written, before he had made his terrible mistake, and become a wanderer.

After hastily satisfying her that he was the genuine La Grange, and profusely apologising for his not having written for so long a time previous to his arrival at Chicago, from Cheyenne, he took up the thread she had dropped, as quickly as possible, and said that he felt sure that Harry would retrieve himself soon, and return the money, as he had no bad habits and everything would be all right again.

'But yet, Mr La Grange,' she continued, 'it makes me shudder whenever I think of all my brothers being away off there on the Rio Grande, among those terrible people!'

'But, you must remember,' he replied, encouragingly, 'they are strong men, and can well defend themselves under any circumstances.'

'Harry is strong and brave, I know,' answered Miss Taylor, rather admiringly; 'but brother Robert is not fit for such a life. Why, he is but a boy yet.'

'Ah, a younger brother,' he thought, making a mental note of it, in order to assist in shaping his conversation after which he said aloud: 'I almost forgot to give you this note.' He took the piece of envelope out of his note-book, as if it had been sacredly guarded, and handed it to her.

Miss Taylor read the hastily written lines with evident emotion and after studying a moment, as if endeavouring to reconcile matters, while her face was being searchingly read by an experienced detective, she rose and, apologising to him for the absence of her father, who was in New York, on business, and of her mother, who was confined to her apartment, a confirmed invalid, she asked to be excused so as to show the note to her mother.

The instant the door closed, my son had seized the album, which he had located during the preceding conversation, and rapidly turned its leaves to assure himself that he was not treading on dangerous ground. He found a half-a-dozen different styles of pictures of the Captain, including three of the copies taken in Philadelphia of the original Atlanta picture, and felt reassured beyond measure at the lucky turn things had taken. He would have abstracted one of these, but it was impossible, and had barely time to return the album to the table, and himself to his seat, when he heard the woman's step along the hall, and in a moment more she entered the room.

Giving the door a little impulsive slam, as she closed it, Miss Taylor at once came to where my son was sitting upon the sofa, and seated herself beside him. She said that her mother was anxious beyond measure to learn how and where he had met Harry, how he was looking, and what he had said.

The imagination and resources of the able detective are fully equal to those of the most brilliant newspaper reporters, and a pleasant and plausible fiction was invented, how he (as La Grange, of course), having taken a run from Louisville down to New Orleans, by boat, was just landing at the levee, when he suddenly came across Harry, who had hastily told him all; how great had been his transgression, how deeply he had regretted it; but that now he was situated in his business matters so that, if let alone, he would be able to return to Kuhn Brothers every dollar which he had taken, and have a fine business left; how it had been necessary for him to come to New Orleans on imperative business, and that he should not come east of the Mississippi again under any circumstances. He further said, that Harry seemed hopeful; that he had stated that his younger brother Robert was well and enjoying the frontier life; and that, further than that, he had no time or disposition to talk, as he was on the very eve of departure for Texas, only having time to write the little note concerning the photographs.

Miss Taylor excused herself for a moment to convey the truthful intelligence to her anxious mother; and on her return suggested that they go through the album together at once, and attend to the photographs, an invitation which was accepted with unusual readiness.

Every gentleman who has had the experience, and there are few who have not, know that looking over an album with a beautiful woman who has some interest in her companion, is a wonderfully pleasant diversion. In this instance it was doubly pleasant, for it meant success to my son, whose zeal is as untiring as my own when once on the trail of a criminal.

'I wonder why,' asked Miss Taylor, as if wondering as much about Mr La Grange as about any other subject; 'I wonder why Harry desires those photographs destroyed?'

He was turning the leaves for her and as La Grange, of course, had a perfect right to take plenty of time to explain the matter soothingly and sympathetically.

'But do those horrid detectives track a man out and run him down, when, if he were let alone, he might recover from his misfortune, and right the wrong he has done?'

Mr La Grange remarked that he had heard that some of them were very much lacking in sentiment and sensibility, and would go right forward through the very fire itself to trace the whereabouts of a criminal; and all those little things helped, he could assure her.

She began to see how it was, she said, but suddenly firing up, she shook her pretty fist at some imaginary person, exclaiming: 'Oh, I could kill the man who would thus dog my brother Harry.' And then, after a little April shower of tears, quite like any other woman's way of showing how very desperate they can be under certain circumstances, began slowly taking the Captain's pictures from the album, commenting upon them, and then handing them to the bogus La Grange to burn, who would occasionally step to the fire-place for that purpose, where he would quickly substitute miscellaneous business cards, which answered the purpose excellently.

An hour or two was passed with Miss Taylor in conversation upon various topics which might lead the really estimable young lady to divulge all she knew about the Captain, or concerning his whereabouts and business, which was certainly not much.

It appeared that immediately after the embezzlement, and while at St Louis, Taylor had telegraphed to his brother Robert to meet him at New Orleans at a certain time as he was going into business in that section and should need his services, for which he would be able to pay him handsomely. The brothers had met there and had proceeded to some other point, the Captain claiming that it would be injudicious to make that fact known as he had also sent a full and complete confession to his parents of his embezzlement from Kuhn Brothers, which he had directed them to burn, and which he finished by requesting his family not to write to either himself or his brother for some time to come; or at least until he should indicate to them that it would be safe to do so and under no circumstances to give any person an iota of information concerning himself or his brother.

My son left Miss Taylor's hospitable home with a pang of regret for the deception which had seemed necessary in this case; for whatever may be the opinion of the public regarding the matter, a detective has often quite as large and compassionate a soul as men of other and apparently more high-toned professions.

So long as intelligent crime is the result of a high standard of mental culture and a low standard of moral conscience, conditions which now exist and have for some years existed, intelligent minds must be trained to battle criminals with their own weapons; and these two questions, of speedy detection of crime and swift punishment of criminals, will be found quite as essential to a preservation of law and society as lofty arguments or high moral dissertations on the right or wrong of the expediencies necessary to bring wrong-doers to immediate and certain justice.

As soon as I had received a full telegraphic report of the success of the Philadelphia experiment, I directed him to proceed to Louisville, where he would be met by operative Keating from Chicago, who would bring letters of introduction from myself to Colonel Wood, commanding the First Infantry at New Orleans; Captain White, chief of the detective force of that city; General Canby, commanding the Department of Texas, at Austin; Col. Hunt, Chief Quartermaster of the Department of Texas, and other army officers, requesting them to render my son and his assistant any aid in their power should the necessity for such assistance arise; the requisition from Governor Foulke, of Dakotah Territory, for Henry G. Taylor, upon Governor Pease, of Texas, and general instructions concerning his conduct of the search for the handsome captain after he had got beyond mail and telegraphic communication.

I was sending him into a country which was at that time in many portions utterly unsafe for the securing of a criminal should the pursuer's mission become known, so as to allow the person desired time to apprise his friends of his danger, or give him even an opportunity to rally any number of acquaintances for defence; for the reason that, as Texas had become a sort of refuge for ruffians, they became clannish through the general peril of being pursued each experienced and would, as a rule, on the slightest provocation, assist in the rescue of any person under arrest, not knowing how soon it might be their turn to cry for help. I have invariably sent my sons into danger with the same expectation that they would do their duty regardless of consequences, as I have had when sending other men's sons into danger. Happily I have never mistaken their metal and, in this instance, felt sure that I could rely upon him to exercise both discretion and intrepidity in exigencies to which his long experience and careful training have at all times made him equal.

The two detectives met in Louisville, and at once proceeded to New Orleans, where they arrived early in the morning of 7 January, 1868, and were driven to the St Charles Hotel. No time was lost. While my son presented his letters to different parties, and made cautious inquiries regarding the recent appearance in New Orleans of Taylor, Keating in the character of a provincial merchant, investigated as far as possible the business houses dealing in stock, leather, or wool, as to whether any such person had made arrangement for consignments from the interior or seaport Texan cities. No trace of their man was found however, until my son was able to get at the register of the St Charles Hotel for the preceding three months, which was attended with some difficulty, on account of the crowded condition of things at that house. Any detective, or other expert, will understand how much time and patience are required to discover one signature from among ten thousand, when that one may be an assumed name, and perhaps five hundred of the ten thousand be so similar to the one sought, that a disinterested person, could scarcely be convinced it was really not the person's handwriting desired; but after a good deal of trouble and searching, the names of 'H. G. Taylor & Clerk', were discovered on the last half line at the bottom of a page under date of 30 November, 1867, which by constant wear and thumbing in turning pages, had been nearly defaced, but which, in his handwriting, beyond a doubt told the story of their presence.

Further inquiry of the clerk on duty at that time, and with his memory refreshed by a glance at Taylor's photographs, developed the facts that he had certainly been at the St Charles on the date shown by the register, and that he was accompanied by a young man about nineteen years of age, who was recognised as Taylor's clerk.

The peculiar register then kept at the St Charles Hotel in New Orleans was also instrumental in assisting the detectives. It gave the guest's name, residence, hour of arrival, and hour of departure, with name of conveyance at arrival and departure, in the following manner:

H. G. Taylor and Clerk \ Mobile \ 12pm \ Ped 2 Dec \ 7am

This told anybody curious about the matter that H. G. Taylor and clerk, assuming to reside in Mobile, arrived at the St Charles Hotel, New Orleans, at noon on Saturday, 30 November, 1867, either afoot or by some mode of conveyance unknown to the clerk of the house, and that they left the house in an omnibus at seven o'clock on the morning of the third day following.

Naturally the next inquiries were directed to ascertaining to what boat or railroad lines omnibuses could be ordered at that hour of the morning; if different ones, then to discover who had driven the particular omnibus which conveyed Taylor and his brother from the hotel and then make an effort to learn to what point they had been conveyed. This, however, proved less difficult than had been feared; for it was found that on the morning in question the omnibus had gone from the hotel to but one point, and that was to the ferry connecting with Berwick Bay route, by the New Orleans and Opelousas Railroad and the Gulf, to Galveston, although a large number of passengers had been booked, and it was impossible to ascertain whether Taylor and his brother had actually gone that route or not, though everything was in favour of that presumption.

The death of General Rosseau had caused quite a commotion in New Orleans, and it seemed a pretty hard matter to get anything further of a definite character in that place. I therefore instructed my son and Detective Keating to proceed slowly to Galveston, stopping at Brashear City, where Taylor might have diverged, supposing he had taken that route with the other passengers from New Orleans, and to particularly search passenger lists aboard any lines of boats, and all hotel registers, before arriving at Galveston, so as to have the work done thoroughly nearest the base of operation. I knew that for any party to get on the wrong scent in that vast state, thinly settled as it was, with no means of quickly conveying needful intelligence, was to enter upon both a needless waste of money for my patrons, and an objectless and wearying struggle against insurmountable obstacles for my detectives whom, whatever may be said to the contrary, I have never in a single instance needlessly or injudiciously exposed to privation or danger.

In Brashear conductors of trains were applied to, the hotel and omnibus men were questioned, the postmaster was appealed to, and even the passenger-lists of the boats which had been in port, and to which they were able to gain access for a period of three months, had been searched in vain. Every trace of the man seemed lost, and I was appealed to for a decision as to whether they should proceed to Galveston by boat, with the presumption that Taylor had taken passage under an assumed name, or take a few days' trip up along the line of the New Orleans and Opelousas Railroad and seek for information of their man at different points through Central Louisiana.

I decided on the former course, and they accordingly embarked from Brashear immediately after the receipt of my telegram of instructions, on the handsome steamer *Josephine*, the only boat whose books they had had no opportunity of examining and, having received my telegram but a few minutes before the steamer left, were obliged to do some lively running to reach it. In anticipation of a message from me to take that route, my son had directed Keating to settle the hotel bill, and with both valises in hand wait at a convenient corner where, should William receive a dispatch from me of the character expected, within a certain time, they might yet make the boat. Everything transpiring as my son had hoped, they were just in time, after a lively run, to be hauled up the gang-plank by two stalwart negroes, and were soon steaming down the bay and thence out to sea.

As the two ascended to the cabin they were congratulated by the officers of the boat and many of the passengers on their graceful and expeditious boarding of the steamer, and being something of objects of interest on account of the little incident, they concluded not to lose the opportunity to blend the good feeling evoked into a thoroughly pleasant impression, and consequently took the shortest way to accomplish that desired end by at once walking up to the bar where the assembled gentlemen, to a man, apparently in compliance to general custom, seemed to understand that they had been invited before a word had been uttered by either of the detectives, so that when my son asked, 'Gentlemen, won't you join us?' it was an entirely superfluous request. On either side, behind, and extending a solid phalanx beyond, the 'gentlemen' had already joined and were describing the particular liquor that in their minds would do honour to the occasion in the most lively and familiar manner possible, and interspersing their demands upon the leisurely bar-keeper with such remarks as 'Gen'lemen had narrow 'scape'; 'Gen'lemen made a right smart run of it'; 'Gen'lemen not down from Norlens (New Orleans), reckon come down Opelousas route'; and other similar comments, but invariably prefacing each and every remark with the stereotyped word 'Gen'lemen', which men were, without exception, assumed to be in that country at that time, at least in conversation. Any neglect to preface a remark with the word laid one liable to be come immediately engaged in a discussion regarding the propriety of the use of the term, behind navy revolvers, rifles, double-barrelled shot-guns, or any other available pointed or forcible means of argument.

After the thirst of the crowd, which upon a Gulf-roasting steamer is something terrible to contemplate, had been in a measure assuaged, my son excused himself, and with Keating repaired to the office, remarking to the clerk: 'I presume you would like to transact a little business with us now?'

'Any time to suit your convenience,' returned the clerk, but getting at his books with an alacrity which showed that he would be a little more willing to attend to the matter of fares then than at any other time.

William handed him an amount of money large enough to pay for both the fares of himself and Keating from Brashear to Galveston and, while the clerk was making change, said by way of getting into conversation with him, 'I'm afraid we're on a fool's errand out here'.

The clerk counted out the change, inked his pen to take the names, and then elevating his eyebrows, although not speaking a word, plainly asked, 'Ah, how's that?'

'Well, you see,' replied the detective, 'we're hunting a man that's had right good luck.'

'He can't be in these parts,' replied the clerk, with a slightly satirical smile. 'Names?' he then asked.

'James A. Hicks and Patrick Mallory.'

'Where from?'

'Pittsburgh.'

'Which is which?' asked the clerk, in a business tone of voice.

'I am Hicks, and that pretty smart-looking Irish man by the baggage-room is Mallory,' was the reply.

'Your age and weight?' asked the clerk mechanically, at the same time looking at my son keenly, and getting the rest of his description at a glance.

These questions were properly answered, and as the clerk was noting them he asked, 'Might I ask what was the gentleman's good luck?'

'Certainly, he has fallen heir to a coal mine in Pennsylvania, and we are endeavouring to hunt him up for the executors of the estate.'

'Ah?' said the clerk, driving away with his pen. 'Will you be so good as to ask Mr Mallory to step this way?'

My son stepped up to Keating and remarked aloud, 'Mr Mallory, Mr Mallory, the clerk would like to see you', and then as Keating stepped to his side, remarked as if for his better information, 'He knows your name is Patrick Mallory and that we are from Pittsburgh, hunting Taylor, so he can come home and enjoy the property the old man left him; but he wants your entire description.'

'Quite so,' said the quick-witted Irishman, dryly.

'You've got me, now,' said Keating, winking familiarly at the clerk, 'when we came over we went under; and so many of us was lost that those saved wasn't worth mention as to age, ye see; but concerning heft, why I'd not fear to say I'd turn an honest scale at a hundred an' sixty.'

The clerk smiled, but concluded not to ask Mr Mallory from Pittsburgh any more questions.

As soon as he had made his notes, however, William told him that he had examined the lists of all other boats plying between Brashear and Galveston, save those of the *Josephine*, and requested him to look through them, concluding by describing Taylor, and stating that he might register either as H. G. Taylor and Clerk, or under an assumed name, as he was somewhat erratic, and through family troubles, not necessary to explain, he had got into a habit of occasionally travelling incognito.

The clerk readily complied with his request, scanning the pages closely, and repeating the name musingly as if endeavouring to recall where he had heard it. By the time he had got on with the examination of a few pages, William had selected a photograph of Taylor, and on showing it to the clerk the latter seemed to have a certain recollection of having seen him, but a very uncertain recollection as to where, or under what circumstances. He went on repeating the name, however, turning back the pages with his right hand and tracing the names back and forth with the index finger of his left hand, occasionally looking at the photograph as if to assist in forcing a definite recollection, but without any result for so long a time that Messrs. Hill and Mallory of Pittsburgh became satisfied that their last hope before arriving at Galveston was gone, when suddenly the clerk carelessly placed the picture beside a certain name and in a manner very similar to a dry-goods clerk on securing a successful 'match' in two pieces of cloth, quietly remarked: 'Yes, can't be mistaken. There you are.'

'Then we've got him!' exclaimed my son, in the excess of his gratification, shaking the hand of Mr Mallory, from Pittsburgh.

'It's a joy,' said the latter, beaming.

'Think of the immense property!' continued my son.

'And the surprise to his friends!' murmured Keating.

'The surprise to himself, I should say,' interrupted the clerk.

'Quite so,' said Mr Keating.

It appeared that Taylor and his brother had missed one or two boats at Brashear from some cause, but had finally taken passage on the *Josephine* on 7 November, and as the detectives had not been able to ascertain whether the *Josephine* had carried the fugitives or not, on account of her being belated by adverse weather, and was now returning to Galveston, after having had barely time to touch at Bra- shear, they had felt that perhaps they might be upon the wrong trail, which, with unknown adventures before them, had been peculiarly discouraging; so that now, when they ascertained that his apprehension was only a question of time and careful work, they could not repress their gratification.

Nothing further worthy of note transpired on the voyage from Brashear to Galveston, save that the trip was a pretty rough one, and they finally arrived in the latter city, hopeful and encouraged, notwithstanding the unusually dismal weather, which seemed to consist of one disconnected but never-ending storm. The 'oldest inhabitants' of the place contending with great earnestness that 'it 'peared like's they'd never had nothin' like it befoah!'

Arriving in Galveston early Sunday morning, they went to the Exchange Hotel, and after breakfast set about examining the hotel registers of the place, ascertaining that Taylor and brother had been in the city, stopped a day or two, and then, so far as could be learned, had gone on to Houston. They were satisfied he had made no special efforts to cover his tracks, although he had not made himself at all conspicuous, as the difficulty encountered in getting those who would be most likely to recollect him, to recollect him at all, clearly showed. It was quite evident that he had not anticipated pursuit, at least of any nature which he could not easily compromise, and intended going into some legitimate business under his own name, and with his brother's assistance.

Before he could be arrested in Texas, however, it would be necessary to secure Governor Pease's warrant, which obliged a long, tedious trip to Austin, the capital of the state; nearly the whole distance having to be done by stage, which at that time seemed a forbidding piece of work, as it had rained every day of the year, so it might be a question of helping the stage through rather than being helped through by it. Besides this, according to my son's reports which gave a true description of things in Texas at that time, everything beyond Houston had to be paid for in gold, as sectional sentiment and counterfeiting had pronounced a ban upon greenbacks; and not only in gold, but at exorbitant prices: hotel rates being five dollars per day; single meals from one to two dollars; railroad fares eight cents per mile; and stage rates nearly double that amount with no assurance that you would ever reach a destination you had paid to be conveyed to, all attended by various kinds of danger, among which was the pleasant reflection that you might be called upon at any time to contribute to the benefit of that noble relic of chivalry, the Ku Klux Klan, who at that day were particularly busy in Texas.

All of these pleasant considerations made the departure from Galveston for Austin, in a Pickwickian sense, unusually agreeable.

At Houston they discovered from different persons, including the postmaster, that Taylor had been there, but had made inquiries about points further up country; and the general impression was that he had gone on, though at Brenham, the terminus of the railroad, where they arrived Monday evening, they could find no trace of him.

The next morning, when my son arose and looked on the vast sea of mud, a filthy, black earth below, a dirty, black sky above with nothing but driving rain and wintry gusts between while the lackadaisical Texans slouched about with their hands in their pockets, with only energy enough to procure tobacco or 'licker', their sallow faces, down-at-the-heels, snuff-dipping wives desolately appearing at the doors and windows, only to retire again with a woe-begone expression of suspended animation in their leathery faces, he fully realised the force of the remark attributed to General Sheridan, and more expressive than polite: 'If I owned Texas and hell, I would live in hell and sell Texas!'

The stage was crowded, and the dreary conveyance splashed and crunched on until noon when dinner was taken at Wilson's Ranche, a long low, rambling, tumbledown structure, which, like its owner, who had at one time been a 'General' or something, and now retained the thriving title out of compliment to his departed glory, had gone to a genteel decay with a lazy ease worthy of its master's copy. The dinner was one long to be remembered by the detectives, as it was their first genuine Texan dinner, and consisted merely of fat boiled pork, and hot bread of the consistence of putty cakes of the same dimensions, which, when broken open after a mighty effort, disclosed various articles of household furniture, such as clay pipes, old knife handles, and various other invoices, probably playfully dumped into the flour barrel by some one of the half-score of tow-headed, half-clad children, which the 'General' and his buxom helpmeet had seen fit to provide for torturing another generation with rare Texan dinners at a dollar a plate.

It was a full-day's labour getting to Le Grange, but thirty-five miles from Brenham, where they arrived at ten o'clock, tired and exhausted from the day's banging about in the stage and out of it, for they were obliged to walk many times in order to rest the jaded horses so that they could get the rough to La Grange at all; but before retiring made all the inquiries necessary to develop the fact that their man had not been at that point.

The next day, Wednesday, was rather more trying than the previous one. Two miles out of town the stage got 'bogged', and the entire load of passengers were obliged to get out and walk through three miles of swamps, the stage finally sticking fast, necessitating prying it out with rails. After this Slough of Despond was passed, the Colorado River had to be forded three times, and then came a 'dry run' which now, with every other ravine or depression, had became a 'wet run' and was 'a booming' as the drunken driver termed it between oaths. There was at least four feet of water in the dry run, and the horses balking, the buckskin argument was applied to them so forcibly that they gave a sudden start, and broke the pole off short, which further complicated matters. My son, being on the box, sprang to the assistance of the driver, and stepping down upon the stub of the pole, quickly unhitched the wheel horses, so that the stage could not be overturned, and then disengaged the head team, finally appropriating a heavy wheel horse, with which he rode back to Keating, who was perched upon a rear wheel to keep out of the water, which was rushing and seething below, sweeping through the bottom of the stage, and at every moment seeming to have lifted the vehicle preparatory to sweeping it away like feathers, and also holding on to the baggage, which he had got safely upon the roof of the stage. Taking him aboard his improvised ferry, after securing the valises, he rode to the muddy shore, forming with his companions about as fine a picture of despairing 'carpet-baggers' as the South has ever on any occasion been able to produce. The bedraggled passengers ascertained that the next town, Webberville, was several miles distant, and that there was no house nearer, save on the other side of the rapidly rising stream; and as night had come on, the best thing that could be done was to penetrate the woods, build a rousing fire, and shiver and shiver through as long, wet and weary a night as was ever experienced.

There was never a more longed-for morning than the next one, and the moment that the sickly light came feebly through the mist and rain, and straggled into the dense cotton-wood trees, where the discouraged passengers had a sort of fervent outdoors prayer-meeting, they started forward for Webberville, hungry, drenched, and so benumbed as to be scarcely able to walk. It was five miles into town, but one mile of that distance stretched over a quagmire known and described in that section as 'Hell's half-acre'; and the truthful inhabitants of Webberville related of this delectable ground that during the rainy season its powers of absorption were so great that it would even retain the gigantic Texan mosquito, should it happen to take a seat there.

This bog was impassable to the travellers, who finally bartered with the owner of a hog wagon to be carried over the marsh for a silver half dollar each. This was far better than remaining on the other side, and they finally trudged into the town more dead than alive.

Fortunately for the detectives, the brother of ex-Governor Lubbock, of Texas, was one of the party, and as they had all become so thoroughly acquainted, as common misery will quickly make travellers, he took my son and Keating to the residence of Colonel Banks, a merchant of Webberville, whose good wife never rested until she had provided the party with a splendid meal, something with which to wash it down, and beds which seemed to them all to have been composed of down.

After they had a good rest, the passengers for Austin were got together, and explained the situation of things. The creek the other side of Webberville was a mighty river. The driver thought he could possibly get the stage across, but was certain he could not do so with any passengers or baggage to make it drag more heavily; but he thought that if once on the other side, they might get to Austin the same day. William was anxious to push ahead, and looking about town discovered a rather venturesome negro who owned a monstrous mule, and at once entered into negotiations with him for the transfer of the party and baggage, sink or swim. So when the stage arrived at the creek, the baggage was unloaded, and the stage successfully forded the stream. But as the water covered so broad an expanse, was so deep and rapid, and altogether presented such a forbidding appearance, the passengers refused to try the mule experiment unless William, who had proposed the mode of transfer, and had secured the novel ferry, which stood with the grinning negro upon its back ready for passengers, would first cross the Rubicon to demonstrate the convenience and safety of the passage. So, handing the captain one of the valises, he mounted the mule, which after a few whirls, a little bucking, several suspicious sidewise movements, and a shouted 'Ya-a-oop, da, Daniel! done quit dis heyah foolishness!' plunged into the current without further ceremony.

The passengers saw that Daniel and his master were up to a thing or two in that section of the country; and after seeing Keating cross the stream in safety also, they one by one ventured upon the transfer, which was finished without accident, but with a good deal of merriment; and the coloured clown paid even beyond his contract price, the stage was enabled to go lumbering on to Austin, where it arrived at a late hour of the same day.

Rain, drizzle and mist; mist, drizzle and rain. It seemed all that the country was capable of producing; and the same preface to the befogged condition of the English chancery courts used by Dickens, in his introduction to *Bleak House* with a few of the localisms expunged, would have fitfully applied to the condition of things in Texas, which afterward culminated in a flood which swept everything before it.

In Austin, though the seat of the State government and the headquarters of the military department of Texas, full of legislators, lobbyists, officers and soldiers, everything had the appearance of having been through a washing that had lasted an age, and had been prematurely wrung out to dry, but had been caught on the lines by an eternal rain day. Involuntarily with the spatters and dashes of rain and the morning wind, Longfellow's 'Rainy Day' came drifting into the mind, and the lines:

> The day is cold and dark and dreary;
> It rains, and the wind is never weary;
> The vine still clings to the mouldering wall.
> While at every gust the dead leaves fall.
> And the day is dark and dreary!

were never more appropriate than when applied to any portion of Texas during the months of January and February, 1868.

The very first man my son met in the office of the hotel, the next morning, was a member of the Legislature from Besar County who, hearing his inquiries of the clerk concerning Taylor, informed him that he had been introduced to him in San Antonio a few weeks previous; that he was in company with a much younger man whom he presented as his brother, and that he had ostensibly come to San Antonio to make some inquiries concerning the hide and wool trade. Whether with an idea of settling at that point, or whether he could yet be found in San Antonio, he was unable to state.

In any event this was cheering news; for it assured my detectives that their long and weary search would not prove unavailing; and William directed Keating to make himself useful about the different hotels and hide and stock dealers, as it is a detective's business to work all the time, and the slightest cessation of vigilance after the beginning of an operation might at the most unexpected moment cause the beginning of a series of circumstances eventually permitting a criminal's escape. He himself sought out General Potter, who escorted him to General Canby's headquarters, where he was most cordially received, and not only given an order for military aid, should it be required, but General Canby himself went with him to the capitol and introduced him to Governor Pease, vouching for the reliability of any statement made in connection with the business which had brought him so far from home as, while I had charge of the secret service of the Government during the war, myself and sons had had an intimate acquaintance and personal friendship with him.

Governor Pease frankly stated to William that the affidavits were rather weak, and that should some of the 'shysters' of that state, who did a thriving business in *habeas corpus* releases, get an inkling of his business and the nature of the papers, they might give him a deal of trouble, even if they did not get his man away from him eventually. He said he would make the requisition as strong as possible, however, and expressed his hope that the reputation for ingenuity in devising and executing expedients possessed by Pinkerton's men would be more than sustained in this instance. General Canby terminated the interview by giving the document approval over his own signature.

My son thanked them both for their kindness and withdrew, only too anxious to get to where his man was before any information that he was being sought for should reach him, and either scare him beyond the Rio Grande, or enable him to act on the defensive, as only a man can act who has plenty of money, plenty of friends and, as we already knew, a great plenty of bravery on his own account.

Soon after he had returned to the hotel, Keating came in with undoubted information that Taylor had a permanent residence at or near Corpus Christi; that either he or his brother owned a sheep ranch near the coast, not far from that city, while the other dealt in hides and wool there; and that one or the other penetrated into the interior as far as San Antonio, soliciting consignments.

My son at once concluded that it was the Captain who had done the dealing, as well as stealing, and whose money and business ability had been brought to bear upon the trading at Corpus Christi, and upon the ranch in the country near it. The brother, though probably entirely innocent of complicity in the robbery, or even a knowledge of the source from whence the money had come, only being used for a convenient repository for his ill-gotten funds in case of Kuhn Brothers following him before he was ready to meet them.

He therefore decided to get through to Corpus Christi in the very shortest time in which the trip could be made via New Braunfels, San Antonio, Victoria, and Port Lavaca, hoping that he might be able to pick him up along some portion of that route, as it was quite evident he made frequent trips in that direction; and should he seem to be going much farther into the interior, which would be improbable, as San Antonio at that time was quite a frontier city, arrest him at once, and hurry him back to Galveston along the route he was already familiar with; but, should he be going toward the coast, to let him take his own course, keeping him well in hand until he had reached Corpus Christi or some other seaport city, and, waiting a favourable opportunity, arrest him and get him aboard a boat before he could recover from the surprise.

Not a half hour before they left Austin, he fortunately met Judge Davis of Corpus Christi, who was there attending some political convention, and who gave him a letter to his law partner at home, should his services in any way be needed, as I had been of some service to him on a previous occasion; so that when my two detectives left Austin on the seventeenth of January, they felt perfectly satisfied of ultimate success, though the same terrible experiences as to staging were again encountered.

It required the entire day to traverse the few miles between Austin and Blanco Creek, where they secured a sort of a supper. At Manchell Springs, the stage pole being again broken, they were only able to proceed after improvising a tongue out of a sapling, chopped from the roadside with a very dull hatchet. At Blanco Springs a good rest was taken, and the driver, having the day's experience in his mind, objected to going further that night; but the detectives insisted that they had paid their money to be taken to a certain destination and, as they had shown a disposition to more than earn their passage besides, no excuse for their detention should be offered.

After a good deal of grumbling, fresh horses were got out, a new pole put in the stage, and the procession again took up its weary march over the then most horrible of roads, crossing the innumerable brooks and runs which now pushed torrents into York's Creek. All night long they slushed and splashed, and tramped and cursed; though the rain had ceased for a time there was but little light from the sky, which seemed full of black heavy clouds ready to burst asunder, to again drench them and swell the torrents afresh. My son, Keating, and a man sent along from Blanco Creek, took turns trudging along ahead of the lead-team and, with lanterns, picked out the way. Often they would be misled where the ground was so bad as to almost defy a passage over it, when the patient animals behind them, steaming from the toil of straining along with nothing but an empty coach, would stop, as if guided by a keener instinct, where they would quietly remain until the united search of the three men had discovered the road, when the intelligent creatures docilely plodded along again.

And so, through seemingly bottomless quagmires; over corduroys, where the shaky ends of timbers, struck by a horse's hoof, would mercilessly splash those walking beside the useless vehicle or suddenly relieved from the weight of the ponderous wheel, would fly upwards to heave gallons of slime upon the coach; labouring around the bases of far-extending mounds of sandy loam; descending into unexpected and sometimes dangerous depressions, along creeks, and plunging into streams, where drift and changing, sandy bottoms always made it a question whether the coach could ever be got across; they marched only as Sherman taught soldiers to march, or as honest detectives will crowd all obstacles between themselves and their duty, and came with the gray of the morning to the beautiful, forest-shaded Guadaloupe.

Fording this river without nearly the trouble presented at some of the petty runs and creeks which had been passed, they came to New Braunfels with the sun, which had shown itself for the first time since their arrival in Texas, and which also shone upon the first city which had shown any of that wide awake 'go-aheaditiveness' and thrift so common to nearly all northern cities.

The reason that New Braunfels differed so materially from the ordinary Texan towns lay in the fact that it was almost exclusively settled by Germans; and it was a welcome sight to the detectives to be able to enter a place where, from suburb to centre, up and down long, finely-shaded avenues, it was plain to be seen that the most had been made of everything.

From the pleasantest cottage of the extreme suburb, and past the more pretentious residences, every home being provided with an exterior bake-oven, the same as in Germany, Pennsylvania, or portions of Wisconsin and Minnesota; to the shops, stores, hotels and public buildings, every yard, in many instances, fenced with stone gleaned and cleaned from the soil and, for that matter, every spot upon which the eye rested showed that thrift and not whisky-drinking ruled that place. That fact alone entitles the little Germany city to respectable elevation from the obscurity which has heretofore surrounded it.

As nothing at this point could be learned regarding Taylor, though leaving the town and its extraordinary attractions with some reluctance, they immediately proceeded to San Antonio, the roads to which place were quite passable, and arrived at that city Friday afternoon. I had telegraphed to Colonel Lee, of San Antonio, to hold himself in readiness to assist my son and Keating, on the score of personal friendship, whenever they might arrive there, not knowing, from the terrible condition of the roads, at what time it would be possible for them to reach that point, and he, being ignorant from what direction they might come, where they might stay, or under what name they

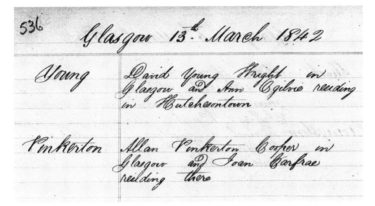

An extract from the Old Parish Records of Glasgow, showing Pinkerton's marriage to Joan Carfrae (by kind permission of the Registar General of Scotland).

Pinkerton (left) with Abraham Lincoln. Pinkerton ran the Union's spy network during the Amercian Civil War and went under the pseudonym Major E. J. Allen.

Allan Pinkerton, when operating as chief of the Union's Intelligence Service, with his men near Cumberland Landing, Virginia. Pinkerton is the one smoking a pipe in the background.

The detective force that Pinkerton started with Chicago attorney Edward Rucker—mainly to deal with railway thefts—developed into the North-Western Police Agency, and later Pinkerton's National Detective Agency, with Pinkerton taking sole control in 1853. Their wide open eye and motto 'We Never Sleep' became synonymous with Pinkerton's.

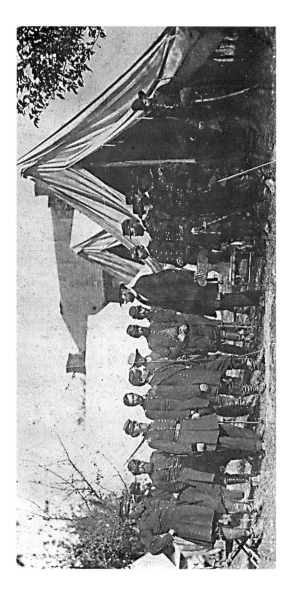

This photograph was taken at General Porter's headquarters of the 5th Army Corps, on the occasion of the Battle of Antietam, October 1862. To the right of Lincoln is General McLellan, for whom Pinkerton ran the Intelligence Service. In the back row, wearing a brimmed hat, is a young captain called George Armstrong Custer.

Timothy Webster, 1860

Allan Pinkerton, *Harpers Bazaar*, 1884

IN MEMORY OF
ALLAN PINKERTON
BORN IN GLASGOW SCOTLAND
AUGUST 25TH 1819
DIED IN CHICAGO ILLINOIS
JULY 1st 1884
AGED 65 YEARS
A FRIEND TO HONESTY
AND A FOE TO CRIME
DEVOTING HIMSELF FOR A GENERATION TO
THE PREVENTION AND DETECTION OF CRIME
IN MANY COUNTRIES, HE WAS THE FOUNDER
IN AMERICA OF A NOBLE PROFESSION.
IN THE HOUR OF THE NATION'S PERIL HE
CONDUCTED ABRAHAM LINCOLN SAFELY
THROUGH THE RANKS OF TREASON TO THE SCENE
OF HIS FIRST INAUGURATION AS PRESIDENT.
HE SYMPATHIZED WITH, PROTECTED AND
DEFENDED THE SLAVES AND LABORED
EARNESTLY FOR THEIR FREEDOM,
HATING WRONG, AND LOVING GOOD, HE WAS
STRONG, BRAVE, TENDER AND TRUE.

The Allan Pinkerton Memorial at Graceland Cemetery, Lakeview, Chicago, Illinois might register, had caused an advertisement to be inserted in the San Antonio Herald, of which the following is a copy:

PERSONAL
WHENEVER THE SON OF A.P., of Chicago, may arrive in San Antonio, he will learn of something to his advantage by calling upon Lieut. Col. Lee, at the Mengler House.

Keating's sharp eyes first saw the item at the supper table of the Mengler House, where they were stopping, and they both learned, by listening to the conversation about them, that the Colonel was sitting at the same table.

After supper William made himself known to Colonel Lee without attracting attention, the latter kindly offering him any help needed, after which inquiries of a guarded character were instituted for the object of their search. The landlord of the Mengler House stated that Taylor had called upon him about three weeks before to inquire for letters, but as he was stopping elsewhere little attention had been paid to him or his questions; all of which William had reason to believe absolutely true, on account of the strong corroborative testimony which would lie in the statement of any landlord that no civility was shown to a man who quartered at any hostelry save his own.

The next morning he called upon Chief of Police, H. D. Bonnet, who extended every imaginable courtesy, went with him to the offices of the different stage-lines, and insisted in examining their lists for some time previous with a view to ascertaining what direction Taylor had taken when he left San Antonio; introduced him to the Mayor and Chief Marshal, and even went with him on an extended tour through the old Mexican quarter of the town; but no other information was secured save through the German landlady of a hotel, who was as positive as her limited knowledge of the English language would allow her to be, that Taylor had stopped at her house without registering at all, and had gone directly from San Antonio to Port Lavaca or Corpus Christi on horseback which, after all, in the exceptional condition of the weather that year in Texas, seemed quite probable.

It was evident nothing was to be gained by remaining any longer at San Antonio, and was quite as plain that all possible expedition should be used in getting on to the coast.

As if the fates were ordained perverse, the moment the two left San Antonio a steady drenching rain again began to fall, and as the stage was crowded, the discomfort of those within could not very well be increased. About twelve miles from San Antonio the driver succeeded in tipping over the stage, and giving the occupants 'an elegant mud varnish all over', as operative Keating aptly expressed it.

The driver remarked that he was 'going up the new road', but some of the more profane passengers swore that if so, he was hunting it three feet under the old one.

On arriving at Lavernia station the dismal announcement was made by the lean, long stage agent, who seemed never to have done anything from time immemorial save sit in the door of his tumbledown hovel to make dismal announcement that 'the Cibolo (pronounced there 'C'uillou') is just a scootin' and a rippin' up its banks like a mad buffler bull! Ye'll all be back to stay at my tavern all night.'

It was the contemplation of this man's pure cussedness, as he sat there doting on the big bills he would charge when the Cibolo should drive back a stage load of hungry travellers, that nerved them to push on at all hazards and attempt a crossing at some point where the Cibolo 'scooted and ripped up its banks' with less ardour than across the regular route to Victoria; but on reaching Southerland Springs, seven miles distant, it was found that it would be necessary to wait until Thursday morning, when they might possibly make a passage, as the stream was running down to within something like ordinary bounds very fast.

Thursday afternoon came before an attempt to ford the stream was made, when the driver agreed to land the passengers in the middle of the stream on an immense fallen tree, from which point they could reach the other side, when they might be able to get the empty stage across also.

The trial was made, and was successful so far as landing the passengers was concerned, but while this was being done the wheels of the coach sank deeper and deeper into the mucky bed of the stream, and though but a few minutes had elapsed, the strange action of the water had caused deposits to form about the coach so rapidly that it became firmly imbedded, and could not be moved by the four horses attached. At this juncture an old farmer came along, who carried the evidences of some of his propensities strongly marked in his face, which was a thin one, like his conscience, but with bright tips on his cheek bones and as red a nose as ever the devil-artist in alcohol tipped with crimson. No importunities or amount of money could prevail on him to assist the discouraged travellers with his fine mule train but a pint of good whiskey, to be delivered the moment the stage had been drawn from its peril, with a small drink by way of retainer, accomplished what would not have been done in any other manner, and set the travellers joyfully on their way again. They journeyed on at a snail's pace until one o'clock Friday morning, when they arrived at Kelly's ranch, kept by Bill Kelly, uncle of the 'Taylor boys', notorious for their connection with the Ku Klux and various other gangs of villainous desperadoes.

The family were unceremoniously awakened, and at once good-humouredly proceeded to provide the ravenous passengers with something to eat; after which they made a 'shake-down' on the floor, into which substitute for a bed everybody turned, and slept late into the morning, awakening stiff in every joint and scarcely able for that day's journey, which, with its complement of accidents and delays, took them safely over Esteto creek and into Yorktown early in the evening. Here the detectives secured certain information that Taylor had been in Corpus Christi the week previous, and was undoubtedly there at that time, as Texas by this time had become a network of resistless streams, almost impassable quagmires and far-reaching lagoons.

Late the next morning they left Yorktown, having taken on a passenger of no less importance than ex-Confederate Governor Owens, of Arizona. He was a pleasant, voluble old fellow, and my son at once fell in with his ways, and treated him so courteously that it perhaps averted a greater disaster than had at any previous time occurred.

Governor Owens was largely engaged in the Rio Grande trade of supplying frontier points with provisions and merchandise, and was just on his way to Indianola on the coast, where he was to meet his

Mexican freighters, comprising thirty wagons and carts, of all characters and descriptions, driven by the inevitable lazy greaser. Even as
late as 1867-8, a vast amount of freighting was done between St Paul,
Minnesota, and Fort Garry, Manitoba, in the famed Red River carts,
driven by the inevitable, lazy half-breed.

William, knowing the position held by Governor Owens during a
portion of the war, and realising that an ex-office-holder will never lose
his tenderness for the political regime which made him titled, assumed
to be a Mississippian, from Vicksburg, with an Irish acquaintance, on
a trip of inspection through Texas and, so far, terribly disappointed
with the State.

During those periods when, owing to the depth of the mud, the
passengers were obliged to walk, they would fall behind or walk ahead
of the stage, when they would chat pleasantly upon general subjects.
On one of these occasions Governor Owens eyed his companion
sharply a moment, and then asked: 'Can I trust you, sir?'

'Certainly.'

'On the word and honour of a gentleman?'

'Yes, and an honest man, too,' William answered.

'I believe you; thank you. You know stages are robbed out this
way?'

'I do.'

'Did you ever see it done?'

'No; nor have I any desire to be around on such an occasion,' he
replied, laughing.

'I reckon you hadn't better, either,' said the Governor earnestly.
'It wouldn't make so much difference if they would do the work a trifle
genteelly, in a gentlemanly way; but the fact is, we have low fellows
along our Texas stage-lines. They have no regard for a man's family.
Why,' he continued, warmly, 'they'll just pop out from behind the
trees, or up through some clumps of bushes, ram a double barrelled
shot-gun, loaded to the muzzle with slugs and things, into the coach
from both sides at once, and just blaze away until all that are not killed
outright are scared to death. There's nothing fair about it!'

William expressed his curiosity to know if the drivers were killed.

'Drivers? Never, sir, never. Why, those ruffians are too smart for that. Let it be known that they have begun killing drivers, and there isn't a stage company in Texas that could send a coach past the first timber. They couldn't afford to kill stage-drivers, for the moment they began it, that would be the end of staging.'

My son expressed his thanks at learning so much of the business principles of these land pirates, and the old gentleman continued: 'You see, it takes a peculiar kind of a driver for a Texas coach. You want one, first, that can drink right smart of whiskey, for the water isn't good along some of these branches. You want one that can swear a hoss's head square off, too. He's got to be a coward, or he would help put this robbing down; and yet, he has got to be rather brave to drive right along up to a spot where he knows he is to see his passengers butchered! And that,' continued the Governor earnestly, 'is just what I want to talk to you about, as I feel sure that I can trust you.'

The Governor then explained to him that a certain member of the Ku Klux, whom he was sorry to say was too intimate with those roadside plunderers, had informed him that morning, just as he was leaving Yorktown, that preparations had been made to rob their stage at a point between Clinton and Mission Valley; and that he very much desired some organisation among the passengers for defence, as he himself had upwards of thirty thousand dollars, to be paid out at Indianola for goods, and to his freighters for wages.

On the receipt of this alarming intelligence, my son took the responsibility of informing the rest of the passengers what might possibly be expected; and, as Governor Owens had six fine carbines, which he was also taking down to Indianola for the protection of his freighters on the Rio Grande, preparatory to any attack that might be made.

About six miles from Mission Valley the stage route traversed a low piece of bottom-lands covered with timber, and a considerable growth of underbrush. A corduroy road had been built through the place, and as the coach was obliged to be driven slowly across it, the locality offered particularly fine inducements for a robbery of the character described by the Governor; so that the precaution was taken of walking along with the coach, three on either side, with carbines ready for instant use. Just before entering the timber, two men were seen prowling about and, evidently fearing their actions might cause suspicion and frustrate the plan they had in view, made a great effort to appear to be two respectable hunters in search of only wild game. Before leaving the timber at the other side, two more persons were seen, who, evidently, not having been given any signal, had come as near to the stage as they dared, to ascertain for themselves why their comrades had failed in their calculations; but skulked away after seeing the force which grimly trudged along, guarding the empty vehicle, into which the passengers were glad enough to climb when the clanger was gone by, and be carried with sound bodies and whole pockets to the supper which had been some time in waiting when they reached Mission galley.

Dinner the next day was taken at Victoria, from which city William and Keating expected to be able to go by railroad to Port Lavaca, only twenty-eight miles distant. They were doomed to disappointment in this, as the railroad had been abandoned since the war, either the Union or Confederate soldiers having taken it up bodily and turned it upside down, like a gigantic furrow, from Victoria to the sea.

After many years somebody had come along and turned it back, but to this day the steam-engine has never thundered over it again. The most that has ever been done having been to drag an occasional freight car over the road by the not peculiarly thrilling application of mule power and, so it was said, a handcar, worked by a gang of negroes, was used for transporting passengers, the trips being made back and forth whenever a load could be got, and not before.

As they were obliged to remain for this new mode of conveyance, their time was entirely unoccupied, and they could not but have leisure to make something of a study of Texan life as it then existed, and on Sunday afternoon were witnesses to one of those little episodes which sometimes make extremely lively certain periods that would otherwise remain hum-drum and ordinary.

The bar-room of the hotel had been crowded all day, and a good deal of liquor had been drunk, while there had also been a large amount of money lost and won over cards, so that there was that feverish, explosive condition of things which always follows large winnings or losses at games of chance, although there had as yet been no disturbance of a serious character.

At one of the little gaming tables, John Foster, county clerk of Victoria County, and another person, named Lew Phillips, who had been one of the Andersonville prison-keepers during the war, but had drifted out to Victoria and had secured charge of a large livery-stable there, were engaged at a game of poker, when Foster was heard to quietly say: 'See here, Lew Phillips, you stole that card!'

'You're a liar!' was retorted, with an oath.

The two men were up over the card-table in a twinkling, looking at each other, and both very white.

'Apologise!' demanded Foster, still quiet, but with a terrible earnestness in his voice.

'I don't do that sort of business, you white-livered coward!' shouted Phillips.

Without another look or word, the two parted, one passing out one door and the other out of another, while the crowd in the hotel canvassed the matter as coolly as though there had been no difficulty worth mentioning, while a few quietly laid wagers on who would get the first shot.

In about fifteen minutes more, Foster was seen returning with a double-barrelled shot-gun, and Phillips, who had a wooden leg, came stumping up another street, with an immense navy revolver in his hand. It was noticeable that the space between the advancing men was made very clear, so that nothing should interfere with their sociability. In a moment more, Phillips had fired at Foster, and evidently hit him; for, as he was bringing his gun to his shoulder, his aim had been badly disturbed, and before he had time to fire, Phillips had fired again and wounded his man the second time. Foster now leaned against a porch column, desperately resolved to get a good aim, his antagonist, all the while advancing, attempted to fire again, but missed this time, the cap refusing to communicate the deadly flash to the chamber of the revolver. There was a blinding flash from Foster's gun, accompanied by a thunderous report, and the two men fell almost instantaneously.

Foster had discharged both barrels of his weapon, heavily loaded with buck-shot, at Phillips, the entire charge having entered his wooden leg, and sent him spinning to the ground, like the sudden jerk and whirl of a nearly spent top, the recoil of the gun also 'kicking' Foster flat as a Tennessee 'poor white's' corn pone.

The 'gentlemen' who had been looking on and quietly criticising the little by-play, now rushed forward and surrounded the combatants, the anxiety of each of whom was to be assured of the other's death; or, in case of his being alive, to have someone to be the immediate bearer of tender regards and profuse expressions of friendship; thus terminating satisfactorily to all parties what the chivalrous inhabitants of Victoria informed my detectives was called a 'stag duel'; the most common and effective method known for settling the little difficulties liable at any time to occur among gentlemen. The only conditions imposed by custom being that neither party shall offer to shoot in a crowded room, or be allowed to fire at his opponent unless he is also prepared, when other citizens who may be using the streets at those times withdraw from them as rapidly as consistent with the proprieties, when the occasion is immediately made interesting to the participants, who advance and fire upon each other as rapidly as a liberal practice in this and other 'codes' of taking human life will permit.

As the next sensation to a 'stag duel' in Victoria was the arrival of the 'train' from Lavaca, in the shape of the hand-car manned by four burly negroes, who with the original superintendent of the road had formed a soulless corporation with which nothing could compete. It was not long before the detectives had secured seats with four other passengers, making ten persons in all, to be conveyed twenty-eight miles in a broken-down hand-car over probably the most villainous excuse for a railroad ever known.

The fare was six dollars in gold for each passenger, which might seem to have a shade of exorbitance about it when it was considered that the accommodations consisted of two very insecure seats, constructed over the wheels, upon each of which three persons might cling with a constant expectation of being jolted off by the unevenness of the road, or of falling off from sheer fatigue in endeavour to cling to the ramshackle boards beneath them.

'All abo'd!' shouted the negro conductor, with all the style and unction of the diamond-pinned aristocrat of a New York Central train. Then, as the 'train' started out of Victoria the passengers and the admiring lookers-on were greeted with the following song, tuned to the 'Ra-ta-tat' of the wheels upon the rails, and sturdily sung, or chanted rather, by the jolly but powerful crew:

> Heave ho! Away we go.
> Winds may wait, or de winds may blow!
> Heave ho! Away we go.
> For to cotch de gals at Lavac-o!

In the sense that this mode of travelling had the charm of novelty and the thrilling attraction of danger combined, it was a success. There was freshness and variety about it too, for whenever one of the negroes had 'done gin out' the conductor would call for volunteers from among the passengers, and give the demand a peculiar emphasis by the remark, 'Takes brawn 'n sinyew to pump dis hy'r train into action 'n de Lo'd never did make no men out o' cl'ar iron 'n steel!'

The argument was so forcible that someone would work with the negroes while the 'clean done gone' man and brother rested and meditated upon 'catchin' the gals of Lavaca!' which the song brought out so feelingly.

Besides this, new interest would be added to the excursion whenever the wind was favourable for a mast, to which a sort of 'mutton-leg sail' as they termed it, would be attached. The conductor would brace himself and would lengthen or shorten the sail as was most judicious, and then the hand-car ship would speed along the billowy tract like a majestic thing of life for a mile or two, when the party were again forced into a realising sense of the plodding nature of the means of transit, which, after all, at times became monotonous.

On one of these occasions of momentary fair sailing and enthusiasm, they were also favoured with a down grade of quite a stretch, and as everybody was happy at the wonderful rate of speed acquired, while the negroes were singing snatches of songs in the gayest manner possible, a 'spread' of the track let the car upon the ties, from which it leaped at one bound into the swamp, completely immersing several of its occupants in the muddy slime.

No damage was done, however, as the spot where everything and everybody alighted was too soft to cause anything to be broken, and after righting the car, they were able to repair the disaster as much as possible.

William and Keating safely arrived in Lavaca early in the afternoon, were at once driven to Indianola, where they cleaned up, including a most welcome bathing and shaving, at the Magnolia House. From here they embarked on a little schooner carrying the government mail from the coast; were becalmed in Aranzas Bay, and late during the night of the twenty-seventh of January the light from a quaint seaport city danced along the waves of its beautiful harbour, and welcomed the worn-out but indefatigable detectives to Corpus Christi.

Going ashore, the two proceeded to a sort of hotel or boarding-house on the beach, where they found Judge Carpenter, formerly of Chicago, who had become district judge there, and who, on learning my son's name, inquired if he were not a relative of Allan Pinkerton the detective.

He replied that he was very distantly related, which was a literal truth at that time, when the Judge, claiming an acquaintance, proffered any assistance which might be desired, whatever his business. The courtesy was courteously accepted, but no questions were asked concerning Taylor.

After breakfast the next morning, they strolled up-town with Judge Carpenter, when passing a Mr Buckley's store, Keating, while catching step, took occasion to nudge my son, who carelessly looked into the place, as any stranger might, and there saw the object of his long search pleasantly chatting with one of the clerks; but they walked on quietly with the Judge as far as the post-office, when he kindly introduced them to another Mr Taylor, the postmaster.

After a few moments' pleasant conversation, William asked the postmaster if he could direct him to ex-Sheriff John McLane's residence. It proved to be but a block distant, but on inquiring there, it was ascertained that he was absent at his store, farther down-town. He was the only person in that city, besides Keating, whom my son felt that he could trust, as I had not only previously rendered him service, but also held him in the light of a friend; and he had already been requested by me to render him any service in his power, should William pass that way, so that he knew the first thing he should do was to go to him, explain his business fully and secure his immediate advice and assistance.

Finding him, he told him that he did not feel justified in arresting Taylor unless the mail-boat in which he had arrived was, in some way, detained for an hour. McLane said he would attend to that, and brought Captain Reinhart to the store, but not telling him why the delay was desired, arranged for the same, and at once hunted up Sheriff Benson, so my son delivered the warrant and demanded the prisoner.

Benson at first hesitated, expressing the utmost surprise, as Taylor was a fellow-boarder, and he could not realise, so he said, that he was other than a brave and chivalrous gentleman, and began to question the validity of the requisition, but William told him that there was the order of Governor Pease approved by General Canby, and that he did not propose to be dallied with or imposed upon in any manner.

Seeing that my son had come too far and under gone too many hardships to be trifled with, he went with him to Buckley's store, where they found Taylor, who was given into the detectives' hands, though utterly astounded and completely unnerved at the idea that the strong hand of the law was upon him.

In this condition, and before he could collect his scattered senses and decide to make a legal resistance, which would have caused my son a vast amount of trouble, if indeed it had not resulted in the liberation of the elegant swindler, he was placed on board the schooner.

After they had left Corpus Christi behind, William began a system of soothing argument, with the end in view of convincing Taylor, who was now be coming nervous and restless, and evidently ashamed of being carried away so ingloriously, that it would be the best thing for himself, his brother, and even his people in Philadelphia, to go along quietly, without creating any disturbance, as, should he do so, he would treat him like a gentleman in every instance; but should he give him any trouble whatever he would be obliged to put him in irons, and not only treat him like a criminal, but would serve him roughly in every particular.

Taylor saw that he was in my power, and that I had put two men after him who would have gone to Cape Horn for him, and that his only chance of escape lay in strategy.

He had the perfect freedom of the boat and, when he desired, chatted with the captain and the crew, who were not apprised by my son of the character of his new companion, and everything was done to make him comfortable.

At first he kept entirely to himself, but of a sudden his manner changed entirely, and he became particularly pleasant, especially to the captain of the boat; and as they were nearing the little barren Saluria Island, at the entrance to Matagorda Bay, William accidentally overheard the captain say to Taylor, 'The tide is high enough, and I will be able to run close to the island'. This caused him to have no particular suspicion of Taylor, as the remark might equally apply to a hundred other subjects besides the one to which it did; but in a few moments after he noticed the schooner, which had hugged the island pretty closely, now suddenly take a still closer tack, and rapidly neared the barren coast.

Feeling alarmed lest the helmsman was not attending to his duty, my son yelled: 'Captain, what under heaven do you mean? Don't you see that in another moment you'll have us beached?'

He had scarcely uttered the words when Taylor was seen to spring into the waves, and then disappear, and the boat at the same moment stood off from the island, as if in obedience to the warning my son had given.

The truth flashed into his mind in an instant: here, after this hard, unremitting toil, the discomforts, the annoyances, the dangers, everything through which they had been obliged to pass, after their hopes for success, just when they were beginning to feel the pleasure of work well done, and be able to experience the genuine satisfaction it is to any man who is honest enough to acknowledge it, in securing the regard of the public for assisting in its protection, the commendation of one's employer for good sturdy care for his interests, and the self-respect one gains in doing one's duty, even if it has led him a hard life, they were to be cheated and outwitted. Half crazed, my son, with anger and indignation, and a perfect flood of humiliating thoughts filled his brain in the first great question, 'What was to be done?'

His first impulse was to plunge in after him, and in pursuance of that impulse he had freed himself of his boots and coat, when, seeing

Taylor rise to the surface and make but little headway against the tide, which was ebbing strongly, he called to the captain to round to, and began firing with considerable rapidity, so as to strike the water within a few feet of the man who was so unsuccessfully struggling against the tide, but whom he could not blame for making so brave and desperate an effort to free himself.

He was provided with two magnificent English Trenter revolvers, which will carry a half-ounce ball a fourth of a mile with absolute accuracy; and as he could use it with great precision he could easily have killed the man in the water. Both the captain and Taylor were terribly scared, and as Taylor held up his hand, and yelled 'I surrender!' the balls were cutting into the water all about him savagely.

The captain shouted, 'For God's sake, don't kill the man! Don't you see I'm rounding to?'

Keating, who had been almost worn out from the Texas trip, had been sleeping in a bunk below, and had been roused by William's firing and the strange motion of the schooner, now came on deck rather thinly clad, and the two detectives covered Taylor with their revolvers; while the captain, himself at the wheel, handled the schooner so that it was only necessary for him to keep himself above water in order to float with the tide against the side of the boat, when my son, rather too indignant to be particularly tender, grabbed him by the hair and his luxuriant whiskers, drew him aboard, and soundly kicked him into the cabin, where he began crying from excitement and fright, even going to such depths of discouragement that he begged for a revolver with which to kill himself. Which being handed him by my son for that purpose, he very properly refused, and was put to the purpose of drying his clothes like a truant school-boy.

It was my son's intention to take the steamer at Indianola for Galveston immediately upon arriving at the former place; but on account of a heavy 'Norther' which had blown all day Friday, the steamer had been obliged to put out to sea, and the party were consequently compelled to put up at the Magnolia House, and wait there until the following Monday. It required all the detective's shrewdness to keep Taylor quiet, as he had learned from some source that the creation of Wyoming Territory, which occurred a short time before his capture, had caused Cheyenne to be a city of quite a different territory than when the requisition was issued, which would have amounted to so grave a technical flaw that the requisition would not have held against a *habeas corpus*.

Court had just set at the place, and Indianola was full of lawyers, hungry as vultures for just such a rich case. By constant persuasions, partial promises, leading to a hope, that a compromise might be effected at New Orleans, and dark hints of irons, and that, should his brother come on there and create any disturbance he would be immediately arrested as accessory both before and after the crime; with constant drives out into the country, rambles down the sea-shore, and every pretext known to the mind of the ingenious detective, everything was managed successfully; a receipt for nearly two thousand dollars in specie secured; the turning over of the money to Taylor's brother stopped. Taylor himself taken to New Orleans without an attempt at rescue; and receiving a dispatch there from me to the effect that a compromise could not be for a moment considered, the party left that city Thursday, 4 February, arriving in Cheyenne six days later, my son accounting for his prisoner to the authorities into whose hands the case then passed. The last being seen of 'Harry G. Taylor, the Man from Somewhere', being behind the bars of the guard-house at Fort Russell, where he had been placed for safe-keeping previous to his trial. I have related these facts, not so much to show any startling phase of crime, as to give the public a single illustration, out of thousands upon my records, of how men must overcome every known obstacle leading the hard life of the detective.

For someone who prided himself as a stealthy undercover observer and master of disguise, Pinkerton never fails to inform his gentle readers when he is recognised by a malefactor, the implication being that his features were well-known throughout America. His distaste for 'blockade runners' (who had tried to circumvent the cordoning of the rebel South during the civil war) is evident in this tale set in 1868.

⊰ A Bogus Baronet and His Victims ⊱

The good people of the city of Boston were greatly exercised, at a certain period during the war, over the doings of one Sir Henry Mercer, who came to the surface, made a ripple of excitement, and then passed from sight and thought, giving place to the next sensation, as will be the way of the world until the end of time.

The particular interest centring on Sir Henry Mercer lay in the ease with which he secured his rank, the remarkably good time he had while he held the title, and the general luxurious way in which he enjoyed the prerogatives of rank and wealth including of course several first-class scandals while he was supposed to be their rightful possessor.

Great men frequently spring from humble surroundings, and Mercer was no exception to this desirable way of getting on in the world, which used him rather shabbily at the start, for at the breaking out of the war, himself and wife were found making a very questionable living in a very questionable way in a then very doubtful locality on Sudbury Street, Boston. In fact, Mrs Mercer enjoyed the reputation of being one of those accommodating business ladies who can conduct a cigar-store so as to make it more profitable than the best of men, although the actual sale of cigars would not have supported so modest a salesman as Silas Wegg, before he met old Noddy Boffin, and became avaricious, for she had a way of making appointments for parties, both ladies and gentlemen, who imagined they had not their affinities. Added to this business basis was the employment of two slinking fellows, who were called 'private detectives', and who employed their time taking notes on callers and parties in general who met here, following them, learning all that was possible concerning them, and then, after a little time, taking occasion to call on them at their offices, if they had any, remind them of their 'little indiscretion', and secure whatever might be got, which usually was and usually is in proportion to the cowardice of the victim.

This was the business of Mrs Mercer, while her husband had rather precarious employment as a city 'hummer' for the drygoods house of Laught & Co and was in every way qualified for adventure, possessing a fine appearance, a large amount of self-assurance, and had several languages at his tongue's end, so that after a time he was not only able to bring a large amount of business to his employers, but considerable custom to the Sudbury Street cigar-store, where he had no trouble in inducing country merchants to go wild in their laudable endeavours to study the zoological department of society usually described by that generic phrase, 'seeing the elephant'.

While matters were progressing in this manner with the Mercers, Laught & Co, in their haste to become rich, in 1864 began shipping largely to Nassau, for Florida, goods that would suit the Southern market. They did not run the blockade, but they forwarded the material that was to run it. The shrewd Mercer shortly discovered this secret, and he was not long in using it to advantage; and while acting as agent for the firm, he informed the government of the acts of his employers, and finally obtained the double position of drummer and government detective.

His first disclosures led to the arrest of Laught, who was lodged in jail. While lying there, by some treacherous arrangement Mercer so imposed on his employer that he obtained a power-of-attorney to collect all the debts of Laught & Co at Nassau; and there, as well as in Boston, after this brilliant move, he was recognised as a partner in the firm.

On his arrival at Nassau, Mercer, who now blossomed out as a genuine English Sir Henry Mercer, a partner in the firm of Laught & Co, was received by Mr Henry Adler, the great blockade-runner and agent for the Confederate States, with the most distinguished marks of esteem. After he had concluded his business, and just before leaving for Boston, Mr Adler introduced him to a very attractive young widow, a Northern lady, who had lost her husband, a Southerner, running the blockade. He was of course introduced as a live baronet, and the widow naturally felt proud of such noble society; the result of which was that on the voyage from Nassau to Boston Sir Henry wooed and won her, which wooing and winning was continued after the couple had arrived in Boston, notwithstanding the trifling obstacle remaining in the way behind the cigar stand on Sudbury Street.

When this shadow presented itself, Sir Henry urged that a little matter like that was hardly to be considered. All English noblemen were accustomed to such incumbrances. A trifling annuity would take the cigar-stand party back to England; and it is a fact worthy of record that she did go there, whatever the inducement offered.

It appears that the widow was worth nearly half a million dollars in her own right; and as this was too tempting a capture to permit escaping, Sir Henry pressed his suit with greater vigour than ever, and the day for the proposed marriage was finally set, while the happy baronet succeeded in quartering himself at the widow's elegant mansion.

The lady's friends made a bitter fight against the man, but she seemed completely infatuated, and not until the most powerful efforts were made would she consent to even seem to doubt him by a visit to his 'bankers', which was proposed as a test of the man's being all he professed. When the baronet heard of this proposition, he acceded to it in the blandest terms, giving his lovely bride-to-be a letter, over which was beautifully printed an embossed coat-of-arms in bronze and gilt, to his 'bankers' in New York.

Armed with this reassuring document, the lady proceeded to New York, to find Sir Henry unknown there; and, thoroughly alarmed, swiftly returned to Boston, only to find that the bogus baronet had left on the very next train, taking with him twelve thousand dollars of her money, together with all the silver plate, and that he had started for England, via Quebec, in which city he was arrested. But the fair widow, afraid of the scandal and exposure it would bring about, let the scamp go with her money, plate, and honour; and Sir Henry Mercer, as a sensation, soon passed from public attention, and eventually from sight, but came back again, like a bad penny, in a way which, through my efforts, shut the doors of a prison upon him.

Just four years later, Mr J. M. Ballard, then division superintendent of one of the express companies running in and out of Chicago, called upon me at my chief office in that city, and in a very excited manner told me that only an hour or two previous he had become convinced that an embezzlement, amounting to two or three thousand dollars, had occurred on their route between Chicago and a large city further west.

With what slight information I could secure, I immediately detailed several of my best operatives, and within a short time had secured a happy result to my work, which brought out the following facts: about six weeks before, J. R. Wilson, a pleasant-faced, boyish fellow of about twenty, and a messenger of the express company between Chicago and the city referred to, one of the most important express routes in the country, was introduced by another messenger to one W. S. G. Mercer, proprietor of a Randolph Street saloon and restaurant. Mercer cultivated Wilson's acquaintance assiduously, so much so, in fact, that the two were firm friends within a week or two, and, when Wilson was in Chicago, were constantly in each other's society.

About two weeks previous to the call upon me by Mr Ballard, Mercer, who was none other than the bogus Sir Henry, and who had degenerated from a live baronet to a Chicago saloon-keeper, gambler, and ward politician—about as low as it is possible for one to get— took a trip to the western city with his young friend, and the two had a very gay time of it, during which the crafty Mercer praised Wilson's good qualities, fine appearance, and splendid business abilities, cunningly coming around to delicate insinuations that the boy was having too hard a time of it for one of his good parts, and finally, with devilish ingenuity, hinting at the ease with which a good haul could be made from the company.

This subject was hinted at over wine and cigars, at the theatre and at places where the very devil in men is most easily awakened, until, before leaving on their return, the two had agreed upon a plan by which Wilson should secure all that was possible, without awakening suspicion, on two 'runs', or trips to Chicago, when the money should be divided and the two should fly to Canada, and from there proceed to Europe on a tour of pleasure.

According to arrangements, on Monday morning, 30 March, 1868, Wilson returned from his trip, and, while getting his money-box and books into the express wagon, a business-like looking gentleman stepped up to the car and inquired: 'Is there a valise for me from J. A. Walters?'

'Yes,' replied Wilson. 'You can get it over to the office in a few minutes.'

'Can't you let me have it now? Here's the receipt.'

'All right, then. Fifty cents charges.'

The stranger signed the messenger's book, paid him fifty cents, and walked away.

That valise contained three thousand dollars taken by Wilson, and the party who carried it away so nonchalantly was the ex-Sir Henry.

It was on the next day that Mr Ballard called, and all that I could learn then was that inquiries had been made for amounts by business men which had not come to hand, for a total sum so large that its non-arrival alarmed him; so that my men were on hand at once to follow and observe every movement of each messenger that might by any possibility have been the guilty party.

Consequent upon this arrangement, I discovered that on Wednesday morning, as the train bearing Wilson on his 'out-trip' was about leaving, a certain gentleman brought a well-filled valise to the express car, gave it to the messenger, who consigned it on his way-bill to 'J. A. Walters', a mythical personage of course, and on paying the charges, and taking a receipt in a most business-like manner, walked off whistling; but not alone, for wherever the man, whom I soon found to be Mercer, went, there was an invisible though remorseless attendant beside him.

A certain Chicago gentleman also took a trip on the same train with Wilson, who at every station where the train halted saw that the messenger did not leave it, and after he had arrived at his destination, that he never made an unobserved move.

The reports of the two operatives, condensed, were:

Wilson: restless; excited; has something on his mind worrying him. Sports a brand-new suit of clothes, a handsome gold watch, and a diamond pin.'

Mercer: neglecting business; pretty full of liquor; constantly borrowing money right and left.

This settled the matter in my mind.

Wilson, closely watched by my operative, left on his return Thursday night, arriving in Chicago on Friday morning.

After the rush of the departing passengers was a little over, Mercer, who had been waiting between some cars in front of the train so as not to attract attention, walked rapidly down the track, stepped up to the express-car, repeated the same inquiries as on the former occasion, was met by the same answers from Wilson, paid the charger on the valise and, just as he turned to depart, one of my operatives, who happened to be passing, heard him remark in a low tone of voice: 'Meet me at the Sherman House just as soon as you get through. Room 86.'

Two men accompanied Mercer to that hotel without his knowledge, with orders to arrest him instantly on his making the slightest sign of an intention to not keep his appointment with Wilson. Two more detectives followed the company's wagon, in a private conveyance, to the express office, with instructions to never permit the guilty messenger to escape them, but in no manner to disturb him if he proceeded to the hotel according to appointment. While I at once dispatched a special messenger requesting Superintendent Ballard to meet me immediately in the office of the Sherman House.

By this means in less than an hour all the parties had been brought together, and helped materially to swell the crowd in the rotunda.

I kept Mr Ballard out of sight, as I was apprehensive lest Wilson might suspect his mission, and found that this was the wisest plan, for shortly he came hurriedly into the hotel, and, after standing a moment as if irresolute, walked though and through the office, hazily scanning the face of every man in it, not excepting myself. Then, after going out and looking up and down the street in either direction, as if to be doubly assured that he was not suspected and followed, he returned and hurriedly proceeded to the room designated as No. 86.

Telling Mr Ballard to follow in a few moments, I hastened after the retreating messenger, and arrived at the landing of the floor on which No. 86 was situated just in time to observe Wilson, a few yards in advance, pause before a door, give two quick raps, and enter immediately after.

There were two or three gentlemen in the hall, carelessly conversing together. A stranger to them would merely have regarded them as pleasant, chatty guests, who had met by chance and were enjoying the meeting. They were my operatives; but they paid no attention to me, nor I to them.

Scarcely had the door to 86 closed, when I silently stood beside it, and could easily catch the low, earnest conversation within.

'My dear boy,' said Mercer enthusiastically, 'you did splendidly!'

'I feel like death about it!' said the messenger, with such a touch of genuine remorse in his tones, that I pitied the deluded fellow from the bottom of my heart

'O pshaw! damn them! It's nothing to them, and in two days we will be out of harm's way. But we must get out of this lively. My plan is to get a livery team and drive out into Indiana, and there take the train for Canada. They'll probably have a lot of Pinkerton's men watching the depots, and we will just learn these smart detectives a new trick,' replied Mercer with a triumphant laugh.

By this time Mr Ballard was beside me and, with a slight signal, I had two of the parties in the hall, whom a stranger would have taken for chatting guests, at the door, one stationed silently at either side.

Then I rapped loudly upon the door.

A smothered oath from Mercer, a cry of remorseful surprise from the poor messenger, and a rustle and hurry inside, were the only response.

I rapped again, louder than before, and then finally told the parties that if the door was not instantly opened, it would be forced.

After another rustle and scuffle, Mercer opened the door, and Mr Ballard and myself quickly entered, 1 locking the door, putting the key in my pocket.

Mercer looked me full in the face for a moment, and with the one gasping ejaculation, 'My God! Allan Pinkerton!', sank into a chair; while Wilson, white as a ghost, reeled against the wall, looking from me to Mr Ballard, his superintendent, for a moment, and then, burying his face in his hands, threw himself upon the bed, and moaned in utter agony.

They were at once arrested; and while Mercer was consigned to the county jail to await examination, I had Wilson taken to my office, where a full confession was secured. All the money was recovered, save the few hundred dollars expended by Mercer for the clothing and jewellery with which his dupe was led on to the commission of the second and greater crime.

At the trial which was shortly had, the judge, at my earnest solicitation, mercifully took into consideration the facts of the case, and the messenger, Wilson, was given the least punishment possible; while ex-Sir Henry, whose crime was aggravated ten-fold by his cruel and heartless ruin of a previously honoured and respected boy, was consigned to his rightful sphere of action, where, for ten years at least, he remained an honest and law-abiding citizen of the State of Illinois within its penitentiary at Joliet.

The rest of the tales in this book concern a series of ingenious hustles. In the first, Pinkerton manages to combine a grudging admiration for 'Canada Bill' Jones and for gypsies, 'the merriest, kindest-hearted and most child-like simple dogs on earth'. The story appears in Criminal Reminiscences *and* Detective Sketches *(1878), reprinted as* Criminal Reminiscences *and* The Detectives *(1884) and 'Canada Bill' turns up again in* Thirty Years a Detective *(1884).*

⊣ Canada Bill ⊢

There are some men who naturally choose, or, through a series of unfortunate blunders, drift into the life of social outlaws, who possess so many remarkably original traits of character that they become rather subjects for admiration than condemnation when we review their life and career.

On first thought it could hardly be imagined that one who has been all his life, so far as is known, a gambler and a confidence man, whose associates were always of the same or worse class than himself, who had no more regard for law than a wild Indian, and who never in his entire career seemed to have an aspiration above being the vagabond *par excellence*, could move us to anything beyond a passing interest, the same as we would have for a wild animal or any unusual character among men and women.

But here is a man who, from his daring, his genuine simplicity, his great aptitude for his nefarious work, his simple, almost childish ways, his unequalled success, and a hundred other marked and remarkable qualities, cannot but cause something more than a common interest, and must always remain as an extraordinarily brilliant type of a very dangerous and unworthy class.

Such was 'Canada Bill', whose real name was William Jones. He was born in a little tent under the trees of Yorkshire, in old England. His people were genuine gypsies, who lived, as all other gypsies do,

131

by tinkering, dickering, or fortune-telling, and horse-trading. Bill, as he was always called, grew up among the Romany like any other gypsy lad, becoming proficient in the nameless and numberless tricks of the gypsy life, and particularly adept at handling cards. In fact, this proficiency caused him finally to leave his tribe, as, wherever he went among them, he never failed to beat the shrewdest of his shrewd people on every occasion where it was possible for him to secure an opponent willing to risk any money upon his supposed superiority in that direction.

Having become altogether too keen for his gypsy friends, he began appearing at fairs and travelling with provincial catchpenny shows in England. Tiring of successes in that field, he eventually came to America, and wandered about Canada for some time in the genuine gypsy fashion. This was about twenty-five years ago, when Bill was twenty-two or twenty-three years of age, and when thimble-rigging was the great game at the fairs and among travellers.

Bill soon developed a great reputation for playing short-card games, but finally devoted his talents entirely to three-card monte under the guise of a countryman, and may be said to have been the genuine original of that poor, simple personage who had been swindled by sharpers, and who, while bewailing his loss and showing interested people the manner in which he had been robbed, invariably made their natural curiosity and patronizing sympathy cost them dearly.

Himself and another well-known monte-player, named Dick Cady, travelled through Canada for several years, gaining a great notoriety among gamblers and sporting men; and it was here that this singular person secured the sobriquet of 'Canada Bill', which name clung to him until his death, in the summer of 1877. He was known by everybody throughout the country who knew him at all by that name, it being generally supposed that he was of Canadian birth.

As a rule, three-card monte men are among the most godless, worthless, unprincipled villains that infest society anywhere, but this strange character, from his simplicity, which was genius, his cunning, which was most brilliant, his acting, which was inimitable, because it was nature itself, created a lofty niche for himself in all the honour there may be attached to a brilliant and wholly original career as a sharper of this kind. However many imitators he may have, and he has hundreds, none can ever approach his perfection in the slightest possible degree.

Any deft person, after a certain amount of practice, can do all the trickery there is about the sleight-of-hand in three-card monte, but the game is so common a dodge among swindlers, that unless the confidence of the dupe is first fully secured, he seldom bites at the bait offered.

This must either be confidence, on the part of the person being operated on, that he is smarter than the dealer, if his real character is known; or, in case it is not known, a conviction that he is a genuine greenhorn who can easily be beaten the second time.

It was here that Canada Bill's peculiar genius never failed to give him victory; and it is said of him that he never made a mistake and never failed to win money whenever he attempted it.

His personal appearance, which was most ludicrous, undeniably had much to do with his success. He was the veritable country gawky, the ridiculous, ignorant, absurd creature that has been so imperfectly imitated on and off the stage for years, and whose true description can scarcely be written. He was fully six feet high, with dark eyes and hair, and always had a smooth-shaven face, full of seams and wrinkles, that were put to all manner of difficult expressions with a marvellous facility and ease, all this coupled with long, loose-jointed arms, long, thin, and apparently a trifle unsteady legs, a shambling, shuffling, awkward gait, and this remarkable face and head bent forward and turned a little to one side, like an inquiring and wise old owl, and then an outfit of Granger clothing, the entire cost of which never exceeded fifteen dollars, made a combination that never failed to call a smile to a stranger's face, or awaken a feeling of curiosity and interest wherever he might be seen.

One striking difference between Canada Bill and all the other sharpers of his ilk lay in the fact that he was the thing he seemed to be. Old gamblers and sporting-men could never fathom him. He was an enigma to his closest friends. A short study of the awkward, ambling fellow would give one the impression that he was simply supremely clever in his manner and make up; that he was merely one of the most accomplished actors in his profession ever known; and that he only kept up this appearance of guilelessness for the purpose of acquiring greater reputation among his fellows. But those who knew him, as far as it was possible to know the wandering vagabond that he was, assert that he was the most unaffected, innocent, and really simple-hearted of human beings, and never had been anything, and never could have been anything, save just what he was.

This would hardly seem possible of even an exceptional person among ordinary people, and I can only reconcile this singular case with consistency when I call to mind many of the interesting old gypsy tinkers I have myself known, who, with all their wise lore and cunning tricks were the merriest, kindest-hearted and most child-like simple dogs on earth.

It seems almost impossible that any living person waging such a relentless war against society as Canada Bill did, until the day of his death, could have anything generous and simple about him; but he certainly had those two qualities to a remarkable degree. They were uppermost in everything that he did. It almost seemed that this man had no thought but that his vocation in life was of the highest respectability; that skinning a man out of a thousand dollars as neatly as he could do it was an admirable stroke of business, even if it led to that man's ruin; and that every act of his criminal life was one of the most honourable accomplishments; so that this sunny temper and honest face was an outgrowth of a satisfaction in upright living.

He was certainly different from all other men whom I have been called upon to study. He always had a mellow and old look about him that at once won the looker-on and caused a real touch of warmth and kindliness toward him. His face was always beaming with a rough good-fellowship and a sturdy friendliness that seemed almost something to cling to and bet on, while every movement of his slouchy, unkempt body was only a new indication of his rustic ingenuousness.

One November night, several years since, I started on a hurried trip over the Pittsburg and Fort Wayne road from Chicago to the east, for the transaction of some important business of such a nature that I did not desire the fact of my presence known there. Noticing several eastern and western people of my acquaintance in the sleeper and throughout the cars, before the train started, I quietly entered the smoking car. and took a cigar and a seat in a quiet corner, with the object of avoiding my friends as much as possible, and remaining where I was until everything had got quiet in the sleeper for the night, so that I could safely retire without observation.

Being very tired, after a casual glance at several other persons in front of me in the car, I settled myself snugly in my seat, hoping to be able to get a little nap; but I had scarcely got myself comfortably arranged, when the train halted at 22nd Street, and my attention was attracted by the entrance into our car of a tall, stumbling fellow, dressed in some cheap, woollen, home-spun stuff, that hung about his attenuated frame like a dirty camp-meeting tent around a straggling set of poles.

Pausing just inside the door for a moment, he deposited on the floor a valise whose size and cavernous appearance would have won the heart of an audience at a minstrel show, and then, giving his big hand a great ungainly wave as if to clear away the smoke immediately in front of him, peered into the murky distance, and ejaculated 'Gauldarned thick!'

He probably referred to both the smoke and the passengers. In any event, he sat clumsily down upon the stove, from which he suddenly bounded like a rubber ball, although there was no fire within it. It appeared though it had crept into his bucolic mind that he was sitting on a stove, and that there must, of course, be a fire within it, and, consequently, he must be burned. Whatever impelled him, he and his cavernous valise went ricocheting along the aisle, finally coming up short, like a bucking mule, at about the centre of the car, and there, tumbling noisily into a seat, which, taking into consideration the crowded condition of the coach, singularly enough was vacant.

By this time there was a broad smile on the faces of all the passengers, and many mirthful references were made in an undertone to the wild 'Hoosier', some of which he evidently overheard, but which were received in the best of humour. The subject of such witticism turning a benign and smiling farmer face upon all, but holding on to his big, though evidently nearly empty, valise with both hands, as if indicating that he was quite ready for any good-natured joke with 'the boys' so long as none of them attempted any sharp city tricks upon him which, it could be easily seen from his manner, he had already experienced, and was quite ready to have it generally known that quite a mistake would be made when anybody took him for a 'young man from the country'.

After the 22nd Street crossing was passed. we sped along rapidly, almost the majority of the car seeming to be of that very common class of travellers that are usually considered 'good fellows', who were ready for a jest, whether it were ordinary or of the first class.

We had been bowling along for but a short time, however, before the conductor made his appearance.

His was mere business to collect fares; that was all. He came through the car like an old campaigner, with no favours to ask and none to give.

He got along to where our bucolic friend was sitting without trouble, when that lively individual seemed ready for an argument.

'You're the conductor?' he remarked dryly.

'Yes.'

'You takes the money for ridin' on this machine?'

'Yes; where ye goin'?'

— 'Fort Wayne, God willin'.'

The countryman clumsily produced a bill from out a huge roll, and then remarked:

'Lots of good boys on the train?'

'Dunno; guess so,' replied the conductor. The conductor gave the innocent party his change, when that ubiquitous individual remarked:

'Lots of funny fellows on this train?'

The conductor had passed, but he took the time to turn and say:

'Don't trust 'em, my Granger friend.'

'D—d if I will,' said he, as he took a stronger and firmer hold of his priceless sack. 'D—d if I will, fur I've been thar! I've been thar!'

A roar of laughter followed this sally from the Indiana Granger and I noticed at the time, without giving it any particular attention so far as this countryman and his immediate remarks were concerned, that, at various intervals throughout the car, the laughing which followed his remark was extremely well distributed; but being tired, I received all this merriment as a common occurrence, and, after the conductor passed, fell into a heavy drowse, in which tall Indiana Grangers, brusque conductors, commercial travellers, and the ordinary railroad riffraff danced back and forth through my disturbed dreams.

I was of course unconscious of what passed for a little time, but was eventually disturbed by renewed laughter through the car, and noticed that quite a group had gathered around the Granger, whose members were evidently greatly interested in whatever he was doing and saying; while his great, honest face, all alive with enthusiasm, was wreathed with smiles at being such an object of general interest.

As before stated, up to this time I had given the matter no thought; but when I now heard one of a couple in front of me remark: 'Very quaint character; very quaint character. I believe some of those Chicago rascals have victimized him, and he is telling the passengers about it', which was followed by a request to his companion to 'come along and see the fun'. I immediately understood that we were to be given an exhibition of three-card monte of a very interesting character, and that many of the persons in the car were 'cappers', or those members of the gang who are used to persuade fools to bet upon the game.

My first impulse was to put a stop to the villainy at my personal risk; but I recollected that the very reason which had forced me to take up with the discomforts of the smoking-car, an absolute necessity for remaining unknown, prevented this, and though my blood boiled with desire to frustrate the already ripened and charmingly-working plans of the keen scamps, I was forced to swallow my indignation and content myself with taking up a position where I could get a comprehensive idea of what might follow.

By this time so much interest was being exhibited in the uncouth fellow's manipulations, that two seats had been given him; and there he sat in one corner of the space thus made, with his legs crossed under him like a tailor's, his huge valise lying across this framework in such a manner that a most neat, level, and glossy surface was made. All this with a nicety of calculation really remarkable, while his whole form, manner, and action showed him to be the simplest, most honest of men who, out of the pure goodness of his heart, rough, ignorant, and unkempt as he was. proposed giving the crowd about him his experiences merely for what benefit it would certainly prove to them.

'Yaas,' he said in an indescribably droll tone of voice, 'yaas, them doggoned Chicago skinners cum nigh a ruinin' me. Now, I do 'low them fellers beat the hull 'tarnal kentry. But gosh! I found 'em out!'

Here the Hoosier laughed with such a ridiculously childish air of triumph, that general laughter was irresistible,

He then reached his long, skinny fingers down into his huge valise and brought out a handful of articles of various kinds, among which were a couple of sickle-teeth, tied together with a string, a horn husking-pin, and a 'snack' of chicken covered with bread-crumbs. These caused another laugh, but were suddenly returned to their resting-place and several other dives made into the greasy cavern, evidently to the great discomfiture of the gawky; but he chattered and grinned away, until finally a brand-new pack of cards had been secured.

This was bunglingly opened, the greater portion of the cards slushing out of his hands upon the floor and flying in different directions upon the seat.

To any casual observer it was more than apparent that the poor silly fellow was not more than half-witted, and the fun of it all seemed to lie in his sincerity, which the passengers took for one of the hugest of jokes.

After things had been got to rights which took the clumsy fellow a long time, during which he enlivened his listeners with his idea of Chicago as a city, its people as sharpers of the first order, and the grandeur of his own great state, Indiana, he selected three cards from the pack and, wrapping the balance in a dirty bit of brown paper, put them away carefully in the valise.

The three cards selected were the five of spades, the five of clubs, and the queen of hearts, and the gentleman from Indiana now began his exposition in real earnest

'Why, d'ye know, the durn skunks said they knowed me, 'n' 'fore I knowed what I was a doin' these old friends, as they said they wus, had me bettin' that I could jerk up the joker. Now, yer see, fellers,' remarked the dealer, as he held up the queen, 'they called this keerd the joker, fur why I can't tell yer, lest it's a joke on the dealer if yer picks it up,'

'Of course you picked it up!' remarked a flashy gentleman, who had the appearance of a successful commercial traveller on a good salary.

Such a look as the dealer gave the man.

'Picked it up! Picked it up? My friend, mebby you think you're smart enough to pick it up! Don't you ever squander yer money like I did a-tryin'! Pick her up! Pick up hell! 'Tain't in her to git picked up. She can't be got. Them cussed coons has worked some all-fired charm on that durned keerd, so that no man can raise her. Mebby you kin lift the keerd? She allers wins, she does; but don't bet nuthin'.'

Here the dealer bunglingly shuffled the cards, and made such a mess of it that the effort only brought forth more peals of derisive laughter.

'Now, ye see, fellers,' pursued the imperturbable dealer, 'this is the five uv spades, hy'r is the five uv dubs, and thar is the rip-roarin' female that wins every time she kin be got. I'm jest a-goin' to skin the boys down hum in Kos-cus-ky County; fur it's the beautifulest and deceivenst game out; but,' he added, with the solemnity of a parson at a funeral, 'fellers, d'ye know I wouldn't hev a friend o' mine bet on this yer game fur anything, not fur a good boss!'

He closed this admonitory remark with such a droll wave of his long arm and hand, that a palpable snicker greeted the performance; and the flashy gentleman who had suggested that the greeny must have been able to pick up the card when being entertained by his Chicago friends, bent forward, and after a moment's hesitation over the three cards, which were lying face downward upon the valise, picked up one, which, with an air of triumph, he held aloft for a moment and then slapped down with a great flourish.

This was the 'rip-roarin' female that wins every time!' and his honour, the gentleman from Kosciusco County, Indiana, turned white as he observed how neatly her ladyship could be brought to the surface by one of a miscellaneous crowd.

'Jehosiphat!' he exclaimed, as he grabbed the cards and began another bungling shuffle of them 'Jehosiphat! Stranger, d'yer know I've got pea-green scrip in my pocket as says as yer can't do that agin?'

'Oh, I wouldn't take your money!' the flashy man replied, as he nudged a man near him. ''T wouldn't be fair, you know.'

'Now now, see hy'r, stranger,' answered the Indianian, 'I've told ye already that ye hadn't ought to bet on this deceitful game; but yer is too sassy and bold. Yer thinks yer knows it all, 'n' yer doesn't. Jist wait till I fix the keerds. Thar now! Old Injeanny agin the field!'

The dealer had rearranged the cards in a reckless, fashion; but there they lay, and the passengers crowded closer and closer about the group to see all the fun that might happen.

Slowly and ungainly enough the dealer reached down into the outside pockets of his homespun suit with both hands. Finding nothing there, he tremulously went into his pantaloons pockets; but he found nothing there.

'Oh, he's a fraud!' suggested a big-bellied man near me, turning to a rural-looking fellow at his side. 'Do you know,' he continued warmly, 'you and I could go in together, and clean that 'old Jasey' out if he's got any money. But,' he added, confidentially, to his companion, 'I don't believe he's got a copper and I wouldn't be surprised if he passed around his hat, begging for car-fare, or lodging, or for his supper-bill, or something of that sort, before he leaves the train. Oh, I've seen too much of that sort of thing, I have!'

His companion, whom I had already taken for a country merchant, or something of that kind, as he afterward proved to be, looked nervous, and only replied: 'Wait a bit. Let's see what he can find in his clothes. Perhaps these gentlemen wouldn't let us win anything anyhow.'

I did not catch the answer, only observing that a pretty good understanding had been arrived at between the two. The party from Indiana by this time, after going through nearly every pocket in his clothing, had brought out from an inside vest-pocket a great, rough, dirty-looking wallet that contained, as could be seen at a glance, a very large though loosely arranged package of green-backs, which he had denominated 'pea-green scrip', and which he shook out into his broad-rimmed hat at his side in an alarmingly careless way.

'That's what I got left, after comin' outn' that d—d Gomorer, Chicager!' the dealer said feelingly. 'Stock's down, grass is dry, but I'll be gol-walloped ef I don't believe for a hundred-dollar pictur the female boss can't be lifted agin!'

'I'm your sweet potato just for once, mind you, just for once, for I ain't a betting man. But I'll risk that much just to show you how easily you can be beat at your own game!' remarked the flashy man, carelessly, at the same time covering the hundred-dollar 'picture' with ten ten-dollar bills.

'Can't I go halves on that?' eagerly asked a rough- looking fellow, who stood on a seat peering over the heads of the passengers, and at the same time holding up a fifty dollar bill.

I saw that the scheme for getting outside parties to bet, and divide chances with those who considered themselves 'up to the game', was being given a fine impetus.

'Well, I don't mind, although I'm sure of the whole,' said the flashy party, as he received the fifty dollars nonchalantly.

The honest Granger from Indiana looked dumbfounded at this new evidence of a want of confidence in his ability, but spoke up cheerily: 'Wall, thar's the keerds; yer kin take yer pick!'

Upon this the flash party pushed his way into the open space, sat down opposite the dealer, and, without any further ado, reached forward with one hand and turned the queen in a twinkling, and raked in the money with the other, immediately rising and handing the party who had taken half the bet the one-hundred-dollar bill, and pocketing the ten ten-dollar bills, and then immediately leaving the luckless dealer, to communicate and comment upon his good fortune to his friends throughout the car and tell them how easily the thing was done.

'Gaul darn the keerds, anyhow!' blurted out the dealer; 'the hull cussed thing's gone back on me; but I swon ef I don't keep the fun a-goin'!'

Several small bets were made by various parties, the winnings being almost equally divided; if anything, outside parties getting the best of what was to be got.

Suddenly there was a movement near me, and I heard the country merchant remark to his friend:

'Well, I'll go in five hundred with you. Be careful now, be careful!'

Another 'capper' in the crowd, having a Jew in tow, now bet a hundred dollars, and won, dividing the winnings with that party, who received his share with rapturous delight; and it could be easily seen he was in a fine condition to be 'worked'.

The large man with the country merchant now stopped and turned to his friend, saying in an undertone: 'No, you're a stranger to me, and I'd rather you'd bet the money. We will fix it this way: I'm certain of picking up the card, but I might be mistaken. I'll make two or three small bets first, or enough, so that I can pick up the card. While I have it in my hand, I'll turn one corner under, so that the card, after it is dealt, won't lay down flat. You'll see it plainly, and you can't make a mistake. Now, watch things!'

With this fine piece of bait, the corpulent fellow, who was none other than a 'capper', sat down opposite the dealer and made a few small bets. He lost three in quick succession, but on the fourth trial he turned up the queen, and won.

I watched him closely, for I had overheard him state to his dupe that he would mark the card by turning one corner of the same under toward the face. Surely enough, he did so very deftly, and I noticed that the country merchant had also seen the action, for he immediately stepped forward and took the place made vacant for him.

'Careful now!' said the stout man, as they passed each other.

An answering look from the merchant showed that he considered himself up to a thing or two; and, as he seated himself, he inquired of the ignorant dealer if he limited his bets

'Ye kin jist bet yer hull pile, or a ten-cent pictur, stranger!' replied that worthy, with a silly, childish chuckle, as he tossed the cards back and forth in a seemingly foolishly-reckless way.

The crowd now pressed forward, all interest and attention. There is always an inexpressible fascination about either winning or losing money; the flush of winning communicates itself to every looker-on, while the wild hunger to get back what one has lost has just as firm a hold upon the bystander as the victim; and one feels almost impelled to try his luck, when he sees that the very fates are all against him.

'Two hundred dollars on the queen!' said the country merchant, laying that amount on the old valise. I noticed that a quick look of intelligence passed between the stout man and the Hoosier dealer. The stout fellow was mistaken in his man. He was betting too low. I made up my mind that his look to the dealer expressed all this with the additional advice: 'Let him win a little!'

The money was covered, and the merchant's hands fluttered tremulously over the cards for a moment. But he picked up the queen and won. A buzz of excited comments followed.

'Be ye one o' them Chicager skinners?' asked the dealer. 'Confound it! I'm a-gittin' beat right an' left!'

The merchant was flushed with his winnings. He was evidently flattered by being considered so shrewd as a 'Chicago skinner'. Over behind the front ranks of the lookers-on came a pantomime order from his stout friend, which seemed to me to mean: 'Bet heavy while you are to luck.'

'You don't limit bets?' asked the merchant eagerly.

'Nary time, nary time. Hyr's a hatful of picturs as backs the winnin' keerd, which is always the queen.'

'Well, then,' said the dupe with painful slowness, while the corners of his mouth drew down and his lips became colourless,' I'll bet fifteen hundred dollars I can pick up the queen!'

There laid one of the cards, showing it had been doubled enough to prevent its resting flatly upon the old valise. The merchant counted out the money in a husky voice, making several errors, and being corrected by some of the passengers. The dealer, who might have had just a trace of a glitter in his black, fishy eyes, groped around among his 'pictures' and provided an equal amount. Every person in the car bent forward, and in a painful, breathless silence awaited the result.

'Yer pays yer money, 'n' yer takes yer choice!' remarked the dealer, leaning back in his seat, and whistling as unconcernedly as if at a town-meeting.

The merchant leaned forward. He looked at the cards as though his very soul had leaped into his eyes. He suddenly grasped the card that refused to lie flatly upon the valise, and turned it over.

He had picked up the five of clubs, and had lost !

Something like a moan escaped the poor victim's lips. My own blood boiled to rescue him from this villainous robbery. I could not do it without jeopardizing far greater interests, but my heart bled for him in his misery.

'I'm a ruined man!' he gasped, and then staggered through the crowd to sink into a vacant seat.

Even then he could not be left alone. His stout friend, the 'capper', sought him out and upbraided him for his foolishness in picking up the wrong card and losing his five hundred dollars with his own. He even begged him to try again and, finding that he had a few hundred dollars left out of what he was going to New York to buy goods with, cursed him because he would not risk that in order to retrieve himself and pay him back his money, which the reader will readily understand already belonged to the honest, simple-hearted Hoosier who was manipulating the cards.

But the game went on. The loss of so great a sum of money put rather a dampener upon it; but the 'cappers' came to the rescue with twenty, fifty, and one hundred dollar bets, which were so rapidly won that the Jew was at last 'worked' out of six hundred dollars in two quick bets of three hundred each; and amid a great row and racket which he made over his loss, the voice of the brakeman could be heard, crying out: 'Valparaiso! Twenty minutes for supper!'

Not a minute more had passed, and the train had not even come to a halt, when every one of the nefarious gang had disappeared.

The flashy man, with the look of a successful commercial travel- ler, was gone; the stout man, who had 'stood in' with the country merchant, had gone; the party who had entertained the Jew was gone; and the honest, simple, cheery countryman from Kosciusko County, Indiana, with his cavernous valise half full of loose bills, which he had not even taken time to arrange in the old book for carrying in his side- pocket and who was none other than the notorious 'Canada Bill' was gone. They were all gone, and they had taken from their dupes from eighteen hundred to two thousand dollars.

I could not but pity the poor victims, who were left on the train to brood over their foolishness; but at the same time a sense of justice stole in upon my sympathy. Everyone of these dupes had got beaten at his own game. They were just as dishonest as the men who fleeced them. They would not have risked a dollar had they not, one and all, believed that they had the advantage of a poor, foolish fellow. If he had been what they believed, and they had won his money, it would have been robbery just as much as it was robbery to take their money as neatly and easily as it was taken.

Just after the close of the war Canada Bill, in company with a river gambler, named George Devol, or 'Uncle George', as he had a fondness for being called, started for the South, and began operating in and about New Orleans. This George Devol was himself a character, as he had once been a station-agent of some railroad in Minnesota, and on being 'braced' and beaten out of his own and considerable of the company's funds, had such an admiration for the manner in which he had been beaten, that he turned out a gambler himself, and became quite well known along the lower Mississippi.

The two men, in company with one Jerry Kendricks, did an immense business in New Orleans, in the city, upon the boats, and on the different railroad lines running out of that place. Here, in New Orleans, Bill was the green, rollicking, back-country planter, and nearly always made his appearance upon a boat or a train as though he had had a narrow escape from a gang of cut-throats, but was in high glee over the fact that they had not stolen quite all of his money, and had left him a fine package of tin-ware, two or three packages of cow-hide shoes, large enough for a Louisiana negro, and a side or two of bacon. Old 'Ben' Burnish, a character well known among sporting men in the North, was one of his most accomplished 'cappers' during these days, and the gang made vast sums of money.

But finally 'Uncle George' Devol hoped to get the best of Bill, he was so careless and really ingenuous among his friends; and, knowing that he carried a twenty-five hundred dollar roll, got a man and arranged things to beat him. Through his wonderful faculty for reading people and character, Bill permitted the play, and when his opponent won, remarked quietly: 'George, you sized my pile pretty well, and got things fixed nice. Your friend will find that roll the smallest twenty-five hundred dollar pot he ever grabbed. Good-by, Uncle George!'

Bill having arranged a 'road-roll', or a showy pile of bills of small denomination, was willing to expend that much to ascertain definitely that Devol had played him false, and immediately took leave of him forever.

When the Union and Central Pacific Railroads were in process of construction, this field proved a grand harvest for Canada Bill; and, on leaving the South, where he at one time owned nearly half of a town at the mouth of the Red River, he proceeded to Kansas City, where, with 'Dutch Charlie' as principal 'pal', he certainly must have won from a hundred and fifty to two hundred thousand dollars.

From Kansas City he went to Omaha, and drifted back and forth between these points for some time, never failing to win money where he attempted, becoming a perfect scourge to the railroad companies and travellers, but, strangely enough, establishing the highest regard among all business men with whom he came in contact, hardly one of whom would not have taken his word for almost any amount of money.

The man did not seem to realise what money was worth, and gave it to anybody that might ask it. It has been related by those who should be capable of judging, that Bill gave away, gambled, or foolishly expended, fully a quarter of a million dollars.

On one occasion, in Omaha, some policemen, having a spite against Bill, arrested him and brought him before a police magistrate. He was fined fifty dollars.

Bill, rising in the box, with one of his most droll and happy expressions of voice and face, asked:

'Jedge, who does the money go to?'

'This class of fines goes to the school fund. Why?' replied the justice.

'Wall, I reckon ef it goes to so good a cause as that, you can chalk her up to a hundred and fifty, jedge!' and Bill put down the money and left the court.

But finally his prowess became so great and the winnings of his crowd so large upon the Union Pacific Railroad, that a general order of the strictest terms was issued forbidding any monte-players riding or playing on the trains of the road, and instructing conductors, on peril of dismissal, to eject them from the cars at all risks and with whatever force might be required. It was upon the appearance of this order that Bill wrote or caused to be written, as he could not write his own name his noted impudent proposition to the general superintendent of that road, in which he offered the company ten thousand dollars per annum, if he were given the sole right to throw three-card monte on the Union Pacific trains, and making his offer more attractive by pledging his word that he would confine his professional attentions exclusively to Chicago commercial travellers and Methodist preachers.

It is unnecessary to add that Bill's proposition did not receive the attention which he imagined it deserved.

After this, in 1874, in company with 'Jim' Porter and the veteran gambler, 'Colonel' Charlie Starr, Canada Bill proceeded to Chicago, where, by means best known to this class, he secured an understanding with the police, and at once opened up 'joints', or playing-places, and soon had half the 'bunko' men in Chicago 'steering' for him.

It is estimated that he made fully one hundred and fifty thousand dollars in Chicago; but as he was an inveterate gambler himself, and played into faro banks nearly all he took at monte, he left that city comparatively 'broke,' and, in company with 'Jim' and Alick Porter, went to Cleveland, where his last active work was done.

Countless instances are related of the shrewdness and success of this strange man. Among his kind he was king and I have only given this sketch of him as illustrative of a striking type of a dangerous class, still powerful and cunning, which the public would do well to avoid in whatever guise they may appear.

Canada Bill, after an unprecedentedly successful career of over twenty years in America, died a pauper as nearly every one of all the criminal classes do at the Charity Hospital, in Reading, Pennsylvania, in the summer of 1877.

This yarn is interesting for the details of prisons, the workings of railroads and the punchline (literally!), first published in Criminal Reminiscences and Detective Sketches *(1878).*

⊰ Remarkable Prison Escapes ⊱

I am certain that my readers will be interested in the recital of a few instances within my recollection where criminals, either convicts or prisoners awaiting trial for general offences, have escaped their prison confines in a most ingenious and dramatic manner.

On 8 July, 1878, the city of Columbus, Ohio, was startled by a report that some forty prisoners, confined at the State penitentiary there, had escaped, and were 'making a lively trial for tall timber' in all directions. A visit to the penitentiary proved that the reports were greatly magnified. Only three prisoners had escaped, but these had shown an amount of enterprise in getting outside of the walls that was truly remarkable.

It was found, too, that even the three did not make their escape together, but that one had got out the previous night. He had been recaptured, and was once more a prisoner, although the other two were still at liberty. The one that had been recaptured had occupied a cell in one of the tiers of cell-houses on which the State was then placing a new roof. He managed, in some way, to dig out of his cell and gain access to the roof. A large derrick for elevating stone, used in the walls during the day, stood against the prison, but at night was pulled back quite a distance from it. The prisoner stood on top of the wall, and, calculating the distance in the darkness, made a leap, the like of which has never been attempted by any acrobat on earth, and, after descending at least thirty feet through the air, caught the derrick-rope and slid down the remaining distance, making his escape unobserved.

What nerve and actual bravery were required for this! The convict risked his life more surely than if taking his chances in battle.

The slightest miscalculation, the merest mischance, the least failure in estimating his power for leaping, would have caused him to have fallen a mangled corpse upon the stones below.

But all this daring brought no reward to the poor fellow, for he was captured on the Pan Handle Road, near Summit Station, not ten hours subsequent to his marvellous escape.

The other men did not show as much daring in their escape, but even more shrewdness and ingenuity. They were engaged cutting stone just north of the penitentiary; through the aid of friends they supplied themselves with citizens' clothing, which they secreted in a closet near where they were working, and leaped from this into a sewer leading into the Scioto River. As soon as they reached the bank, they stripped off their prison garb, and, donning their citizens' clothing, strolled leisurely away. For all that is known, they are still leisurely strolling, as they have never been recaptured.

One of the most desperate prison escapes ever known was made from Sing Sing prison on the morning of 14 May, 1875, and would have ended disastrously to more than a score of lives had it not been for the presence of mind of Dennis Cassin, a Hudson River Railroad engineer.

Just north of Sing Sing prison, between the extreme northern guard-house and the arched railway bridge, as you go south, is located the prison quarry, on the east side of the railroad track. From it, over the railroad track, on the west side, extends a bridge over which stone from the quarry is trundled in wheelbarrows by the convicts.

At about eight o'clock, on the morning mentioned, an extra freight train, bound south, slowly approached the prison bridge. The train was drawn by 'No. 89', Dennis Cassin, engineer. They were slowly following the regular passenger train from Sing Sing to New York, which had left a few moments before. As the engine reached the trestle, or prison bridge, five convicts suddenly dropped upon it, from the bridge above; they were led by the notorious Steve Boyle and Charles Woods.

Four of them ran into the engineer's cab, while the other hastened to the coupling which attached the train to the engine. The convicts on the cab, with drawn revolvers, ordered the engineer and fireman to jump off, which they did, when the convicts put on steam, and the engine started down the road at lightning speed.

Their escape was detected almost immediately, and several shots were fired after them by the prison-guard, but without effect. Then began the pursuit. The superintendent of the railroad was notified quickly, when a telegraph alarm was sounded at all points south of Sing Sing. A dispatch was sent to the Tarrytown agent directing him to turn the switch at that station on the river side, so as to let the engine, with the convicts on board, jump the bank and plunge into the river. Danger signals were also ordered to be set on the down track, and prompt measures of every kind were taken to prevent danger from collision with the stolen locomotive. The trackmen in the vicinity of Scarborough saw the engine coming like lightning, or rather saw a vast cloud of smoke and steam and water, whirl by with a deafening roar, and gazed with terror at the frightful speed the engine had attained. At Tarrytown crowds of people were gathered, expecting to see the engine dash into the station, and off the switch into the river; but it did not arrive.

After waiting a short time, the Tarrytown agent sent an engine cautiously up the road to look for the stolen property; and 'No. 89' was finally found, with both cylinder-heads broken, three miles north and opposite the Aspinwall Place.' The boiler was full of water and the steam down. The convicts had left the disabled engine a half mile farther north, and had disappeared into the dense Aspinwall woods, having first stolen all the clothing which could be found in the engineer's and fireman's boxes in the tender.

Engineer Cassin's wonderful presence of mind undoubtedly prevented a large destruction of property and human life. He was surrounded by the four convicts before being conscious of it, and could feel the cold muzzles of their revolvers against his head. Instantly after he realised what had occurred.

'Get off! Get off!' the desperate men shouted. They did get off, and right lively; but Cassin did not turn from his place until he had prevented disaster. Just before the convicts jumped into the cab, he had three gauges of water in the boiler, and had shut off the pumps; but, as he turned to go when ordered, he shoved the pumps full on, the convicts not noticing the movement. The desperadoes undoubtedly pulled the throttle-valve wide open when they started, and for a little time the engine attained a terrific speed; but finally the cylinders got so full that both heads were blown out, or broken, and that necessarily ended the trip.

None of the daring fellows were immediately recaptured, but the eventual return of the leader of the escapade was effected through my office; and how it all came about necessitates a short sketch of Steve Boyle, the leading and most desperate spirit in the escape just narrated.

Boyle is a noted 'houseworker', or house-burglar, and general thief, and has nearly always been brilliant and successful in whatever he has undertaken. His work was principally done in the East, until 1867, when that part of the country became too warm for him, and, in company with his gang, consisting of Bob Taylor, Tom Fitzgerald alias 'Big Fitz' and William, alias 'Black Bill', he removed to Chicago.

Their first operation in that city was very unfortunate for Boyle. They were 'working' a residence in the West Division, and Boyle was 'doing' the rooms and passing the plunder out to his confederates, when, being very weak from a severe attack of the asthma, he made a misstep, stumbled, dropped his revolver, and caused such a noise that in an instant the gentleman of the house was upon him with a cocked revolver in his hand, and effected his capture easily.

As he was then comparatively unknown in the West, on the plea of ill-health, first offence, respectable parents, and the like, he succeeded in escaping with a sentence of but one year's imprisonment at Joliet, Illinois.

His comrades now employed every effort in their power to secure a pardon for Boyle, using large sums of money for this purpose; but this failing, they eventually found a way of conveying money to him within the penitentiary. Whether or not this was more powerful than whatever instruments to effect his escape Boyle may have secured, I cannot say; but, at all events, a plan of escape was determined on, which proved successful. On a certain night, Boyle, at the head of eleven other convicts, made their way from the cells up into one of the guard towers used for the sentry, and thence, in some mysterious manner, which has never since been fully explained, not only made good

151

their escape, but carried away all the arms, quite a number, which were stored in the tower.

Boyle's hard luck seemed about equal to his good fortune and ability to conquer difficulties.

The second day after escaping from the Illinois penitentiary, as he needed money, himself and another of the escaped prisoners were arrested in Chicago while in the act of 'tapping' the till of a north-side German grocery. They were locked up for the night together at one of the North Side stations. Boyle's companion was possessed of a terrible fear that he would be recognised and returned to Joliet.

'Oh, I'll fix all that!' said Boyle jauntily, and forthwith he set to work and gave his ex-convict comrade such a pummelling, disfiguring his face and blacking his eyes, that his own mother would not have recognised him.

Again, Pinkerton takes pains to make it clear that he is well-read and a fan of Dickens. This case from 1866 gives an early consideration of one of the tenets of criminal investigation—find motive, means and opportunity. The stage Irish dialogue is amusing, too.

⊰ An Insurance Conspiracy Foiled ⊱

Of all species of business there is none so liable to the machinations of dishonest persons as insurance. The large sums which are often secured from death or loss, with the undeniable obligations which the companies labour under to cancel their indebtedness, upon the showing of good and sufficient causes for the same, are incentives that have often urged men to employ their ingenuity and villainy in endeavours to defraud insurance companies. There may be something like a law of compensation about this kind of swindling, as the insurance business itself has harboured most accomplished scamps, and presented to the world about as brilliant schemes of commercial piracy as have come to light in any other kind of business. Of these instances Dickens has given us the type in *Martin Chuzzlewit*, in the operations of Montague Tiggs, Anglo-Bengalee Disinterested Loan and Life Insurance Company; and, as an illustration of the consummate plans for defrauding honestly-conducted insurance companies, the following case, where I was fortunately able to defeat an exceedingly clever scheme of fraud, will stand as an interesting illustration of conspiracies against such corporations.

In the month of June, 1866, one Monroe Rigger, a sailor, at that time a resident of Chicago, called at the office of a certain life insurance company, and effected an insurance upon his life for the sum of five thousand dollars. For this policy he paid the sum of thirty dollars. This was an ordinary case of insurance, and comprehended only such accidents and disasters as one is ordinarily exposed to on shore.

A few days afterward he returned to the insurance office, and expressed a desire to have the terms of the policy altered, as he wished to sail upon the lakes during the months of September and October. This permission was granted upon the payment of an extra ten dollars, and a new policy, covering accidents on the lake during those two months, was issued. On the very next day he returned to the office, and informed the officers that he had concluded to sail during the entire season, having secured a position on a vessel, and that he wished the policy changed from a special to an extra-hazardous one, in order to guard against his increased liability to accidents and dangers. Upon the payment of twenty dollars additional, the extra guarantee was granted, and Rigger took his departure. This was the last the company ever saw of him.

On 8 August following, Mrs Susan Rigger, the wife of Monroe Rigger, called at the office of the insurance company, and informed the officers that her husband, who held a policy in their company, had been drowned. This lady was dressed in mourning, and told a straightforward story.

She stated that her husband had been drowned in Lake Erie on the night of 20 July, about fifteen miles north west of Cleveland, while sailing on the brig *Mechanic*, James Todd, master. There was no constraint or indications of dishonesty in her statement. She further said that on the evening in question her husband, acting under instructions from his superior officer, had gone out on the bowsprit of the ship to adjust the rigging; that his foot suddenly slipped, precipitating him into the lake; and that efforts were made to save him, but all in vain.

To substantiate her story, she furnished several affidavits, duly attested and authenticated, corroborating the details of her husband's death. These affidavits were furnished by persons who professed to have seen Rigger fall into the lake, and were signed by the owner of the brig, an old and respectable citizen of Chicago, largely identified with shipping interests, the captain, the mate, the helmsman, and several others, all evidently trustworthy and reliable persons. Their affidavits certainly were deserving of consideration; but, in accordance with their usual custom, the officers desired time to look into the matter, and they dismissed the lady, requesting her to call again.

This was all the information that came to me about the matter, with a request from the company that I should make a speedy and most rigid investigation; and I confess that, when I first gave the subject a cursory examination, I saw nothing about it which did not have a clean and straight appearance. But upon perusing the affidavits, certain little discrepancies therein began to excite my curiosity. I began to see that the name of a certain Joseph Wagner, mate of the brig *Mechanic*, from which it was alleged that Rigger had been lost, appeared with a frequency, which, to say the least, was noticeable.

The affidavits were taken before a magistrate in Buffalo and I at once dispatched a keen, careful man to that city, who soon returned with the information that this Joseph Wagner, mate of the brig, who had become fixed in my mind as in some way mixed up with the matter, if it should be found that it was tainted with fraud, had been chiefly instrumental in procuring the affidavits. He had been present when they were made, had signed one of them himself, had defrayed the expenses of executing them, and had finally brought them to Chicago to Mrs Rigger. Here was a circumstance, trivial enough in itself, easily accounted for on the ground of solicitude for the widow of a deceased comrade, and might seem to have no special relation to the case, but it continued to strongly impress me. I felt that this man had exhibited too great an officiousness. He had been at too much trouble; he had expended too much money for a wholly disinterested party.

Besides all this, the haste which had been exercised in securing the affidavits was worthy of notice. It occurred to me that sailors, as a rule, are easy-going fellows, and they seldom do things in a hurry. The *Mechanic* had hardly reached Buffalo before Wagner had set about securing evidence of Rigger's death. These papers had been immediately forwarded to Mrs Rigger, so that she had been able to call at the insurance office within a very few days after the alleged drowning of Rigger and some time before the *Mechanic* returned to Chicago. In my mind this was another noticeable feature of the case. It might be, I even reasoned, that there had been murder done; that Mrs Rigger had conceived an unlawful affection for this mate, Joseph Wagner; that the two had not conspired against the insurance company so much as against the life of the husband whom the woman had urged to become insured, so that should he happen to fall overboard while in Wagner's company, there would be a snug little sum coming to the two; and that the whole thing, from beginning to end, was a terrible plan to both get rid of an obnoxious person and secure a small fortune.

In any event, I could not but couple the mate of the *Mechanic* and Mrs Rigger in a conspiracy, either against the company, in which case Rigger himself had joined in a conspiracy against the life of the latter; or, indeed, in a conspiracy against the company, in which Rigger had readily joined, but which might not have been wholly understood by him, and which was wedded to the darker crime that had been privately planned by his wife and friend, and too well executed by the friend.

In casting about for a starting-point in detective operations, wherever a crime is to be unravelled, one of the most essential things to be done is to determine what motives probably caused the commission of the crime. When the causes leading to a crime are fully known half your work is done, for you then at once know how to get to work.

I determined to ascertain what relations existed between Mrs Rigger and the mate Wagner. I found that Mrs Rigger lived in a quiet, respectable manner, as befitted the wife of a sailor, and no suspicious circumstance could be developed against her, although I felt that the facts justified keeping a strict surveillance upon her.

The reader will recollect that, on account of Wagner's great haste in securing proof of the sailor's death, there had been both time for Mrs Rigger to make her application at the insurance office for her five thousand dollars, and for me to get a man to Buffalo and return with the information referred to.

I had also taken means to ascertain that Wagner had left Buffalo on the return trip in the *Mechanic* and of the date of her probable arrival in Chicago. So, finding the owner of the brig, I easily made arrangements to be informed of her arrival in port, as well as to ship aboard as a common sailor upon her, on her second trip to Buffalo, should I so desire.

When the *Mechanic* arrived, Wagner, as soon as his duties would permit, went straight to Mrs Rigger's house. He remained inside but a few hours, and made his exit upon the street with a thoughtful, anxious face. In the little time he had been in the house I had taken measures which conclusively proved to me that no criminal intimacy existed between the mate and the alleged widow Rigger, and this clearly demonstrated that no conspiracy by the two against the life of the missing sailor had been entered into.

If there had been a conspiracy, I concluded that it had been between the entire three against the company; and as a persistent watching of the house had failed to discover the arrival of Rigger, who, I hoped, might secretly reappear, I knew that the only way to get a hold upon the shrewd trio was to fall back upon my old and successful plan of placing some person, capable of winning and holding Wagner's confidence, with him. I had already provided for this, as will presently be seen, in the person of an operative named Dick Hamilton who seemed to possess a combination of every known interesting trait of the Irish character.

Generous, brave, faithful, cunning; full of unconquerable antics and irrepressible humour; quick as lightning at repartee or jest; but possessing good judgment; a great traveller and salt-water sailor; and the biggest liar on earth when it came to a cock-and-bull story, or to a match at story-telling: this was the man I had detailed to operate upon Wagner, and that individual, with a worried look upon his face, had not been absent from Mrs Rigger's humble dwelling half an hour when the two had become firm friends.

Wagner, with his worry upon him, had stepped into one of those saloons along the wharves of great cities which sailors and their friends congregate, to get a glass of grog, and, being in a rather ugly frame of mind from receiving the ill-tidings from Mrs Rigger that there was a suspicious delay in the payment of the insurance money, was in no mood for joking. As the place was full of carousing sailors, some silly drunken remark was made to him, which he resented. In a moment the place was in an uproar; Wagner was violently assaulted, and only rescued from a hard drubbing by Hamilton, who laid out the assailing parties right and left, and finally got Wagner away in safety.

He was very grateful of course, and finding, according to Hamilton's story, that he was a salt-water sailor and a great fellow altogether, and had come to Chicago with a little money ahead, not caring where his fortunes took him, a great friendship immediately sprang up between the two. It was arranged, over many and copious glasses, that Hamilton and Wagner should pass the time together while in port, and that my operative should then ship with Wagner on the brig *Mechanic* for the trip to Buffalo and return; when, if everything still went well between them, they would join fortunes and sail regularly together.

The *Mechanic* and its crew remained in port but three days; but during that time enough came to the surface to show me conclusively that I was upon the right track, and that it was but a question of time when my shrewd Irish operative would unearth the mystery, enshrouding the sailor's supposed death.

Hamilton became a welcome visitor at Mrs Rigger's cottage the next day after making Wagner's acquaintance. Not a single thing could be seen to warrant a suspicion of wrong between the woman and the mate, with the exception of several private and earnest interviews between the two, during which an occasional unguarded word was let fall which showed that some new move was on hand. This was made plain on the third day, just before the vessel left, when Wagner and Mrs Rigger visited a lawyer's office and began suit against the company for the payment of the policy. They felt so certain of the strength of their plans that they were either willing that the whole matter should be raked up, or they hoped to force the payment of the money by a show of fight.

In the meantime Wagner and Hamilton got along famously.

Dick, who had become acquainted with the entire brig's crew, from captain to cook, made things lively for them all. A book would not have held the infernal lies that he told, and not all of the sparkling 'Irish Dragoon' contains such irresistible wit and droll humour as he was capable of, on the least pretext, so that before the *Mechanic* sailed every man on board was in love with Dick and congratulating Wagner on finding such a capital fellow for the voyage. Of course Wagner felt flattered and glad at the turn matters had taken, and seemed to begin to place great confidence in his new found friend. When drinking, as is quite common with sailors when ashore, he made great promises for himself and friend, and hinted in various ways that before the season was over he would command a first-class vessel himself, and would make Hamilton no less than mate.

One trip was made to Buffalo without result, so far as the operation was concerned, save that Wagner seemed drawn closer and closer to his companion. They became greater friends than ever; but Wagner had not got wholly ready to trust him. In a hundred ways he endeavoured to test him as to his being one he could trust and use, and during the trip gradually unfolded a scheme to rob a brother-in-law of Mrs Rigger's, an honest and hard-working mechanic in Milwaukee.

The wife of this man frequently visited her sister, Mrs Rigger, in Chicago, and Wagner had in some way learned that the couple, by years of hard labour, had saved several hundred dollars, and kept the same in a certain bureau drawer. As the husband was compelled to leave the house at an unusually early hour in the morning to reach his work, and was so kind and considerate to his wife that he never awakened her, it would be an easy matter to leave Chicago on the late train for that city, watch the party's house until he had left for his daily toil, and then, easily gaining access to the house, secure the money, and return to Chicago on the next train. The whole thing could be done inside of twelve hours, and there was certainly four or five hundred dollars apiece for them.

Hamilton entered into the scheme with all his heart, and suggested so many capital ideas concerning carrying out the robbery, that Wagner was more in love with him than ever; and he hinted at many other schemes which they would mutually profit by.

On the arrival of the brig in Chicago, the plan of this projected robbery was immediately laid before me. I indorsed what Hamilton had done, as a means of winning Wagner's thorough confidence, and also as a measure of establishing the character of the man. I at once arranged matters in Milwaukee, so that when the robbery was attempted, a sham policeman would be on hand to prevent the actual robbery. I believed it necessary to permit this to seem to go on, as I knew that, should the two attempt anything criminal together, this would prove the last bond of confidence required to enable my operative to compel a revelation of his connection with the conspiracy against the insurance company.

As luck would have it, however, the *Mechanic* only remained in Chicago one night and a day, and the robbery of the honest Milwaukee workingman was necessarily postponed. But Wagner was now certain of his man.

There had been two or three interviews between Mrs Rigger and Wagner, which Hamilton could not secure the gist of and, just as the boat was leaving her slip, a small lad brought a large package, evidently containing clothing, which Wagner quickly received and stored snugly away under his bunk.

Hamilton had also laid in a package for this particular trip, but it contained something more to the liking of sailors than clothing. It was two gallons of the best of liquor and, as himself and Wagner were sampling the article; while a grimy little tug was pulling the *Mechanic* swiftly out past the Chicago lighthouse to the broad expanse of the lake, where the regular evening breeze from the land should speed the brig on its trackless way, Wagner, after filling a glass unusually full, touched it against the rim of Hamilton's glass in a most friendly way, and remarked: 'Dick, old boy, you've been the great story-teller of this craft ever since you came aboard her. Before we get to Buffalo I'll tell you a better story than you ever heard.'

'Give it to us now, while the brig is gettin' her wind,' replied Hamilton, with a knowing wink.

'No, no; not yet, not before we get almost to Buffalo. And, Dick, if you're the man I take you for, and the friend I believe you to be, before the last chapter of the story's done, and it'll be only two or three chapters, I'll tell you then there may be a little 'spec' in it for you. This is no gammon story. There's a live corpse in it, and a stiff one to be got!'

'All right, then, me hearty,' responded Hamilton, clinking the glasses again. 'I'm your boy for any lively game, and here's luck to ourselves and both corpses, God rest 'em!'

The liquor was drunk, and the two shook hands heartily, and went on deck.

There never was a finer trip than that from Chicago to Buffalo, 'around the lakes', and this one proved a lovely one to the *Mechanic* and all on board.

Dick was in his happiest vein, and kept everybody on board roaring with laughter with his mad pranks and ridiculous yarns. Through the long sunny days it was story and joke and trick, and yet always so harmless and jolly as to cause no feeling of antagonism or offence, and, through the moonlit evenings, the same round of pleasures, so that the slight labour involved in handling the vessel amounted to nothing but a desirable change from what would otherwise have been a surfeit of enjoyment.

At last, one night, when within a few miles if Buffalo, Wagner came on watch and Hamilton with him. After everything had become quiet for the night, Wagner, after a liberal supply of liquor, in a low, careful tone, told Hamilton the following story: 'You know about the Rigger case? Of course, you have heard the men talk about it, and know that Mrs Rigger has begun suit against the insurance company for five thousand dollars? Well, Dick, we three put that up!'

'Faith, is that where the corpses come in?' asked Hamilton, with a well-assumed look of cunning praise.

'That's it, Dick. I'll come to that shortly.'

"We were just about this distance from Buffalo, about thirty miles, and Rigger and I were on watch. The night was fearfully foggy, and I run her (the boat) into within half a mile off shore. Then I had Rigger go forward and fix a line on the bowsprit, taking pains to have one or two of the crew on deck. He kinder weaved when he got to the timber, and I yelled out: 'Take care, Rigger, mind your footing!' I hadn't more than said that, when up he slips and pitches headlong into the lake! It was all in the game, you know, and he had two life-preservers, a couple of biscuits, and a little compass, fast on him. But I raised a fearful rumpus, got the boats out, and for an hour we tried awful hard to find him, I sending the boats in the opposite direction from which he fell in and struck out for shore. After a time we give it up, and by the time I took hold of the brig again, and set her out into deep water, Rigger was ashore!"

'Tare an' ages! but you're a slick one!' ejaculated Hamilton. 'An' won't the haythen insurance company pay up like men?'

'No, that's just what's the matter. Mrs Rigger has begun suit against them; and now, Dick, I want you to help us out!'

'I'm your buck! What's the game?'

'You remember that big bag I've got under my bunk?'

'Faith, I do!'

'Well, that's the very suit of clothes Rigger wore when he went over. He skipped back to Chicago, changed his togs, and left for California on the next train. We're all going out there after we beat the d—d company out of the money.'

'Yes, splendid!'

'Now, when we get down to Buffalo I want you to help me look up a convenient cemetery, and then we'll dig up some fellow that's been under the sod a month or so, take the body out along the shore and, after mashing it up so the very devil wouldn't recognise it save by the clothes, chuck it in the lake, let it wash ashore, and be found his letters and papers, and all that are in the clothes. And then, by the Eternal, we've got 'em fixed! Are ye in, Dick?'

'In! In! Bedad I'm in for any fun of that kind, and we'll have the corpse in the water, out of it, upon the shore and discovered, before even a fish can get a smell of 'em!'

With a hearty hand-shake and a parting glass of grog, the two turned in as the next watch came on; and I had won the case.

The next morning the *Mechanic* arrived at Buffalo, and Hamilton had not been on shore thirty minutes before Wagner's confession and plans came spinning over the wires to me at Chicago.

I at once laid the information before the company, and requested that its officers permit me to arrest both parties, and that they would prosecute them to the fullest extent of the law, for I have always bitterly opposed any compromise with criminals. But it seemed to be their policy to keep out of the courts and the newspapers and, with what had been got, with which they were highly elated. Mrs Rigger was confronted; and scared and half-crazed with the turn things had taken, she at once proceeded to the Circuit Court, and signed a waiver and release of all obligations held by her against the company.

This much done, Hamilton was recalled by telegraph, and I subsequently learned that Wagner, becoming alarmed at his co-conspirator's sudden disappearance, left the *Mechanic* at Buffalo, never to reappear among his sailor friends at Chicago; while the bogus widow evidently quickly took honest old Horace Greeley's advice, and went West to grow up with the country, for the little cottage was utterly deserted, and 'For Rent' but two days after.

In this tale from 1871, Pinkerton yet again quotes Robert Burns and gives us a case that is tantamount to a 'locked room mystery', one of the staples of detective fiction thereafter. He also manages to have a swipe at 'amateur detectives', in which category he clearly considers everyone else to be.

⇥ Quick Work ⇤

'Bang, bang, bang!'

There was no response to this impatient knocking upon the heavy door of the small Adams Express Company building near the end of the Columbus, Ohio, Union Depot, that night.

There stood the train with all its usual bustle about it, the engine snorting like a spirited steed impatient to be out upon the road again, but the Adams Express clerk and assistant had not made their accustomed appearance. The express messenger, John Gossman, had become greatly alarmed, for but a few moments more elapsed before the train would pass on, and it was one of his guards who had been sent to awaken the two careless employees and hasten their regular visit to the train.

'Bang, bang, bang!' This time louder and more persistent than before upon the heavy oaken and riveted door. But there was still no answer from within.

Then the guard took hold of the door-knob and, throwing his whole weight against the door, shook and rattled it frantically. Still no answer, and the guard rushed back to the train.

'Can't wake 'em up, John. Mebby they ain't there at all!'

Not daring to leave his car, the messenger, now fearing that foul play of some kind had transpired, directed the guard to return to the express building and get into it if he had to break in. In a moment more he was at the door and, turning the knob, as he ordinarily would have done, the door swung readily upon its hinges, and he walked into the room.

It was very dark inside, and striking a match, he went to the gas-light, where he found that it had been turned very low. Letting on the full light, it was seen that the papers and packages lay about the floor in the wildest confusion, while the clerk and his assistant, who were lying in bed but a few feet from the safes, seemed to be in a sort of stupor; for, although the guard had hallooed lustily to them after entering, he was obliged to give them a pretty thorough shaking.

It was evident that the two men had been chloroformed; the sickening, deathly aroma of that drug still pervading the atmosphere of the room and that the company had been robbed. The agent of the company at Columbus, although it was about two o'clock in the morning, immediately informed the officers of the company of the affair, who called upon me, by telegraph, for help, and I was able to put Superintendent Warner, of my Chicago office, upon the ground during the next forenoon after the robbery, with two shrewd operatives in the background ready for any possible emergency which might arise in the case.

Little information had been forwarded with the brief telegram, but I was familiar with the working of the express company's matters at Columbus, and I could hardly imagine how any thief or thieves could approach this building in so public a place, chloroform the inmates, and rob the safes, without attracting notice.

The main office of the company was located in the more business portion of the city, a considerable distance from the depot, and it had been for a long time necessary to keep a clerk and assistant at the depot to deliver and receive express matter. The custom was for the clerk to leave the downtown office at about six o'clock in the evening, proceed to the depot, put everything snugly away in the safes, and then retire until the arrival of the late night trains, being awakened to attend to his duties, by the depot watchman. I could not shake off the feelings which I impressed upon Mr Warner before he took his departure, that this robbery could hardly have been committed without the complicity of some one of the express employees at Columbus.

A searching investigation by my superintendent developed the following facts: on the evening before the robbery, 16 May, 1871,

John Barker, the depot express clerk, left the main office on Broad Street for the depot office at six o'clock, with seventy-two thousand dollars for different points, thirty-two thousand of which was in revenue stamps, and all of which was put into the safes. On the arrival of the late train at twenty-five minutes past two in the morning, the clerk did not make his appearance, although he had been called as usual by the watchman who was not certain that he had been answered, but who supposed Barker had been awakened. The guard had found the door open, as previously explained, and on gaining an entrance, and turning on the light, the keys had been found in one of the safe doors, everything seemed to be in confusion in the office; and Barker and his assistant were still in their bed, apparently stupefied from the effects of chloroform. A bottle still containing a small amount of chloroform was discovered, as also a sponge used in applying it to the faces of the sleeping employees. When they had finally been awakened, Barker was the first to speak, and he remarked: 'Why, we've been robbed!' and, after noticing the package of revenue stamps, 'I'm glad they left that much!'

Both Barker and his assistant acted in an honest, straightforward manner, and readily answered all questions put to them. A casual investigation would hardly have developed anything save that the office was entered, the men chloroformed, and the safes robbed; but a thorough examination did show, among other things, that the bolt on the door had been bent back, as if the door had been forced open. Unfortunately for this theory, however, the butt, which ran from the frame across the edge of the door, had been bent considerably further than necessary, to permit the edge of the door to pass it, while there was no evidence of a 'jimmy' or other instrument having been used to force the door open and thus bend the bolt. It had been done from the inside, and the very important query was: who did it?

This trifling circumstance, which an amateur detective would be likely to wholly overlook, clinched the conviction in both my own and Mr Warner's mind, that one of the two employees in the little office, or possibly both, had some criminal knowledge of the robbery if, indeed, they had not done the work themselves.

While the investigation was progressing the two men were kept under constant espionage, and it was very soon discovered and communicated to me by Mr Warner that John Barker, the express clerk, had a brother named Henry Barker, who had been seen at Columbus, and in a way to indicate that he had made every possible effort to prevent being seen in the city. It was also learned that this mysterious brother was from Chicago. These two facts ascertained, I soon learned, in Chicago, that Henry Barker had borne a rather unpleasant reputation, and had been discharged from the employ of the Adams Express Company, and also from service on the Chicago and Alton Railroad. This might not amount to much, but taken in connection with other circumstances, it looked suspicious.

I was also informed by Mr Warner that the express clerk, when questioned about his brother, at first denied all knowledge of him: but after a time he confessed that his brother had been in Columbus, but was there merely on a little friendly visit! He also laid great stress on the fact that his brother was wealthy, or rather that he had married a wealthy Chicago lady, and had no need to work. Following this out, I found that, instead of the wife of Henry Barker being a respectable and wealthy Chicago lady, she was neither. She proved to be merely the daughter of a noted proprietress of a Chicago house of ill-fame, who had given her the choice of marrying Barker, or being sent to the reform school in that city; and that she was then living a disreputable life in mean apartments, and without a dollar of honestly acquired money on earth.

I judged that all these facts warranted the conclusion that the brothers were guilty of the robbery, or at least, had planned it, and had largely participated in the proceeds of the same. I accordingly intrusted Mr Warner to at once cause the arrest of the express clerk, and use every effort to wring from him a confession, while his assistant and brother should be remorselessly watched and followed, hoping that they might in this way betray some evidence of guilt which would give me the truth of the whole matter.

It is a principle in criminal matters, which almost invariably holds true, that successful detection of crime is in nearly every instance defeated when all suspected parties are at once incarcerated. Let one or two, as the case may be, be held so closely that they cannot be approached or communicated with, and their accomplices will then, if they are watched by keen detectives, always make some move which will betray them. But, if all parties are arrested, all mouths and sources of information are instantly closed, and, in nine cases out of ten, though the authorities may be morally certain that they have the right parties, their discharge or acquittal will be the result, simply because no evidence of their guilt can be secured.

So, applying the result of my experience to this particular case, I reasoned that if the express clerk was arrested, and put where he could secure no assistance and sympathy, his accomplices would at once exhibit a nervousness and alarm which would definitely betray them.

According to this programme, Mr Warner caused John Barker's arrest, formally charging him with the robbery, and intimating that the whole plan of his operations was known, and in every possible way endeavouring to secure from him a statement which would implicate others. But the young man was obdurate, and nothing save that which might be learned from an utterly innocent person could be got from him. He very naively admitted that he could readily see how he might be reasonably suspected; how the bending of the bolt apparently from the inside might be attributed to him, but he argued in the same breath that it might have been done by the party who did the work for the purpose of casting suspicion upon him.

The closest of watching could develop nothing of a suspicious nature against the assistant. He was a simple, hard-working fellow, who seemed to be merely dazed and stunned by the robbery, and it seemingly had not once entered his head that he could be suspected of any manner of complicity in the matter.

But the results from watching Henry Barker, who had married the 'wealthy Chicago lady', were far different.

He endeavoured to keep quietly at home in Columbus, and it was observed that he never left his mother's house for any purpose until after night had wrapped its protecting folds around the city. Neither did he, after his brother's arrest and incarceration, visit him, or attempt in any manner to communicate with him, and I was more than ever satisfied of his guilt.

On the evening of the fifth day succeeding the robbery, Henry Barker suddenly took a train for Chicago. He did not leave Columbus like an honest man, but 'sneak'ed about the depot until the train was well under way, when he sprang aboard, giving my operative all he could do to accomplish the same thing and accompany him. At the way station the detective telegraphed me the condition of affairs, and I had two men at the depot in Chicago awaiting their arrival, one to relieve the man accompanying Barker, and another my son William, to get a thorough look at Barker, so that he might be able to render any assistance necessary.

Barker at once proceeded to his 'wealthy wife's' rooms in a disreputable quarter of the city. Here he remained well-closeted from observation, but so thoroughly guarded that his escape was impossible. Then, with a small valise which his wife had been seen to purchase for him at a pawn-shop near their habitation, he set out leisurely in the morning, considerably changed in personal appearance but perfectly self-possessed and evidently with no fear of pursuit, for the Michigan Central depot.

Arriving here he purchased a paper and a cigar, and smoking the one and occasionally glancing at the other, he sauntered about the locality for a short time, when he walked to the ticket office and purchased a ticket for Canada, via the Michigan Central and Grand Trunk railroads. This much done and he went to the train, took a seat in the smoking-car, and resumed the reading of his paper as pleasantly and nonchalantly as though a reputable business man starting out on a summer trip to the Thousand Islands.

His presence at the depot had been reported to me immediately, and I authorised my son, William A. Pinkerton, to make the arrest. A carriage took him to the depot from my office in five minutes, and he arrived at the train at the same time as young Barker. Following him into the car, he waited until Barker had seated himself comfortably, when William approached him and said, pleasantly: 'Barker, sorry to annoy you, but you will have to delay your trip to Canada until later in the season. The express folks down at Columbus want you.'

He made no resistance at all, but came along quietly, seeming to feel grateful that he had been arrested in a gentlemanly manner.

He was then placed in the carnage which had conveyed William to the depot, and my son, taking a seat beside him, and an officer riding on the box with the driver, the whole party were in my private office in a few minutes.

He made no noise and seemed in no great degree alarmed. He submitted to being searched with the best of grace, not over fifty dollars being found upon his person. I was beginning to fear we had made a mistake, when I ordered one of the men to remove the lining of the valise. Barker grew deathly pale when I said this, but he said nothing.

This precaution rewarded me by discovering, neatly secreted within the lining, fourteen thousand dollars. Even then he had nothing to say, and I concluded to let him think the matter over for a little time while on the train to Columbus, which he, an officer, and myself were on board of the same night, Barker pretty well ironed, more for the effect I hoped it would have on him than from any fear that he would attempt to escape.

I gave strict orders that no word should be spoken to the man by any person, and engaging a stateroom of the sleeper for our party, shut him and the officer within it, compelling the officer to sit there like a sphinx, looking wise as an owl, but uttering never a word.

Late in the night, Barker could stand the silence and suspense no longer, and he begged piteously of his guard to permit him to speak to me. For a time he silently shook his head, but at last called me, when the poor follow broke down altogether, begged piteously for mercy, and revealed where twenty-five thousand dollars of the stolen money could be found buried in a vacant lot next that occupied by his mother's house, and gave me the whole particulars of the robbery, which I telegraphed in advance to Mr Warner, who, with this aid, had secured a like full and free confession from the incarcerated express clerk, before our arrival at Columbus at noon of the next day.

The robbery had been planned by Henry Barker, and was the simplest thing in the world after his brother, the clerk, had consented to his share in it. The door was conveniently left open; the assistant was given a heavy dose of chloroform; then the clerk himself opened the safes and selected the packages of value for removal. Then the appearance of general confusion was arranged, and after the bolt had been bent to give the impression that the door had been forced from the outside. Henry had given his brother a mild dose of chloroform, and departed with every dollar that the office contained, twenty-five thousand of which he had buried, and fifteen thousand of which he had taken with him from Columbus, it being the intention of the express clerk to join his brother in Canada when the storm had blown over a little.

But: 'The best laid schemes o' mice and men gang aft agley!'

The two robbers were subsequently given four years each in the penitentiary, while the company was highly elated that I had been the means of recovering for them thirty-nine thousand dollars, out of what seemed an absolute loss of forty thousand dollars, and that, too, all within eight days.

Pinkerton loved to tell tales of stuffed shirts punctured and self-importance confounded, which undoubtedly endeared his tales to the readers. The setting is 1871.

◄ The Cost of Business Arrogance ►

Some time in September, 1871, there was presented at the banking house of Henry Clews & Co, in New York City, a draft for the sum of $55 dollars. In the usual course of business, the draft was stamped thus:

> ACCEPTED
> Payable at the Fourth National Bank
> HENRY CLEWS & Co

Two or three days afterwards, the draft was presented to the Fourth National Bank for payment. The figure had been altered to $5500, but not so as to attract attention.

The man who presented the check, however, was so nervous that the suspicions of the paying teller were aroused. He detained the man who presented the draft and sent a messenger to the house of Henry Clews & Co, to see if it was good. After some trouble the messenger forced an interview with the junior member of the firm. That young gentleman seized the check, drew it through his jewelled fingers and said: 'Young man, there's our stamp on that draft right before your eyes. If that stamp was a bear, it would bite you. Tell your paying teller that time is valuable to me, and if we are to be interrupted in our business hours through his stupidity, the Fourth National Bank will have to make some other arrangements so far as Henry Clews & Co are concerned!'

So saying, he seized a pen, and before the messenger had recovered from his surprise and could tell him of the suspicions of the teller of the Fourth National, he wrote across the face of the check:

> Good for $5500.
> HENRY CLEWS & Co

This he handed to the young man, again rebuked him for bothering the great firm of Henry Clews & Co, and vanished.

The messenger returned to the bank, and the paying teller indignantly paid the money without more question. The gentleman who altered the figures went on his way rejoicing, and but two days afterwards the firm of Clews & Co discovered the fraud.

They had lost exactly five thousand four hundred and forty-five dollars for the exhibition of a little arrogance.

This is 'the one who got away' and Pinkerton's exasperation at the unjustified verdict (as he felt) shines through. It's unclear whether Pinkerton was involved in the case, but if he were, he may be settling a score here.

A Curious Case of Circumstantial Evidence

A curious case of circumstantial evidence was tried before Judge Paxon, in the New York Court of Quarter Sessions, some time since. A shoe manufacturer, named George Bruder, was tried for the alleged theft of three thousand dollars, which was in charge of a bank messenger, named Brooks. The latter left the Security Banking House with certain securities and money for the Clearing House, and on the way stopped at the shop of the shoemaker named, to pay a bill.

The messenger laid his pocket-book and the package on the counter, and placed his arm upon them while he wrote out a bill. When he got to the Clearing House, a count of the securities and money was had, and then, for the first time, it was discovered that there was a deficit of three thousand dollars. The messenger at once returned to Bruder's shop and made known his loss. The shoemaker denied having seen it, and a search was made of the place. Had the case rested here, there would have been very little upon which to base a belief that the shoemaker handled the money. The Commonwealth called a witness to prove that he was in the shop of George Bruder, the day after the loss, when his daughter came in bearing a package of money, saying that the shop-boy had found it in the cellar; whereupon the defendant claimed that it was his, that he had put it there for safe-keeping, and that he supposed his dog had dug it out of its place of concealment. The shop-boy also testified to finding the money in the cellar, to which he had gone to chop wood. The package of money was upon the ground, and was done up in an a most precisely similar manner to that of the bank package.

There was proof that Bruder had a fire-proof safe in the store, which made it all the more strange that he should have his treasure lying around loose in the cellar. The only evidence offered by the defence to meet this case was that of good character, and the fact that he did not keep a bank account. The jury were together for some time, and then rendered a verdict of not guilty.

I think it would not be possible to make out a stronger case on circumstantial evidence than here presented. The remarkable fact of a package of money of the same amount, and in every other particular closely resembling the lost one, being found in the cellar by the shopboy the day after the alleged loss, and the shoemaker's explanation that he supposed his dog had found it and dragged it from its place of concealment, would be, it seems to me, strongly indicative of guilt. But the little instance is simply one of thousands which every year contrive to throw a strange fascination and interest of possibility and doubt around all cases of circumstantial evidence.

Allan Pinkerton clearly had a sense of humour that his rather stern portraits fail to capture. This story is set in the Civil War period, when Pinkerton was operating under cover as 'Major E. J. Allen', and ostensibly told against himself, affords Pinkerton another opportunity to remind us that his very name struck fear into the hearts of all wrongdoers!

A Private Assurance Company and a Public Insurance Company

This sketch relates to an insurance company and an assurance company. The former got the worst of it, and the latter were the worst.

The insurance company in question was the Royal Fire and Life Insurance Company of Liverpool and London, whose American office was, at the time I write of, located at 56 Wall Street, New York. The Assurance Company was composed of the eminent Dan Noble, Jimmy Griffin, Frank Knapp, and Jack Tierney, 'sneak'-thieves; and while New York was their general headquarters, it may be truthfully said that their operations extended into all cities of the United States, while their risks were high and their profits very large.

Dan Noble himself has always been noted as a brilliant and gentlemanly rascal of the confidence game and, at about the time he organised the company of precious rascals referred to, was at the height of his business prosperity as professional 'sneak'-thief. Noble never did much of the actual 'sneak'ing himself, but he was a most brilliant general of these matters and was nearly always successful in, first, planning a huge robbery; second, in bringing the right parties together to assist in doing the work; and, third, in having immediate and direct charge of ail the neat little work of the robbery itself.

Even as far back as during the early period of the war Noble was a noted criminal, but had always, through his splendid appearance, ready money, and fine generalship, managed to elude the several clutches of justice grasping for him from all directions. In those instances where he had been compelled to taste the legitimate fruits of his villainous life the bitter experience had been short and was, through the lavish use of his money, rendered as little disagreeable as possible.

Accidentally, I was the cause of a little practical joke on Noble, which, although it occurred many years since, still clings to him with unusual freshness, and which created great merriment among sporting and criminal classes of the more polished order; and even today, among this class, whenever 'Dan Noble's steerers running old Pinkerton into a faro-house' is mentioned, a laugh at Dan's expense is the result, and, referred to in his presence, is invariably as good as an order for a bottle of wine.

The incident referred to happened in this way: during the war, while I was at the head of the Secret Service of the Government, although here, there, and everywhere, my real headquarters were with General McClellan in the field, although official business frequently took me to Philadelphia, Baltimore, Boston, and New York.

On one occasion, when I was in the latter city for the purpose of seeing Colonel Thomas Key, whose headquarters were then at the Fifth Avenue Hotel, having not as yet established my large New York agency, I took quarters at the St Nicholas, on Broadway.

I had arrived late in the afternoon, with the intention of seeing the Colonel during the evening, which would permit of my return to Washington the same night or, at least, the next morning; and, having secured a hearty supper and purchased a cigar, for I was a great smoker then, I strolled aimlessly and leisurely about the rotunda and public rooms of the hotel.

I had been enjoying this solitary promenade but a few minutes, when one of two gentlemen came up to me with extended hand and smiling face and, heartily grasping my hand, which I readily gave him, most enthusiastically ejaculated: 'Why, Colonel Green, this is a pleasure! When did you get in? Why, here, Edwards, you know the Colonel?'

'Certainly, certainly,' promptly responded that gentleman. 'We had no idea of meeting you here, Colonel. Are you stopping at the St Nicholas?'

Of course I understood the whole matter in an instant. The game was old, very old, and besides, I knew the men. My first thought was to have the couple arrested, but I saw a capital chance for a little fun at the expense of the two, who were regular 'steerers' for the house where Dan Noble was dealing a faro game, and pretty fair confidence men. So I permitted the game to go on, and, assuming an air of opulent rural simplicity, responded: 'My friends, you have the advantage of me. I don't believe I'm the man you're lookin' for.'

'Why, you're Colonel Green, aren't you?' persisted the scamp, with a beaming face and a look which was intended to convey the impression that he would forgive any pleasant raillery like that from his dear old friend, the Colonel from Hackensack.

'No, you're wrong,' said I, pleasantly. 'My name's Smith, Major Smith, of the Quartermaster's Department.'

'And you positively say that you're not Colonel Green?' said the roper, with a very handsomely gotten up look of perplexity, wonder, and amazement stealing over his features.

'Not much,' said I, tersely.

'Well, I'm damned!' he retorted, turning to his friend. 'Edwards, I never made a mistake like that before in my life!'

'Well, I have, once or twice,' remarked Edwards, thoughtfully. 'But by Jupiter! It is the most remarkable likeness I ever saw, most remarkable!'

'Remarkable! Well, I rather think so. Why, Major Smith beg pardon, would you favour me with a light? Thank you. Do you know, I've sold this Colonel Green goods right along for fifteen years, every season, until this. But come, let's sit, and you must pardon me for being so rude. Here's my card. I am the "Preston" of the firm and this is my friend, Mr Edwards, same business, but another house. Do you know, I'd have bet an even thousand dollars that you were Colonel Green?'

'Yes, and I'd have gone you halves on that. What department did you say you were in, Major Smith?' asked Edwards, carelessly.

'Quartermaster's,' I replied. '"Swindling the Government", the newspapers call it.'

'Indeed!' ejaculated the roper-in calling himself Mr Preston, attentively noting every word I uttered.

177

'Yes, I am over here to New York now for a thousand cavalry horses.'

Now, it would take a good deal of money to buy a thousand cavalry horses; and Mr Preston's eyes fairly sparkled as he thought of the rich lead he had struck. I was dressed roughly, was very much tanned by exposure in the field, and undoubtedly looked the character of the rough Quartermaster's Department man I had assumed to perfection, and I led the two men to believe me easy prey.

'Let's have another cigar, Edwards, and then take a stroll up to the clubhouse,' said Preston; and then addressing his conversation more particularly to me, he asked: 'Major Smith, won't you walk up with us? We merchants have got a cosy little place up here a few blocks, where, after the business and downtown banging of the day are over, we can go and have a quiet, sociable time, all by ourselves. Won't you take a walk up with us?'

'Well, I don't mind,' I implied reflectively. 'But I can't stay long, for I've got to attend to part of my buying to night.'

At this remark, indicating to Preston that I probably had a good supply of ready money on my person, as well as large resources, being an army contractor, his eyes snapped again, and I could just imagine the fellow devouring me in his mind and thinking: 'Oh, won't we have a sociable time carving up this old stuffed turkey. Oh, won't we though!'

A moment later we were on the street, and within five minutes were entering what appeared to be a most elegant private mansion, on the east side of Broadway, and but a few blocks from the hotel.

'Fine place you have here,' I observed, as we stood in the vestibule, and the alleged Preston stepped to the bell-knob and gave it a pull.

'It's one of the most complete club-rooms in the country. The boys have good times here occasionally.'

While he was replying to me, I distinctly heard the soft tinkle of another bell besides the one that the 'steerer' had rung, and I at once conjectured that it was a signal, given perhaps by Preston's companion, to those within, that another fool with a fat purse had been captured, and that everything should be ready within for a proper reception of him. Although I had not the slightest fear of personal harm, I dexterously whipped out my revolver from my hip-pocket and slipped it down into my front pantaloons pocket, where I conveniently held its handle with my light hand, quite ready for anything that might occur, and with my hands in my pockets and my hat on the back of my head, quite countrified in appearance, I strolled in after the two precious scamps.

It is needless to give my readers any detailed description of the place into which we were now ushered. It was a magnificent gambling-house, and that was all there was of it.

When we had arrived within, quite a pleasant scene was presented. To one uninitiated it would have appeared to be just what the 'roper' stated that it was: a business-man's resort, where he could enjoy himself among clever companions. Here sat a group of persons talking of stocks and bonds, and gravely discussing the effect of certain war movements upon securities; at another place were a couple chatting on social topics; and, again, a little party seemed to have some connection with newspaper matters. Everything was beautifully arranged to create a fine impression upon a rural stranger, and, as the bank-note reporters used to say, was 'well calculated to deceive'.

In the rear room of the suite stood a regular faro table, and several gentlemen were gathered about this, chatting and laughing, and occasionally making a play, After introducing me to several of the inmates and relating the incident bringing us together, which he termed 'a most ludicrous though agreeable error', Preston led the way toward the gaming-table.

I did not follow him immediately but, with my hand still in my pockets, and my hat still upon my head, I lounged about the place in a very lawless and country fashion, curiously examining and handling different articles of bijouterie and ornamentation, and occasionally asking information about the cost or quality of any article which struck my fancy, as it appeared, of whoever might be standing near me.

Finally Preston carelessly remarked: 'Come, Major, step over here and have something.'

'Well, I believe I will,' I replied, making a lunge toward the magnificent sideboard. A half-dozen other persons followed, and were introduced in a high-sounding manner, while the spruce negro attendants served to each of us such liquor as we might fancy; and I recollect that the whisky I got was some of the finest I ever drank.

During this pleasant diversion I heard the voice of the elegant Dan Noble, who was dealing the game and right here let me say that I could not have, for my life, told whether it was faro, keno, or any other game, for I never played a game of cards in my life, and never expect to, urging the 'cappers' and 'steerers' to lose no time, but bring me to the table and begin the operation of inviting me; while they, evidently somewhat impressed with my stubbornness, protested in low tones that there was plenty of time, and that they would 'work me' shortly.

After this refreshment, I resumed my appearance of curiosity, and again began my strolling; while several of the pretended gentlemen crowded around the gaming table, and made heavy winnings all of which of course was for the purpose of arousing my curiosity and tempting me to join the game; while, without appearing to do so, I noticed that the keen, sharp eyes of Dan Noble followed me wherever I went, and he appeared anxious to try his hand at fleecing me so thoroughly that I would remember it so long as I lived.

The appointments of the place were simply magnificent, and I took my own time to examine them, while the two 'steerers' I had met at the St Nicholas, by every manner in their power, persistently sought to induce me to join the parties playing; and I could not help enjoying a hearty laugh internally, so hearty, in fact, that I could at times scarcely repress a roaring-out burst to see the ingenuity of the men so handsomely yet so fruitlessly exercised, while I mentally noted the interest exhibited by their confederates and the chances they seemed to take in their own minds as to the probability of gaining my supposed wealth from me, although they each and all, true to their habits and profession, made a great effort to support the character of being elegant business or other gentlemen, at leisure for the evening, and bent on having a good time themselves.

Finding that I resisted all these ingenious attacks, recourse was again had to the sideboard; but this time, to the dismay of the gamblers, I only took a cigar. The cigar was as fine as the liquor and, enjoying its splendid aroma, I now straggled up to the table.

Everybody was now in high spirits. Jokes and wit flowed freely, and the betting began to run high, those risking their money very singularly winning largely; while the magnificent Mr Noble, slick and trim as a bishop, and with a solitaire diamond as large as a big hazelnut gleaming from his shirt-front, greeted my presence among the gentlemen around the green cloth with a nod and a smile of welcome.

'Gentlemen, won't you please make room for Major Smith?' said Noble, with a voice as sweet and pleasant as a blooming country schoolma'am's. Instantly at least three chairs were made ready for my occupancy.

But I stood there very provokingly disinclined to be made a victim of and remarked, extremely innocently after a little time: 'Well, I guess I won't play any tonight. I don't understand the game.'

Immediately I was appealed to from all sides with, 'Do, Major; just one play, Major!'

'Major, try your luck with the rest of us!' and all that sort of thing.

Noble himself remarked pleasantly: 'You must remember, Major Smith, that we are all gentlemen here!'

At this I looked at Dan a few moments in a quizzical, comical way and finally, as if suddenly being struck by a remarkable recollection, I blurted out: 'Come over here, dealer, and have a drink, and then I'll tell you something funny.'

There was a noticeable confusion about the table. Everybody was surprised and some bewildered. Noble at first hesitated but as I led the way to the sideboard he followed me mechanically, and his face began to express wonder, perplexity, chagrin, and even rage, in rapid succession. Several of the gamblers followed, and the liquor was swallowed by all in silence. Scarcely had I set my glass upon the sideboard, when Noble said, in a perplexed, curious, and half-alarmed tone: 'Who in hell are you, any how?'

I seized him by the hand, and gave it a squeeze that made his fingers crack, from which he writhed as if hurt.

'Why, Dan Noble, don't you remember me? You ought to, Dan! How long since you came from Elmira? Are you going to get out of that scrape, Dan? You don't know how glad I am to see you, Dan!'

181

and I gave his hand another powerful grip, that made him squirm again.

'But damn it, who are you?' he said hotly.

'Come over here, Dan, and I'll tell you,' and I jerked and dragged him aside, and then whispered in his ear: 'Allan Pinkerton.'

'You know me now, Dan,' I continued uproariously. 'You see I know you, and you!' I roared, grasping the hand of Jim Laflin, the gambler. 'How long have you been away from Chicago, Jim? I'm damned glad to see all you good fellows! And you, Sears,' said I, crossing to another gambler whom I knew. 'How's luck been with you lately? And you, and you, and you!' said I rapturously, nodding to half the people in the place, and calling each one of them by name, and clinching the knowledge of each by some little reference to their previous criminal acts. 'Why, boys, this is a surprise to me; so glad to see you all, you know. Perhaps you're all a trifle surprised. But don't mind me. I'm just a common sort of a fellow. Come, Dan, old boy,' said I, turning to Noble, who stood there as though a bombshell had exploded in the room. 'Let's all have a good, sociable, friendly old drink together.'

'But you don't want me, do you?' gasped Noble tremblingly, after the liquor had been drank, with many toasts to Mr Pinkerton, instead of to 'Major Smith, of the Quartermaster's Department.'

'Oh no, not just now; but remember, Dan, if ever I do want you, it will not be a hard matter to get you.'

'I know that, I know that,' said Noble, in a conciliatory tone. 'But are you after anybody else here?'

'Oh, no, I guess not; not just now, anyhow. It would be a pity to disturb a party of so eminent gentlemen bankers, newspaper men, society people, etc; and, as I have had a very pleasant call, I think I'll go and attend to buying those thousand horses.'

My identity had leaked out by this time to all, and several of the scamps took occasion to slip out; but most of the inmates gathered about me with great protestations of friendship and admiration; and, after lighting a fresh cigar, I left the place, having caused the greatest sensation it had ever known, and left to Dan Noble the legacy of a practical joke that his criminal companions will jest him upon to the day of his death.

But his ingenuity and ability to plan and assist in the execution of 'sneak' work were of the highest order, as the robbery of the Royal Fire and Life Insurance Company of Liverpool and London evidenced.

On 10 December, 1866, all New York was thrown into a great state of excitement by the announcement that the office of the company in question had been robbed of a quarter of a million dollars; and the public interest in the matter was none the less when the manner of the robbery became known.

A meeting of the American directors of the company had been announced to be held at their office, at noon of the day in question, and at about half-past ten o'clock of the same forenoon a tin box, usually deposited for safe keeping in the vaults of the Merchants' Bank, and containing about a quarter of a million dollars in Government bonds and negotiable securities, had been sent for, to be used or inspected by the directors in the event of any change in stock, as was the usual custom at such meetings

The box with its contents was placed in the vault opening from the inner or back room of the office of Mr Anthony B. McDonald, the agent, and the inner iron door of the safe closed, but not locked.

At about a quarter past eleven two well-dressed and apparently respectable men called and, expressing a desire to be informed regarding the conditions of life insurance, were shown into Mr McDonald's apartment.

One of them, a young man about thirty years of age and having the appearance of an able commercial traveller on a fine salary, immediately entered into conversation with the agent; and, taking a seat on the opposite side of the table, inquired the terms on life policies, stating that he and several other individuals wished to effect an insurance on their lives, as they were about leaving to go down the Mississippi to New Orleans on a quite extended trip for their different houses.

He then made some remarks, to the effect that they were undecided as to whether they would take a traveller's risk or insure for a life period, and stated that, as he had just been married, he felt an additional anxiety to secure his wife against prospective poverty.

During the time this business-like conversation was going on, the other gentleman, from occasional timely remarks, indicated to Mr McDonald that he was one of the commercial travellers desiring insurance, and that the person talking to him was the spokesman for the whole party. After a little time, while the agent and the inquirer after rates and terms were busily employed together, the friend remarked that he thought he would step out for a few moments, and would return shortly.

The vault was situated to one side and to the rear of where Mr McDonald was at work upon his tables and statements, and the young man who remained entered into the business so arduously that Mr McDonald made some calculations from a table of risks to satisfy his inquiries regarding the policies for his friends.

During this time the young man who had left resumed his careless manner of walking about the room and minutely examining the pictures and other articles of ornamentation hanging upon the walls.

After a little time he made some casual remark about not being able to keep a certain appointment unless his friend excused him then; and, after agreeing to meet him at a later designated hour at the house of a prominent business firm, he bade the two gentlemen good-day and left the office.

A few minutes later the gentleman who had been such an interested inquirer in insurance matters, after thanking Mr McDonald for his kindness and attention, and promising to consult his friends and call again after so doing, also withdrew.

The meeting of the directors was held according to the call. Those gentlemen gravely considered such matters as required their attention, and finally desired an examination of the bonds and stocks. The tin box was sought; but lo! it was gone. The greatest consternation prevailed; but it was soon seen that the company had been robbed in a most brilliant manner, and that the two gentlemanly pretended travellers, who wished to provide for their wives so tenderly, were the skilful 'sneak-thieves' who did the work.

Now, Dan Noble had planned the whole matter, knew that the directors' meeting was to be held, knew that the tin box which travelled so frequently between the insurance office and the Merchants' Bank contained bonds or other valuables, and also had learned all about the habits and methods of conducting the inner office.

He therefore organised a 'gang', as it is called, consisting of Frank Knapp, Jimmy Griffin, and Jack Tierney, to do the work. Himself and Jack Tierney were to do the 'piping' on the outside, as also to hold a carriage in readiness, either to remove the plunder or enable the 'sneaks' to escape, should their object be discovered before it should have been consummated.

Frank Knapp represented the inquiring commercial traveller, and Jimmy Griffin was the 'sneak' who represented the friend who was compelled to go out, and then, after his return, was unable to remain on account of keeping a certain appointment.

Knapp took a seat at agent McDonald's table, so that the latter's back was toward the vault, and then Knapp shrewdly kept him so thoroughly engaged that he paid no attention whatever to the supposed friend, who, with an overcoat thrown lightly over his arm, carelessly walked about the place, apparently whiling away the time in a cursory examination of the ornaments on the walls.

During this sort of thing Griffin slipped into the vault, noiselessly opened the safe, abstracted the tin box containing the bonds, arranged his coat over it neatly, and then came back, standing within two feet of the agent and Knapp when he stated to them that he would have to go out for a few minutes.

He went out, gave the box and the overcoat to Noble and Tierney in the carriage, the latter instantly leaving and then, after a short delay, returned to the insurance office to make his excuses and leave the second time.

The leaving of Knapp has already been described, and no one can question that the scheme, in its planning and cool, leisurely execution, was one of the most perfect and brilliant in the entire annals of crime.

Knapp and Griffin at once fled to Canada, being urged to that course by Noble, who only gave these men twenty-seven thousand dollars out of a booty of over a quarter of a million; and this unfair deal at last led to troubles between the thieves, resulting in Noble's arrest, conviction, and partial punishment for this particular crime.

Fifty-five thousand dollars' worth of the bonds were recovered by the company, on payment of a premium or reward of fifteen per cent.

Noble eluded punishment for over four years, but was finally convicted at Oswego, New York, in February, 1871 his great wealth, entirely secured by crime, having been utterly exhausted in his long battle with justice.

He was sentenced to ten years' imprisonment at Sing Sing, but escaped from there in 1872, having served 'prison time' but a little over one year, and then fled to Europe, where he began anew his career of crime. He attempted to perpetrate a daring 'sneak' job on the Paris Bourse in 1873, on a broker's office, but was caught in the very act, convicted, and sentenced to five years' penal servitude, which full time he served, only being liberated in the summer of 1878, just in time to attend the Paris Exposition, and continue his brilliant conspiracies. But, as I have said, wherever Dan Noble goes, or whatever luck he may have in a criminal way, the story of his 'steerers running old Pinkerton up to his brace game' will always remain a practical joke upon him, which can never be run away from and never shaken off.

The most remarkable statement in this story is that Pinkerton, who takes pains always to prove what an early riser and hard worker he was, would 'ride in my carriage... for from two to four hours of every afternoon'. His distaste for 'cases arising from marital difficulties' is also illuminating.

⚔ A Bit of Detective-office Romance ⚖

Of the tens of thousands of strange and interesting incidents connected with prolonged and far-reaching detective service, undoubtedly that portion containing the richest veins of romance, the brightest humour, and the deepest pathos, is comprised in the demands made on the detective agency for numberless kinds of assistance by men and women who are unfortunate enough to become complicated in family troubles involving the supposed unfaithfulness of the husband or the wife.

I wish to say, at the beginning of this bit of romance, that I am bitterly and irrevocably opposed to touching that kind of work. No honest and honourable detective will soil his hands with it. For thirty years, and through hundreds of thousands of applications for the services of myself and my men, I have shunned and avoided it for the unclean, poisonous thing that it is. In all modesty, and for the purity and honour of the detective service of America, as one who has spent the best half of his life in its elevation and bettering, I wish to, here and at all times, urge upon those younger and less experienced than myself, who may be at the threshold of their life-work, the absolute necessity of turning a deaf ear to applications for this class of assistance.

There may be, there often are, exceptions in this regard, where men and women, from the highest and most honourable of motives, desire and have a right to certain information, which may more thoroughly establish a wife, a husband, or a near friend in their regard and esteem, or permit a decision which, though hard and heart-breaking to make, is the only dignified and honourable thing to be done, when the one under suspicion proves himself or herself utterly unworthy of confidence or respect. But these are unusual exceptions, and nearly every instance where women apply to the detective to watch the husband, or the husband the wife, the mistress the man, or her 'friend', the mistress, there will be found something disreputable and degrading behind it.

To put detectives on such low errands of espionage is to demoralize them and utterly unfit them for higher work. The detective must have a clean mind and clean hands, or he sinks to the level of the criminal, and is no better than he; and there is no way in which he can become so completely corrupt and unbalanced as to place him where he becomes the spy and the football between animal passion and revenge.

The instance I am about to relate, where I took a case of this kind, is only an exception proving the general rule which I have laid down, and was one so pitiable, and yet so ridiculous, that I cannot restrain a hearty laugh whenever I recall it. It occurred but a few years since, and is still as fresh in my mind as though it happened but yesterday.

One summer afternoon, about three o'clock, a pretty *coupé* halted in front of my present offices on Fifth Avenue, Chicago. The sweet face of a young woman appeared at the window and looked up at the large building with evident trepidation and fear. Even the negro footman, that quickly descended to serve the lady, seemed possessed of a certain solemnity and awe, which indicated at least some well-defined unpleasantness in the household where he was employed, and momentous importance attaching to this visit. Alighting upon the sidewalk, the little lady looked nervously about her, peered into the open door of the fine station on the first floor, where my large night watch, the preventative police, are quartered, where she saw a few officers and patrolmen quietly sitting about on day duty; and then, seemingly quickly satisfying herself that this was not the detective department, hastened rapidly up the broad stairs.

She had determination in her manner; but in every feature of her fine face there was a quiver and tremor that told of acute suffering. It was not common that so remarkably fine-looking a lady, so distinguished in appearance, sought the mysteries of detective service; and, as she swept into the main office, casting a flushed and startled look about her, the groups of sub-officers and bevies of clerks, by long custom grown quick and keen in judgment of such things, knew, without being told, something of what the case might be, and in their minds unanimously pronounced it: 'particularly pitiable'.

My office-boy also taking in the situation at a glance, and seeming to understand that the lady was much confused by the unaccustomed surroundings, at once conducted her into my superintendent's consulting-room, and proffered her a seat opposite Mr Warner himself.

Superintendent Warner, who has been in my employ for nearly twenty years, is a very staid, sober gentleman, one who has a reputation, among my other officers and men, of never looking at a woman save sidewise, and then only for the tenth part of a second (a man who is so proverbially modest in this particular that it is even reported of him that he passes words, when reading, unless certain that they are of the masculine gender). However the very woe that spoke from his visitor's face affected him so strongly that he looked up over his gold-rimmed quizzers from his papers and dispatches, and regarded her curiously with his cold gray eyes for fully three seconds.

Then the handsome, elegantly-dressed, beautiful lady began sobbing and talking.

Superintendent Warner, looking straight out of the window, adjusted his quizzers, and began listening.

The lady, whom I will call Mrs Saunders, after several sobs, which she finally mastered with a great effort, said in a voice of repressed emotion: 'Mr Warner, I am in great trouble, great trouble!'

He could see it; and he hinted as much, resuming his attitude of attention.

'Is it necessary to tell my name?'

'Most certainly.'

'And tell you where I live?'

'Yes.'

'Oh, this is awful!' she said, more as if speaking to herself than the superintendent. 'Well, I live at Indiana Avenue' (a very aristocratic thoroughfare). 'My husband is the senior member of the firm of Saunders, Rice & Co, on State Street.'

Mr Warner knew them very well.

'And you know about our trouble?' she asked, in a way showing that the poor woman felt certain, as people always do, that her grief was certain to occupy the attention of all the world.

'Well, I think it would be better for you to give me your version of it,' he replied quietly, but already nervous at the probable prospect before him.

'Oh, dear! Well... ' she began, with a flushing and paling face, 'my husband is rich. We have a beautiful home; it seemed as though the world was very bright before this!' (Sobs.) ' He always came home to dinner and never, never passed the evening away save with me!'

'How long have you been married, madam?' respectfully asked the superintendent

'Only eighteen short months,' she replied, crying bitterly.

'Have you a child?'

'One darling babe.' Another sob.

'Well?' The superintendent was getting anxious for particulars, and troubled for the result.

'Well, sir, about two weeks ago we had a slight misunderstanding.'

Mr Warner nodded his head, as though he knew what that meant.

'But it wasn't much, sir; truly it was hardly a quarrel. But we began taking our meals separately, each too proud to make any concession, each full of spirit, and thinking the other was in the wrong, but both gradually growing away from each other until finally...'

Here the good little lady paused and blushed deeply. It hurt her to say what was on her tongue, but it had to come.

'Well?' queried Mr Warner, wiping his quizzers and blushing to the very top of his bald head.

'Until we finally occupied sleeping apartments in quite opposite parts of the house!'

Mr Warner saw it was the old story, one that had floated ten thousand times into the office, ever since he had been in it, and he began to fidget about in his chair as the lady resumed her weeping.

'Well, sir, he acts so strangely. He slams the doors, and won't even look at the baby. I hold up in my arms for him to see and, about a week ago, I noticed that he did not get into the house until two or three o'clock in the morning. I couldn't get even a glimpse of his face, but he looked guilty! I hate to tell you this, sir, but I am sure some bold, bad woman is at the bottom of it all. He has been away from home for three whole nights, sir for three long, dreary nights. I know he is with this woman. Oh, sir! I don't know what to do! I don't know what to do! But if you can only some way get my husband to realise what a terrible thing he is doing, and then capture this bad woman, and do something awful, just awful, with her, you shall have any, yes, any sum you have a mind to name!'

Here the poor lady, seeing that there was but little hope for her in my superintendent's face, pleaded piteously, between really heart-rending sobs, that her 'dear hubby' might be brought back, and this horrible woman completely annihilated. She explained how, for several days, she had been dodging about the city herself, to ascertain where the supposed cause of her husband's misdoing lived, and how she might wreak a deserted wife's vengeance upon her, and, finding that she could accomplish nothing, discouraged and disheartened, she had come to my office hoping for help.

Superintendent Warner really pitied his fair visitor, and hardly knew what to do. He glanced for courage along the wall, where one of the framed mottoes from my 'General Principles' for detective work hung in its frame.

The motto read:

These Agencies will, under no circumstances, operate in cases arising from marital difficulties!

He tried to get courage and bravery enough from this, but the misery of the little woman got the better of him and, trying to look very sympathetic and at the same time severe, he stammered out, as he rose to indicate the termination of the interview:

'Sorry, very sorry, madam! But much as I deplore your trouble pardon me for saying this is well, ha-hum, well, one of that kind of cases, you see, where I will have to confer with Mr Pinkerton before giving you any answer of a definite character. I can hold out no hope for you whatever today. Mr Pinkerton will be in shortly. I will lay the matter before him. You may call at the same hour tomorrow. I can give you a decision then.'

The little woman dried her eyes, thanked the superintendent as best she could, and was shown out the private door of the outer consulting-room, Mr Warner murmuring sympathetically:

'Good-day, madam, good-day. Sorry, so very sorry!'

It is a custom of mine, which has been observed without exception for several years, to ride in my carriage, rain or shine, snow or sleet, for from two to four hours of every afternoon. I find not only genuine pleasure in it but health and vigour and, above all, a relief from a crush of business, which, with me, seems never to be done, and to increase beyond measure as I advance in life.

These rides are taken in every direction from my office; sometimes through and through the heart of the city; sometimes to some outlying suburb; and often ten, twenty, and frequently thirty miles straight out into the country. I have thus formed a regular acquaintance with little roadside inns, where I always find my bevy of beggars and vagabonds ready to hold or water my horses, for the change they as invariably expect. I have thus come to know every sign in the city, every alley or by-way, every nook and corner; and, in numberless instances, the almost perfect information so secured of every peculiarity of Chicago and its surroundings has proven of invaluable service in facilitating whatever work of a local nature I might have in hand.

On the day in question I had been out over the roads adjacent to Chicago's beautiful North Shore, and had determined to return through Lincoln Park along the wide, smooth boulevard which borders the white beach where the waves come tumbling in. It was one of those rough, raw days when the clouds go scurrying across the sky, and the water upon the broad expanse of Lake Michigan had a steely-blue colour intervening between the scudding white-caps. The park was deserted, and not a carriage save my own was to be seen down the miles of drive, level as a floor. Turning from the highway into the drive, I saw, a mile beyond, like a dark silhouette against the water, the form of a solitary man, pacing rapidly back and forth upon the sands. Swiftly he sped up and down the shore, like one with no purpose, but impelled by some strong and over-whelming excitement.

As I neared him, he took no notice of either myself or my carriage, and I saw that his face was pale, and that all of his actions betokened great mental trouble. My detective instincts, or curiosity, or whatever it may be called, were at once aroused, and I directed my driver to pass the man slowly. Arriving opposite him, as we were now going in opposite directions, I noticed at once that he was a young business man of my acquaintance.

'Hallo, Saunders!' said I.

'Well, what do you want?' he returned, in a hard, hurt kind of way.

'I want you to get right in here with me,' I replied sternly, knowing that the man required a superior will to manage him.

He got in the carriage and sat down beside me without a word.

'What is the matter, Saunders?' I abruptly asked.

'I'm all gone to pieces,' he answered, with a moan.

'In a business way?' I asked.

'No, at home,' he replied bitterly.

'Now, tell me the truth, nothing else!' said I, severely.

'Well, friend Pinkerton,' he answered slowly, and as though his whole life and heart were in the reply, 'my wife is going wrong!'

'I don't believe it!' I replied, warmly.

'Yes,' he said, after a pause; 'yes, it's true. A few weeks ago we had one of those family quarrels that curse married people. It was a little thing at first, a little thing, just one of those family misunderstandings that bring hell between a couple. I wouldn't give in, nor would she. At first we were very proud, and would not recognise each other. Soon we took separate meals. Then my wife got high-toned, and took a bed in another part of the house. I followed suit, and took my bed as far away from her as I could get it in the house. For nearly a week past she has been spending the days and nights out. I have been trying to get at the secret of her estrangement. For the last three days and nights I have been out constantly. I have had several of our most trustworthy employees watching the house and following her, but I am entirely at a loss; some human devil is taking advantage of our family trouble to ruin her. Pinkerton, I made up my mind to come to you. But I recollected that you never touch these matters, and I had about determined to do something desperate!'

My heart opened at once for the man, and I concluded to break over my rule at any cost, get at the bottom of the trouble, which, I could see, he had only made worse by his attempting to play the detective, and then, if it were possible, show the wife the wretchedness and misery she was causing, and in some way, not then quite clear to me, but which I felt assured would in good time transpire, bring about a reconciliation and peace to the family of my young friend.

I told him this and it made a new man of him at once.

We were soon at the agency, and we proceeded together at once to my own private office. I immediately summoned Mr Warner, and began explaining matters with a view of having him get a thorough understanding of it with me, and then make a detail of men when necessary for thorough investigation.

This had hardly been entered into when I observed that my superintendent was conducting himself very strangely. He 'hummed' and 'hawed,' cleared his throat a half-dozen times as if to speak, but each time seemed to change his mind and repress himself by the greatest effort. On several occasions I came near asking him the reason for his singular action, but refrained on account of the presence of my friend.

No sooner had he departed, with the understanding that I should pick him up at a designated spot on the next afternoon, and before he had hardly reached the street, than Mr Warner burst into such an irrepressible fit of laughter that I could not resist joining him, although I confess the whole proceeding was quite beyond my power of comprehension. When he had sufficiently recovered to explain himself and relate the interview with the beautiful lady an hour previous, the ludicrousness and complete absurdity of the entire situation came over me with such force that I am afraid I was quite as badly affected as my superintendent, and certainly myself indulged in a roar of laughter which must have been heard to the remotest part of the great building, and possibly, as I have capital lungs, beyond into the street.

But my readers may be very sure that the cases were taken.

The next afternoon the lady called, was informed that Mr Pinkerton had deviated from his fixed rule in her behalf, and such necessary information was secured as should give colour to the evident planning of a thorough investigation. Superintendent Warner also gave her such hope and courage as he could; and the little woman went away with the understanding that she should call at the same hour on the next day, and looking much brighter and happier for the hope that had risen within her. He also elicited the fact that her husband had returned to his home early on the previous night, had retired early, and had certainly remained in the house during the whole night.

On the same afternoon I had my young friend in my carriage for an hour, gave him some hint that the object of our search would be captured, possibly by the next day, and in all probability everything would terminate much better than I had at first feared, in fact wholly as it should. I was also able to learn that his wife had certainly passed the preceding night at home. He was sure of it, but did not seem to wish to tell me how. Altogether, he had become sunnier and more hopeful.

On the third afternoon the little woman came as true as time to the minute of her appointment with my superintendent.

'Well, we have the truth of the matter at last. I hope it won't prove too bad!' he continued, reassuringly, as the little lady, woman-like, now that the suspense of it all was nearly over, burst into tears.

'Tell me, tell me all about it! Do tell me! If it kills me, I must know it all!' she sobbed violently.

'My dear madam!' replied Mr Warner in a soothing tone, 'you must compose yourself. I am not at liberty to give you the particulars. I can only say this much: we shall in a few minutes have this party who has caused the trouble in our office. You are to take a seat in one of the parlours. We will then have the party introduced to you, and you can then, having everything in your power, secure a confession as we have done, and extort a lasting pledge!'

With this the lady was conducted to one of the several small parlours, or reception-rooms, near my own private office, frequently found necessary in my business. The room was conveniently somewhat darkened, and, on leaving the superintendent at the door, she said, with some trepidity and evident fear:

'Oh, what shall I do alone with this fiend?'

'Just use your very best judgment, madam,' Mr Warner replied. 'Nothing shall harm you.'

With this the door closed, and the little woman was alone. What were her feelings and thoughts I cannot attempt to picture. One thing, however, was certain; as she paced the floor with a quick stride for the few minutes which should intervene, her fingers worked nervously, as though her spirit and indignation could not be restrained, and that she must wreak vengeance upon the fiend who had come between her and all that she loved.

Half an hour before I had left my young friend at his store. I had informed him that I had 'run in' the party he most wanted to see; that the person was then in my office; that I had extorted a full confession, the details of which, however, I declined to give, as I had determined he should be given an opportunity to confront the person himself and see with his own eyes and hear with his own ears the object of his fruitless detective service and the whole story. He was greatly moved, and said he feared he would do the d——d villain bodily harm. I told him that if he did he would forever forfeit my friendship; and he pledged himself solemnly to confine his indignation and punishment to his unexpected presence and words alone.

The last words of mine to him, as he alighted from my carriage at his store, were: 'Now Saunders, if you bring a revolver or anything of that sort, or in any way break faith with me, I will make you suffer for it. I won't have any scenes in my office!'

I had arranged that he should take a certain course to get to the agency. This brought him to the second floor and near my room by a private entrance, so that there might be no danger of any of his friends seeing him.

I shortly heard his footsteps upon the stairs. He halted occasionally, as if to gain strength for his terrible meeting. At last he entered my room, and said:

'Pinkerton! My God! This is too much! Where... where is he?'

'There!' I replied, pointing to a sliding-door, through which a parlour was reached.

He stepped to the door, put his hand upon the knob, paused a moment nervously then, drawing himself to his fullest height and looking so much the man, every inch of him, that I was proud of the fellow, strode into the room.

There was silence for a moment, I confess that to me it was an awful silence. It was a thrilling moment, and had a thousand times more in it than I ever hoped. Then there was a little shriek, a strong voice tremulously choked and stifled, a rush of a true husband and a devoted wife across what had seemed an impassable gulf, safe and sure into each other's arms.

I did not disturb them. For an hour they were there together. What love had been renewed, quickened, doubt dispelled, hopes brightened, everything that is tender and true in life resurrected and bettered, I cannot tell, but I do know that two more grateful people never existed on the face of this green earth.

And I also know that they both went home in the little *coupé* together, and have never occupied 'separate apartments' since.

This is an interesting combination of dogged detective work and sheer intuition, and the device used to startle a confession out of the perpetrator has all the hallmarks of melodrama.

⊰ An Extraordinary Self-robbery ⊱

One day in December, 1870, the president of one of the Chicago national banks called at my office and desired a private interview with me.

His statement was, that the deputy county treasurer of a county in Iowa, while alone in his office, had been assaulted by some unknown ruffians, nearly murdered, and sixteen thousand dollars taken out of his safe. It was desired by some correspondent of the bank's at the county seat where the assault and robbery had occurred, that the bank president should confer with me and secure my assistance.

Having but these bare outlines of the matter, I could do no more than at once dispatch one of my most able men to the point, with such general instructions as at that time could be given. This man, a keen, shrewd Irish-American named Hanlon, upon whom had previously devised the successful working up, under my direction, of several heavy bank and safe robberies, proceeded immediately to the place. There he met a gentleman named Wooster, who had authorised the operation, and who, being on the deputy treasurer's bonds, was naturally very anxious that the burglars and would-be murderers should be apprehended, and the large amount of money taken or at least a portion of it recovered.

The result of a careful preliminary examination into the matter was telegraphed me as follows: on the night of 9 December, in the year mentioned, a gentleman named Newcomb, desiring to purchase a county bond for some customer, went to the courthouse, where the deputy treasurer, a gentleman named Benton Emery, was accustomed to remain until about nine o'clock, his office being a sort of general rendezvous for a few of the county officials and several business men of the town.

On entering the treasurer's office, Mr Newcomb was startled to find a prostrate form upon the floor. He immediately procured a light, and found a man covered with blood, and apparently dying. Blood was upon the floor and flowed from several wounds of the presumably murdered man. The room betrayed evidences of a severe struggle; the lamp had been thrown upon the floor, and the odour of the oil showed that it had been broken in the fall; the chairs were thrown about and broken, what was more conclusive, and seemed to give some little clue to the mystery, was the circumstance that the door to the safe stood wide open, and papers and parcels were scattered in every direction around it.

Mr Newcomb took all this in at a single glance and, half suspecting what was to follow, found the wounded man to be no other than Benton Emery, the deputy treasurer himself. He was immediately taken home, and in a few days, though he barely lived through the terrible wounds he had received, was able to give an account of the robbery, as it undoubtedly was.

He stated that just after dark two men in oil-cloth coats called at his office, and stated that they desired to purchase some revenue stamps. They asked for five dollars' worth, and tendered a one hundred dollar bill in payment. He took up a glass to examine it and, after scrutinizing it and becoming satisfied of its genuineness, turned to open the safe. No sooner had he done so than one of the men sprang upon him, drawing a dagger, and grasped him violently by the throat. He was unable to utter a sound, but struggled with his assailants, clutching the dagger by the blade. The ruffian drew the dagger through his hand, and inflicted an awful gash, nearly severing the thumb at the ball. Weakened from his struggles with his burly foe and the pressure on his throat, he was compelled to gradually relax his efforts, when he received several stabs in his side. He then fell to the floor insensible.

An examination of the wounds proved that, though they were dangerous, they were not necessarily fatal. There was a gash on the hand, as stated, and four wounds around the heart, which, though deep, were not dangerous. The throat was wounded, and a frightful cut in the head disclosed the skull underneath.

The safe was overhauled, and sixteen thousand dollars, chiefly county funds, with a few small sums placed in the safe by merchants for safe-keeping, had been taken.

Now, these were the outlines of the matter, and it would reasonably be supposed that a bold and outrageous robbery had occurred and a brutal murder almost committed. In fact, hardly any other theory could account for the terrible wounds which Mr Emery sustained.

Some delay had ensued before I had been called upon, so that by the time my operative had arrived in the village Mr Emery had so far recovered from his wounds as to be able to take an active part in the endeavour to detect the perpetrators of the crime. He was a man of wealth, was engaged in no speculations which might have embarrassed him, so that while no possible clue to the robbers could be secured at that time, and with the information I then possessed, the last thought to enter my mind was any possible suspicion that the deputy treasurer himself had the remotest connection with the robbery.

But every other possible theory and clue were finally exhausted.

I reasoned that professional criminals of the sort capable of so daring a crime, in nearly every instance leave some clue by which their character as criminals can be established, and subsequently their identity pretty clearly arrived at. In my thirty years of detective work these things became so marked and fixed that, on reading a telegraphic newspaper report of a large or small robbery, with the aid of my vast records, great personal experience and familiarity with these matters, I can at once tell the character of the work, and then, knowing the names, history, habits, and quite frequently the rendezvous of those doing that class of work. I am able to determine, with almost unerring certainty, not only the very parties who committed the robberies, but also what disposition they are likely to make of their plunder, and at what points they may be in hiding.

I hardly believed this robbery to have been committed by professional bank robbers. This conviction was verified by the fact that the closest inquiries failed to show that any strangers who could not be accounted for had been seen in the village for weeks before. The town, though the county seat, did not contain at that time a population of over five hundred, and in a place of that size the face of a stranger is always closely scanned, and he cannot remain in the place without being quizzed and questioned.

I could not believe the robbery had been done by any of the class of outlaws who generally commit depredations upon express companies, isolated banks, and the like, in the more sparsely settled portions of the West; for a scouring of the country, in every direction, failed to discover the slightest clue to any persons having ridden to or from the place, or reached or departed from it on foot or by any manner of conveyance.

This consequently narrowed the investigation to the townspeople of the place itself. So here I directed my operative to dig away persistently, and leave no stone unturned toward the solving of the mystery. But it was of no use; the history, antecedents, occupation, habits, and financial condition of every male person in the village was secured, and where any person was found who might have, by the remotest possibility, been connected with the affair, he was made to give a thorough account of himself.

But alas this course utterly failed to develop anything material to the case, and I found myself balked in every direction.

One day, while sitting in my private office, puzzling my brain over the matter, and going through and through my operative's reports from beginning to end, with the vain hope of picking out of it all some slight thread upon which to hang even a theory of the robbery, I came to this sentence in one of the reports:

Mr Emery is ceaseless in his efforts to assist me, but seems to be very much opposed to my going so hard upon some of the people of the village, as he constantly insists that it was done by professional robbers from a distance.

In the mood I then was, my mind continually reverted to this. Why was Mr Emery so solicitous about his fellow-townsmen while there remained the barest chance of the robbers being found among them? And why did Mr Emery desire to constantly impress my operative with the idea that the robbery was done by professional robbers from a distance?

Pass this paragraph as often as I might, I always came around to it, stopped at it, and began asking myself these questions about it. I could not rid myself of the feeling, the longer I studied over it, that the impression was gradually but surely becoming fixed in my mind, there was behind all this a motive. Now what was that motive? I felt that the suspicion which was gradually creeping into my mind was unjust to Mr Emery; but the line of investigation it suggested, and which I now determined upon, was the *dernier ressort*.

I therefore immediately instructed my operative to continue his investigations as zealously as ever, but to at once devote more attention to noting every act and expression, as well as the manner and bearing of Mr Emery, without in the slightest degree betraying to the deputy treasurer his double duty. The result of this was, that in a few days I had before me reports which fully justified the course taken.

Emery seemed to be worried and anxious, and to relax his interest in endeavouring to track the robbers. There was a great load of some kind upon his mind. He appeared to have relapsed into a listless condition, from which any newly-proposed plan by my operative would waken him into a state of genuine nervousness and excitement, and it soon came to be his half-expressed desire that the operation should be abandoned.

At this point I decided to further test my new theory of the robbery. I arranged that an anonymous communication should be forwarded to the place from Dubuque, intimating that two suspicious characters could be found at a certain designated place in that city, whom the writer had reason to believe were the two persons that had committed the robbery. The descriptions sent tallied exactly with those given of the robbers by the deputy treasurer himself and accordingly my operative and Mr Emery set out for Dubuque to endeavour to secure an identification of the suspected parties.

But my operative found it hard work to even get him away from home. He protested that he had no faith in anonymous letters, and would wager any amount that it would all prove a fool's errand; and although he finally consented to make the trip, nearly every remark made by him concerning the matter tended to show that Mr Emery knew as well as I did that no robbers of his treasury were to be found in Dubuque.

I had instructed operative Hanlon to insist both that the parties were to be found, and that, if there was anything like an excuse for doing so, he should arrest the men and take them back with him. When this was said pretty forcibly and decidedly, Emery seemed to be utterly at a loss for an opinion; but finally, as if overwhelmed by the possible complications which such a course might involve, very hotly urged the injustice of such a step. Finally, just before reaching the city, he came out flatly, and said that he had been thinking the matter over, and had come to the conclusion that, if the real robbers were brought before him, it was very doubtful whether he would be able to identify them at all!

All of this and much other, tending to show a guilty knowledge of the robbery on Emery's part, and a great anxiety to be rid of the whole matter, was telegraphed me from Dubuque. I instantly decided to arrange a ruse by which Emery could be brought right into my office, where I could watch him, converse with him, perhaps play upon him a little, but, at all events, where I might be able to form a better judgment of the man, and conclude whether he was in any way connected with this affair, which, in looking at it from any standpoint, I could not but regard as very mysterious.

I could scarcely imagine what connection Emery had with the matter. I confess that I suspected he had robbed himself. But how were the horrible wounds that had nearly caused his death to be accounted for? Surely no sane man in Emery's position in life would cut his hand nearly off, stab himself a half dozen times most desperately over and about the heart, and lay open his skull as a fearful sabre stroke would do!

I could hardly imagine any solution to the mystery. Possibly he had not been guilty of the actual robbery, but perhaps it had been done by persons who had since approached him, and represented to him that they were too shrewd to be punished and, having convinced him of this, for a liberal share of the stolen funds, secured from him a pledge that he would prevent, as far as possible, the efforts which were being made for their capture. In any event, I had decided that Mr Emery was guilty of something!

I, therefore, at once telegraphed operative Hanlon, at Dubuque, that the parties he had expected there had got an inkling that their whereabouts had been discovered, had fled to this city; that I had had them arrested, and was now detaining them; and directing him to leave there at once for Chicago with Mr Emery, whose presence would be absolutely required. This done, I set about preparing matters at my office so as to give colour to the genuineness of the arrest when Mr Emery arrived.

I selected two stalwart men from among my force, and, by change in dress and sundry other little manoeuvres, made them answer the description of the supposed burglars who had robbed and nearly murdered Mr Emery. They, were heavily ironed and strongly guarded, and certainly, under the circumstances, presented a very hard and desperate appearance.

The next morning operative Hanlon and Mr Emery arrived in Chicago. The very moment I set my eyes upon the man I knew him to be guilty. He was a gentleman of fine appearance naturally, but in every movement of his person, in every feature of his face, in every changing tone of his voice, in every startled look from his downcast eyes as they met my own, there was as strong an evidence of guilt as I ever I had looked upon, and as true a proof that Emery was the criminal as though he had been a robber, had robbed and half-murdered another man, and come into my office under arrest rather than as a guest. I saw all this at once, and endeavoured to reassure him with the belief that we had at last captured the right parties. He hoped so, he said, and this was all that could be got out of him. Soon we proceeded to the apartment where the pretended desperate criminals were guarded.

They played their parts well, and made every possible apparent effort, without overdoing the matter, to prevent recognition. Emery was white as a ghost when he was brought before them. He seemed at an utter loss of knowledge how to act, but finally ventured to say that, while he might have seen them, he could not swear to their being the parties.

Returning to my private office, I invited Mr Emery to a seat, directed the door to be closed and, seating myself before him, remarked pleasantly: 'Mr Emery, we are having pretty hard luck in this matter?'

'Very!' he replied, with a dry throat and a good deal of huskiness in it.

'What would you say, Mr Emery,' I remarked, with a meaning smile, 'if I should tell you that, although you fail to identify the parties under arrest here, I now have the perpetrator of this crime within my office.'

His face grew livid and white by turns, and his eyes seemed starting from their sockets.

'Yes,' I continued, with great severity; 'and what would you say if I would show you the man in this very room?'

'Where? where?' he gasped, giving a startled look in every direction.

'There! there! See him! Look at him!' I almost shouted, turning him at one motion in the revolving chair where he sat and bringing the poor fellow squarely in front of a huge pier-glass, and then forced him squarely upon his feet against it by main strength.

I never saw a more ghastly face than that of this self-robber's.

He sank into his seat and gasped: 'For God's sake, Mr Pinkerton, you don't mean…'

'You know what I mean, Emery. You know it! Now out with the truth, like a man!'

There is but little more to tell. Emery now knew that I knew he committed the robbery, and the poor man went right at it, confessing the whole matter in a few minutes.

It was to the effect that he had no need for the money, was wealthy and beyond any possible want for life, but, being there in the office, shut up with so large a sum of money so long, he had first thought of the ease with which he might be robbed. Then, revolving this in his mind so frequently, he finally conceived the idea of robbing himself. At last this became a sort of all-absorbing idea with him, which he could not by any possibility shake off, until actually, to give himself relief from it, he stole the money, hid it under the side-walk in front of the office, broke up the office furniture, and scattered papers and things, so as to give an evidence of a struggle, and at last inflicted upon himself the terrible wounds from which he had nearly died in order to give colour to the story he was obliged to tell of being assaulted.

But the saddest part remains to be told. Emery was put in charge of the same operative, and returned to Iowa a prisoner, where he had left three days before a respectable citizen and a trusted officer. The money was all found just where Emery had said it was hidden. But the shame and disgrace of it all was more than the deluded man could sustain, and the second day after his arrival home he ended all his troubles by committing suicide; this tragedy terminating one of the strangest incidents of my detective career.

And finally… in 1884 Pinkerton wrote the best How To book for aspiring criminals, counterfeiters and 'coney-men', Thirty Years a Detective, subtitled A Thorough and Comprehensive Exposé of Criminal Practices of all Grades and Classes. The extracts below, detailing the tools and procedures of burglars, should be required reading for anyone taking a vocational qualification in housebreaking or other ne'er-do-wellery.

Methods, Tools, and Implements of the Burglar

In all cases of robbery, it is necessary to have someone of their number conveniently and safely stationed on the outside, who is to give the alarm in case of danger. The usual method of arranging this very necessary matter is for the burglars to secure a room on the opposite side of the street, as near to the bank to be operated upon as possible, and this room is generally on the second or third floor, and in the front of the building. When the night arrives for active work, the confederate is stationed in this room, from the window of which he drops a fine strong cord. This cord is then taken by the robbers and carried across to the second story window of the bank, and then continued through to the point where the work upon the safe is to be done. After the burglars have entered the building, either by fake keys or any prearranged mode, if the string is in the second story, a hole is bored through the floor and ceiling, and thus let down into the spot where the men are at work. One of the burglars then fastens the end of this string to his hand or arm, the slightest pull from the other end is the signal of danger and the men then make their escape as best they can. This is the plan generally adopted by the burglars, and it has worked successfully in almost every instance.

In attempting to open a safe, there are several modes which may be adopted according to the necessities of the case—wedging, drilling, the use of the screw, or by blowing with powder. This latter plan, however, is but seldom used of late years by professional burglars, as the noise of the explosion is apt to be heard outside and thus give the party away. The most approved plan is to open the safe with the least noise, and to do this the door of the safe must be forced. This operation requires tools that are both strong and fine, and they must be manipulated by men who understand how to use them. One of the most ingenious and forcible of these contrivances I will attempt to describe at length. This instrument consists of a plate of steel ten-inches long, eight-inches wide, and about one-and-a-half inches in thickness, in which are fastened two upright pieces of steel which are to act as the support for the upright brace.

This bed-plate is screwed securely to the floor in front of the door of the safe, by six large screws. The box in the centre, as I have stated before, is the 'slot' which is to receive the upright post or brace. This brace is of peculiar construction and is made entirely of steel. It is three-feet-six inches long, about four-inches wide and an inch thick, with an extra piece of steel of the same thickness, and about four-inches square, fastened to the top. In the centre of this brace there is an opening about an inch wide and nearly a foot long. The following diagram will afford a correct idea of this brace.

The foot of this upright is placed in the 'slot' in the box in the base and then tightly bolted through, the centre hole B fitting snugly in the box. In order, however, to make this more firm and to brace it for the pressure it is required to sustain, another smaller plate is screwed to the floor behind E and a strong brace is fitted into this and rests under the angle formed by the additional piece of steel upon the top C. When set up, the brace with its various component parts presents the following appearance.

From these comparatively light materials the burglars have now constructed a brace that is capable of resisting the pressure of tons. In the above cut it will be noticed that there is another attachment, which is a box-slide, also made of steel, the face of which is provided with a number of counter-sunk centres.

This box is arranged so that it will slide up or down upon the upright brace at will and can be fastened to its place with a screw (E2). With this brace duly placed in its position the burglar is now ready to commence work upon the door of the safe. The next implement is the feed-screw drill, which resembles the following figure.

One end of this drill is placed against the sliding box upon the brace, and the other, which holds the drill, is adjusted to the spot where the hole is intended to be drilled into the door of the safe. H shows the feed screw of the drill, which as the drill cuts into the iron at G, extends the length of the brace, and thus keeps the drill in its position. With this drill, it is claimed that an inch hole can be bored through the best wrought iron safe door in ten minutes. After this hole has been successfully bored, the upright is then unshipped from its first position, and instead of a brace it must now perform the duty of a lever. For this purpose a steel screw with a peculiar notch in the head of it, is used.

The upright is then placed horizontally across the front of the safe; the head of the screw is inserted into the hole bored into the door and wedged tightly in, the shoulder being on the inside of the door plate. The thread of the screw is then passed through the opening in the centre of the upright, and is made secure with a nut upon the outside. This fastens the upright, or lever, as it has now become, tightly to the safe door. By this operation the double or shoulder end of the upright is brought into position near to the lock of the safe. In this end, it will be noticed, there is an inch hole K, with a screw thread worked into it; into this hole therefore a strong steel screw, an inch in diameter, with a strong square head is inserted, and this screw is then turned by means of a stout steel wrench.

The screw being placed so as to bear directly upon the side of the safe door, and the wrench being turned by two strong men, it is thus pressed against the door with terrific and unrelenting force, and something must inevitably give way inside, and this is generally one of the bolts. Sometimes, however, the bolts hold too strongly, and though they may be loosened, the door will only be opened perhaps not more than half an inch. This affords an opportunity for the introduction of another powerful instrument in the hands of the burglar, namely, the 'compound jimmy'. This is an implement made of fine-tempered steel, and in two sections, each section about two to one-half feet long, and generally of one and one-half to two inches thick, square, and tapering to an edge at the end.

With this instrument, supplemented by the combined strength of two muscular men, the door is soon forced open, and the property of the bank is at the mercy of the plunderers.

The operations detailed above are such as are used on safes and vaults with but a single door. If in a vault, this method simply overcomes the outer door, and the burglar will find that he has not yet reached the treasure, for that is contained generally in an iron chest inside of the vault. The tools which previously were so efficacious are now found to be too heavy for this new task, but the burglars are prepared for this emergency, and lose no time in renewing their work. A small number of steel wedges are now produced, and starting in one corner they proceed to drive them in, with muffled copper hammers, within a few inches of each other. Ten or twelve of these wedges are inserted in this manner, taking care to drive each of the upper ones as the lower one widens the breach, and loosens their power. When the wedges have produced an opening large enough to introduce the 'compound jimmy', that instrument is inserted, and the doors yield to the pressure that is brought to bear upon them. There is no resisting this terrific force, and the contents of the safe are soon exposed.

There is another method which has been put into practice upon single-door safes with a great deal of success, and which has frequently caused suspicion to test upon some innocent young clerk in the employ of the bank. The operation is simple and only requires correct calculation.

All safes are supposed to have three bolts; one at the top, one at the bottom, and one at the centre, but all are connected by one bar, and as a consequence, if one bolt is knocked out, the others share the same fate and are rendered useless. The task therefore is for the burglar to calculate the position of the centre bolt, and the point at which this bolt would come out upon the outside, and then to drill a hole in the manner above described directly opposite this point. When the hole has been drilled through to the edge of the bolt, they insert a steel punch, and then with a good strong blow or two with a heavy hammer the bolts are completely demoralized. The safe is then opened, the money extracted, the safe closed, the hole in the side plugged up, and no one is able to tell without a thorough examination just how the work was done.

Several modes of blowing a safe with powder have been used, but the easiest and more general one is to drill a hole into the lock, and then force powder through this hole and explode it, which would result in the destruction of the lock and the removal of all obstacles.

In this process very frequently gun-cotton and nitro-glycerine have been used as the explosives, and an ingenious sort of syringe is used for this purpose.

Another method of 'blowing' a safe with powder is to putty up all the crevices of the safe compactly except two points. At one of these points the air pump is applied, which exhausts the air within the safe, and at the other point the powder is drawn in by the force of the suction, caused by the pumping out of the air at the other outlet. By this means the doors of safes have been forced literally from their hinges by the effects of the

explosion. It has also been a practice to draw the temper of hardened irons with the ordinary blow pipe, consisting of a spirit lamp and a tube, such as jewelers use.

This is quickly done, after which the safe may be drilled with a common steel drill. Astute burglars make a practice of thoroughly acquainting themselves with all the particulars of the construction of safes, as well as of their locks, and many safes have been opened by drilling out all the riveting of the inner lining, and of the bolts and lock which fasten the same to the outer shell of the door, the position of these rivets being obtained by exact measurement from the outside. Some safes are so constructed as to give no receptacle for powder or blasting material, excepting in certain apertures of the lock, but so well acquainted with their peculiar internal arrangements do the thieves become, that they are able by measurement from the outside, to know exactly where to place their drills.

The most obstinate safes have been made to yield to the ordinary jack-screw, which is applied in two ways, either by drilling a hole in the door, generally about three-quarters-of-an-inch in diameter, then with a screw tap, cutting a thread for a slightly tapering screw, which by a lever is made to fit tightly into the hole. An attachment is then made with the screw and jack, the latter being supported by a rough frame, and held from the safe by timbers placed against the jambs, when the shell of the door is pulled out by main force, breaking the rivets.

The other method of using the jack-screw is to force the door inward, breaking it into pieces that are easily removed by the 'jimmy'. When an abutment for the jack-screw cannot be obtained by placing timbers against a solid partition other object, a brace is obtained by securing one end of a long timber to the floor, and blocking up the other end, so as to be in a position, central to the door of the safe. Against this and the door, the jack is placed. A great many fire proof safes throughout the country have been opened simply by the pick and 'jimmy'. With safes that are manufactured of ordinary plate iron, all that is necessary is, first with several well directed blows with a pick to make an aperture just sufficient to receive the sharp end of the 'jimmy' in one corner of the panel, then with the 'jimmy' the iron is ripped and torn out the whole length of the panel, thus exposing the filling—the latter is picked out in a few moments—the bent end of the 'jimmy' is then inserted behind the bolt, and the same pried back by main force, breaking the wards in the lock. This operation has frequently been performed in from fifteen to twenty minutes.

Thieves have adopted a good many, ingenious ways of picking locks, and some of them have attained a delicacy of feeling, by which they have been able to determine with fine instruments the exact distance it was necessary to raise each tumbler; but of later years many of the locks have been specially constructed with the view of foiling anything of this. Tumbler-locks requiring large keys have been opened by forcing around in them a blank steel key, breaking the wards and forcing back the bolt. The combination of some locks, it is claimed, can be ascertained by filling each of the apertures, to receive the pivots, with wooden pins excepting one, in which a small particle of fulminating powder is exploded. Then by withdrawing the pins the exact length of the wards is determined by the amount of discolouration on these pins.

The combination of the dial lock can be found by placing under the back of the dials a small peculiarly manufactured ratchet, so that at every reverse motion of the knob, a small puncture is made on the plate upon which it moves, or upon a disc of paper especially secured to it for the purpose of receiving these impressions or punctures.

A celebrated burglar in getting at the contents of the vault and safes of a noted bank had two of these combination dial locks to open, and did all his work in one night.

In all cases of bank robberies, the final work is generally done between Saturday night and Sunday morning. The tools used by professional bank thieves are those commonly used by mechanics—excepting the 'jimmy', which for the heavier work is made in several sections to be screwed together when required for use—being then about the size of the ordinary crow bar.